B. L. MacKinnon

RHESUS NEGATIVE

AUSTIN MACAULEY PUBLISHERS™
LONDON · CAMBRIDGE · NEW YORK · SHARJAH

A CIP catalogue record for this title is available from the British Library.

ISBN 9781786124265 (Paperback)
ISBN 9781786124272 (Hardback)
ISBN 9781786124289 (EBook)

www.austinmacauley.com

2nd Edition
First Published (2016)
Austin Macauley Publishers Ltd.
25 Canada Square
Canary Wharf
London
E14 5LQ

Gratitude!

For want of me the world's course will not fail:
When all its work is done, the lie shall rot;
The truth is great, and shall prevail,
When none cares whether it prevail or not.

From: *Magma Est Veritas*, by Coventry Patmore

Prologue

To be clear: I am irked at my having to write *any* of this. The very *thought* of having to do so is distasteful to me. It is not my *sort of thing*, not my calling. I am not thus minded. The subjects that interest me are those that I have at least a *chance* of making some *rational* – or near rational – sense of, and of deriving worthwhile satisfaction from.

However, there is nothing engaging that ensues from the profound sorrow which inevitably follows upon the killings of one's parents, and other inequitable losses. With the unremitting infliction of further abuse and the passage of more, precious, lost time, there comes only renewed *will* to regroup and 'fight' for justice. It is not any conviction that the pen is mightier than the sword that motivates me to write: just an inability to reconcile use of 'the sword' with my ongoing – although, thus far, often unsuccessful – attempts at living life according to original Christian teachings. There therefore remains only the *word*.

I first compiled and uploaded an account of these life events to the web in 1996, in half-hearted response to a (then) thought-provoking remark made to me by a writer: 'If *you* don't write it, someone else will; and the truth will not be their first consideration.'

The website was hacked almost immediately, the text taken offline, and quickly replaced with a much-altered, truncated and otherwise corrupted version that, upon reading, I found to be, variously: shocking, perplexing and unintelligible. A second uploading of the original text some months later, resulted merely in its being taken offline again, with even greater haste, by a source that I was – back then at least – lacking in the skill set necessary to run down and identify. The doers of the clandestine deed did not even bother trying to replace it with *anything* that time. By then, I suspect that they felt that they did not *need* to. Over the years since, all but one of the remaining floppy disk copies of the original text have been stolen from me. Recently, I took a trip by car and ferry and, finding myself uncertain of the permanence of the gifts of early youth, I donned *Optifade* and proceeded to retrieve that copy (still sealed and dry, since 1999, in a little 'Peli Case') from a remote cave on an island off the west coast of Scotland. It has been that single remaining copy that I have used as a template for developing this update.

Mid-May 2015

I had emerged just about even – by my initial assessment – from a particularly nasty late-night scrap with four of Professor Sir Roddy MacSween's thugs. '*Sir*': that could *still* raise a smile – if only a sardonic one – in me, even at an awful moment like *that*. Maybe, just *maybe*, in some Wodehouse-imagined inter-war *England*, or in the political commentary of the occasionally estimable Peter Hitchens, could such 'Honours', arguably … *conceivably* … if *romantically*, have been Kitemarks of deserved distinction for essentially good, honest and genuinely talented individuals; but at least one hopeful sign for this benighted isle is that there are ever-growing numbers of individuals who recognise that those 'honours' have long-since – if not *always* – served merely as identifiers of rogues, scoundrels, and worse: *much* worse.

Anyway, *honour* in *my* philosophy is to God alone. In remembering *that*, I realised that the consideration had been

10

specious. It was, in any case, and in the next instant, superseded by the apprehension that my 'initial assessment' had been wrong: I had taken a particularly severe blow to my back, midline at around T11/T12, and suddenly I had the strong sense that I was bleeding internally. I hoped that it was not my descending aorta.

Back at the flat, I crawled into bed. Tomorrow, or the following day, would come the 'break-in': they always had keys or other means of 'clean' entry, supplied courtesy of a client/victim of MacSween, currently in an executive position with East Dunbartonshire Council's Housing and Community Services department. "Better be out for that!" I thought. "Even if I make it to the *active* dream and on until morning, I won't be in any shape to defend myself for at least another few days." I *had* to make it, though. Thoughts of those reprobates making merry over the spectacle of my corpse were thoughts that I simply could *not* countenance. There was nonetheless still that persisting, creeping disquiet that my will was beginning to fail me.

If I *were* to survive until the inevitable oft-repeated 'sweep' for the papers and other records that they were so intent on divesting me of − not to forget the one desktop PC, two laptops, one MacBook, one iPad Air 2, one iPhone 6, and six other assorted tablets and mobiles that they had taken from me, sometimes forcefully, over the preceding three years − then there would be 'stage three' to contend with: a visit from some so-called 'journalist'. Sadly, for me, no thumbsucker-generating Woodward or Bernstein had this ever been, but rather, just like that *policeman* − one of the four individuals from my unfortunate encounter less than half an hour before, who was primarily distinguishable by his unsuitability for the task − another foot soldier from the power-*worshipping*, 'media' supportive limb of this country's Power Infrastructure, into which MacSween, by means of sustained and uncompromising blackmail, had gained entry. His effective role once *in*, may have been minimized to the order of zero. However, his profligate and malign misuse of the finite resources afforded him by the 'honour', may as well have been limitless: focussed and concentrated as they had been upon my late mother and myself until – and continuing *since* – his hoodlums had killed her in 2008.

In January of this year, following yet another home invasion – like the written bank statements of yesteryear, they come 'quarterly', and I happened to be *out* for *that* one – they sent one Gavin Madeley of the *Daily Mail*. A would-be wag of my acquaintance, who had read the ensuing article, described Madeley to me as one of that newspaper's 'barely-literate character assassinating hacks', who 'would have difficulty negotiating his way through English 101' (my confidant is an American). His assessment of the journalist may have been accurate, but it was of little comfort to me though.

Ensconced in my bunk, there was no 'conventional' descent through the hypnagogic. I simply blacked out. Thankfully, though, a passive dream eventually came.

Tall and lean and noble he stands: poised and seeming self-possessed, as he rocks gently, with calming, subtle pitch and yaw, upon his silver board in this Astral void. An apparent Archetype, manifest as one like Norrin Radd, who for those of you familiar with the *Classics* …

Between the ages of eight and ten or eleven, I occasionally indulged myself in any editions that I might happen upon of a particular American comic book. Its character came to embody and personify the quality of physical invulnerability for me; and I infer that this is why, to date, this nonesuch so manifests.

He looks askance at me, and as he moves to speak, the dream, like his board, begins to 'wobble'.

"Wait!" says I. "I'm *done* this time. I have no more heart for this. I have written my letter to her … well, *two* as it turned out; and well intentioned as that was, what if, in doing so, I have compromised her integrity? I'm ready to let go now, anyway. So, let it *wait*."

"*Wait?*" he catechizes, his demeanour abruptly darkening and his intonation uncharacteristically booming, stentorian and menacing. "Are you *kidding* me? Did you just say *wait*? Wait for *what* exactly? Wait for what might be only another few minutes of life, because you're just *so fucking* weak that you just can't stand to go on: can't *stand* to see it through?"

The internal haemorrhage pains me fiercely now, even in the dream, which proceeds to wobble more. But with alacrity, I realise that the surfer would not use foul language, and I immediately go lucid. I scramble for effective means of stabilising the dream, and following the advice of Harold von Moers-Messmer, I first look at the 'ground'. But there is none below my feet. *Last chance*! I glance, once, at my hands; flip them over and then back again; and then glance again. They are not *quite* the same second time around, so I am reassured that I am still lucidly dreaming. I rub them vigorously together and the dream begins to stabilise.

I see the 'real' surfer: no *phantasm* now, but the *true* Archetype, emerging. He smiles benignly, and as he makes three strides towards me along the chrome-silver mirroring surface, the long board appears to absorb up through his feet and into the substance of his body. With that, his silver hue evanesces, becoming new skin tone of radiant porcelain white, as though illuminated from within. A mark, akin to a wound or a half-opened eye emerges on the lower part of the middle of his forehead, as fronds of bright, white, flowing, energetic light appear behind and above him. To my oft-tellurian mentality, they suggest spectral *wings*. It *is* he: of that, I remain sure; but as neither *silver* nor *surfer* is he manifest any longer.

Over many years, I have grown accustomed to his extraordinary appearance, and he chooses *this* unfeasible juncture to reveal this even more *astonishing* form.

"*You* have not the *heart*?" he enquires, genially, firmly and unsmiling, his orotund, euphonious voice carrying canorously across the void between us; as his accompanying penetrating 'look' (synaesthesic and *so* vivid) conveys anticipation of my answer.

His words move me to think of the now long-absent augmenter of my heart: my head at rest upon the alabaster expanse of her chest, all those years ago: *yet* … but a seeming *moment* since. My astral head sinks forward with the unremitting grief of the loss of her, and I see that my skin, just like the lately transformed 'surfer', has uniformly taken on that same pale flawless tone. On the instant, the long tapering fingers of this present figure's extended hand are pressing upwards, under my mandible.

"Chin *up*! You cannot be so *lazy* that you would abandon the realm she yet inhabits. There is today, you know, a *one hundred and two* year old woman in Germany, who, denied her chance of completing her studies in Medicine by the Nazis, is, at long last, about to graduate. You are yet but less than *half* that span. Would you, here, and *finally*, capitulate to no less a *Nazi* and his cohorts, who have for so long stymied *your* progress? Would you really yield, at last, to such *awful frights*?"

"*No*," I reply, falling to command as I would to none but one other, and I raise my head again.

"Then go *heal* brother. Go heal!" says he, and is off faster than light: as fast as *thought* itself. And at the last, just a remnant of his voice, fading and echoing: "I hope that you did not take the bloom from her cheek as well! Cover your eyes and go heal!"

"*Soon*!" I attempt to holler back, but in fact merely muttering and heart sore: "Soon."

Inside the lucid dream, I close my eyes – to let my subconscious know that I mean serious business – and I say:

"When I open my eyes again, I will see a replica of my Aura hanging in front of me. Damaged areas will be extremely obvious to me. This replica of my Aura will be tied to my real Aura; any changes I make to the replica I will also make to my real Aura."

By saying exactly what I intend, in this way, I make it the truth. Upon opening my eyes, I go from Lucid Dreamer to Active Dreamer. In the air in front of me, there is a glowing shape, just slightly larger than my own body. I can see that some parts (including the area where I took the hard blow) are *very* wrong. Furthermore, the whole aura is dim and 'thin'. I know anew what I had already realised: that I am in *dire* trouble.

I say aloud:

"I call the powers of the universe to provide me with the power of healing," and I clap my hands together twice. As I clap them the second time, my hands start glowing with a warm, comforting golden light. I reach out and touch the damaged parts of my Aura, and say:

"Heal me now."

The golden light: pure energy of healing pours from my hands, and into the Aura. It first flows into the particularly dim, damaged areas, like water into a dip, and quickly fills them up. Once all the damaged parts are filled up, I put my hands on the Aura, and just pour golden light into it. The Aura expands and becomes brighter and stronger all round. Once it stops getting larger, then I remove my hands and say:

"It is done." And I clap my hands once again. As I do so, they stop glowing. I step forwards and up into the Aura. It fits all around me, like a glove, flares up slightly, and then vanishes. This is my repaired Aura meshing with my Astral body, and locking in with my physical body.

I am suddenly relieved, as I now know that no matter how awful I may feel when I awaken, I will, at least *awaken*; and however bad my injuries were, I shall now quickly recover.

It seems that I was not quite so ready to die after all.

When I was aged no more than five, a kindly primary school teacher once pointed out to me that it was 'not the *done thing*' to change tense over the course of a (very) short story that I had been set to produce as homework. I have not forgotten the lesson, but in the astral realm at least, there does indeed seem to be 'no time like the present': nor, indeed, *any* time like the present.

On awakening, I could hardly move for the first few minutes. The pain, both of the general and localised varieties – with one substituting for the other, moment by moment – felt close to intractable. I stared, vacantly, for a few more minutes at the items on the shelves beside my bed: a wristwatch, a little tub of proteolytic enzymes, with curcumin; Vitamin D-3 and K-2 spray, and a bottle of trace mineral drops. For once, however – and just when I needed it most – there was no carafe of water.

I began to contemplate: first, how *thirsty* I was and next, how *if only* the vast majority of the people of this world were not so audaciously dispossessed of existent-but-concealed medical knowledge and resources that might otherwise elevate them from a latter-day *medieval* age, *then* the notion of *magick* might be rendered *redundant* in a world where marvels, although commonplace, would be held to be the inevitable result of *unhindered* medical advancements. Then, *more or less* satisfied that no matter *what*, there would always be *hope* for a brighter future, I became sufficiently energized to get myself first *vertical*, and thereafter on the move towards the bathroom.

The mirror could not have been more brutal in its imparting of how faithful the translation of adopted skin tone had been, between dreaming and waking life. And if I *had* once taken the bloom from her cheek, it was nowhere to be seen that morning.

With a Herxheimer's reaction well underway, and with the anticipation of more to come throughout the next two or three days, all that I could usefully do was reach for my skin brush.

As I did so, my gaze returned to the mirror. I held it there for a little longer, not because of any desire to keep looking at the reflection of my sorry – but at least now *improving* – physical state, but because the insistently emergent pinpoint of a thought had rapidly burgeoned, such that I was strongly inclined not to ignore it.

Although I felt quite well *mentally*, how could I be entirely sure that, after *all* that I had been through, throughout *so* many years, I had not become, for want of a better term, *crazy*?

I continued to look long and hard at my reflection, in spite of the mounting perturbation that the question – while it remained *unanswered* – visited upon me. Eventually, it came to me that the one modicum of reassurance in *that* regard was that I *had asked* the question.

It was, indeed, two further days until the 'house call'. Fortunately, I was out. *Unfortunately*, they snapped (what turned out to be) a key in the outer lock of the flat door, after having taken my spare keys from a kitchen drawer. It seemed to be a 'set-up', to force me into calling the police: something, which for reasons that I have already hinted at – and will expand further upon later – I have been inclined to do only *very* rarely these past years. One of the uniformed police officers who arrived (*eventually*, some ninety minutes after I had called it in) did indeed prove to be very 'difficult'. His face was an easy 'read' though, and it was readily apparent that he had been 'prepared' (drilled), in advance, for the task. However, I got through it easily enough. Even the inevitable clear up of the trashed lodgings was something that I had grown accustomed to. It was another four days until they sent the journalist: a young woman, and as exceptionally persistent a shouter, and knocker of the door as any of her ilk. I reached for my headphones. Mozart's L'allegro Con Spirito from the Sonata for Two Pianos in D Major has long proven reliable for calming and focussing the mind in hectic times.

The same acquaintance who, not so long ago, commented on the 'hack', recently sent from the *Daily Mail* – for the second time since 2004, as part of a wider oft-repeated attempt to torment and discredit me – proffered, in the course of the same conversation, that my 'case' has proven something of an ongoing embarrassment for Glasgow University. I was somewhat sickened by what he said, but nonetheless managed to hold back on rising to the provocation. He scrutinized me studiously for another long moment, and seeming to find no satisfaction from my expressionless demeanour, he softened somewhat, and continued, musing:

"I suppose there may be *some* correlation with G.U. having descended ever-further down the league tables since the mid-nineties … the loss of academic reputation … the concomitant metamorphosis into little more than a laundering operation for foreign money, which is, largely, reinvested into some of the foulest (if highly profitable) activities of the military-industrial complex."

"It *is* rather a *long* time to rest on the laurels of the likes of Lind," I ventured.

"Who was *he*?"

"*James* Lind: one of the criminally unsung figures of the so-called Scottish Enlightenment; yet, perhaps in his own way a greater contributor than Hume, Smith *or* Watt."

"'The *Scottish* Enlightenment', you say? *That* had to be a quickly-fusing bulb. None of it helps *you* any, though, *does* it? You're still in the same bind."

In view of my coffee house companion being a solicitor, and of our long-standing acquaintance, I decided to 'go adversarial' for just a moment, if only to give vent to a small measure of my mounting ire:

'Perhaps if they'd just come clean, and tell the *truth* …'

And so to my *own* truth.

I ought to state at the outset that my most frequently adopted model of time-space has, for many a year, not been a linear one. I do not, however, hold that to be a failing. On the contrary, in view of my life experiences to date, it is a model that has served me well this past quarter of a century. *Where* and *when* to begin though?

Chapter One

It was an overcast morning in late May 1993, as bolstered to intended purpose, I made my way through the school gates and down on to the concrete yard. I was just over a week short of my thirtieth birthday.

Much is made of the power of scents and odours to evoke long-forgotten sensations, but I suspect that, in addition, some element of the *unexpected* is required to effect such reawakening. I, however, had every expectation of the same old smells, as each was carried towards me: stale schoolyard mud squelched underfoot and wafted upwards, followed a little further on by that peculiar 'school dinner' aroma, which pervaded and demarcated a wide area around the canteen, at the corner of the old building.

There was certainly no sense of *renewal* for me here; only, at *best*, the prospect of a year's drudgery, compounded by fear.

Pausing at the entrance to the main hallway, I again tapped momentarily into the motivation that had brought me to this. *Memory*, and that benchmark God-given arbiter, *conscience*, combined to reaffirm that I was somehow doing a *right* thing: maybe the only remaining *possible* thing, given that I was a being endowed, as all others, with a sense of justice. I pulled the heavy swing door ajar and walked inside.

Along the corridor a little way and on the left, I arrived at the office door of Mrs Holmes, a deputy rector. It stood half-open and, just inside, two women were talking quietly. The younger of the two caught my eye over her colleague's shoulder and smiled.

"Hello, I'm Brandon Lee," I said.

"Ah yes, *Brandon*! I'm Mrs Holmes. If you wouldn't mind waiting in the computer room, I'll be with you in just a few minutes."

A few days before, I had made the appointment by telephone with this still pleasant and, as yet, seemingly unconcerned woman.

The computer room to which she escorted me was long and narrow, and furnished with old tables which bore the ink and penknife inscriptions of yesteryear. I sat and waited at one end and, for a moment, stared blankly at the single machine which dignified that particular apartment with its title. In the quiet, I could sense my heart beating rapidly, but I was resolved that I would appear composed.

In a state of never-before-know-to-me cold rage, I had set myself to this undertaking and there was no going back now.

Five minutes later, in her office, Mrs Holmes again displayed the same benign demeanour as before. I presented her with a letter of introduction from one William Lee, an emeritus professor of zoology, whom I indicated to be my father; and a progress report from a Miss M. Hunt, who, I claimed, had tutored me in biology while I stayed near Edmonton, Canada. I further explained that I had lived and travelled with my mother – an opera singer (mezzo-soprano) – since my parents had separated, some years earlier, and that as a result, I had been privately tutored instead of attending regular school.

The one remaining element of my self-contrived background was that our three-membered family had been involved in an automobile accident in Canada, earlier that year. My mother had died as a result of her injuries and my father, while convalescing, had decided to send me, his fifteen-year-old son, from the paternal home in London, to live with my grandmother in Bearsden. His letter further indicated my hope of securing a place at a medical school and his desire that I might be accommodated to study the subjects commensurate with such an inclination.

As I recounted the last of my devised history, our conversation was suddenly interrupted by a lad of surely no more than thirteen, who knocked, entered the tidy office sheepishly and mumbled something about having been sent downstairs for misbehaving by one of the teachers. The formerly charming Mrs Holmes turned suddenly nasty, dispatched the sorry youth along with instructions for his punishment exercise, and then, just as abruptly, regained her calm to bring our first meeting to an end.

I remember first thinking, 'Who'd be a teacher?', but beneath that, I found myself reassured of something that I had gleaned years before: never entirely trust a human being in a position of authority!

A checklist was produced, which included the listing, 'birth certificate'. This she dismissed with, "No, but I'll believe you!" She then indicated that the one extra item of clothing, which I would require would be a school tie, obtainable from a shop at Bearsden Cross. Finally, she asked me to return to her office the following morning, in order that I could be timetabled for my subject classes: English, Mathematics, Chemistry, Physics and Biology. As planned, I would be placed in the fifth year. I had previously determined that this would best afford me the means of gaining a medical school place in the course of a single year, and I certainly did not wish for my belated return to school to last a *moment* longer than I needed it to.

Even in Scotland, university medical schools had, by then – and for some years previously – desisted from taking applicants who had not completed a sixth year at school. *Somehow* though, even *that* was not going to stop me. And even if it *did* turn out to be *Dundee*, it would still be an MBChB from an accredited medical school. "That would *do* in 'the big wide world', *wouldn't it*?" I asked myself. As I made my way back out through the gates, I kept telling myself it would.

But at *least*, none of my earlier fears about ending the day in the local police station, unmasked and *undone* – the humiliated and disgraced adult equivalent of a dim-witted three year old who had lain behind the sofa with his legs sticking out during a game of hide-and-seek – had come true.

I walked away from the school in something of a bemused daze. There was neither a sense of triumph nor even inflated confidence in me, but perhaps just a little relief at having apparently overcome the first hurdle.

That night I lay awake, contemplating the events from years before that had finally led me to this extreme course of action.

Chapter Two

From shortly before my third birthday, in 1966, and until I was twelve, my family lived in Milton, a grey concrete and asphalt *elbow to the face of one's humanity* of a housing estate on Glasgow's north side. My father was a fire brigade driver and we occupied one of the ground-floor flats of a Strathclyde Fire Service apartment block.

I remember growing up in Milton as a frequently arduous adventure, during which I was occasionally forced into 'fight or flight' (I tended to favour 'flight' wherever and whenever it was an option) as necessary means of self-preservation. The whole experience was nevertheless mitigated by a trinity of saving graces: football, schoolwork and weekends away from that hellhole.

My mother worked as a Queen's Institute district nurse and midwife; and most weekends, both parents' respective work shifts permitting, the four of us – I had a younger sister – would pile into our little red Volkswagen Beetle and head up to the caravan (replaced after a few years by a holiday cottage) beside Loch Fyne.

Fishing and hillwalking were the orders of the day. Indeed, some of my most vivid memories of those years are of fishing from the shore with my father. Our elusive quarries were the canny sea trout – little bars of silver, speckled green and black and white made muscle, and invested with super-animated vigour.

I recall being commended by Mr Eaddie, my primary seven teacher, for a poem that I had written following my having espied a shoal of them in the brackish water near the mouth of a burn (stream), where it entered the sea. Only the latter part of it comes back to me now:

> 'Fuzzy elemental wimpling
> Like light-blended
> Bended, agitated when
> By leeching lice
> Or casts of men
> Contradistinguishing
> Torsional springing and
> Polarizing at the brink.'

Poetry was not really my *bag* though. I was more of a *numbers* and *facts* kind of kid: 'near-eidetic memory', according to Mr Eaddie. On reflection, I suspect that he was being uncommonly generous in his appraisal: surprised as he must have been – faced with another class full of boys who were, individually and collectively, preoccupied with little else other than football and the discussion of the previous night's television – that even *one* amongst them would have had a stab at writing a poem.

By virtue of their unpredictable behaviour, the sea trout were as difficult to land as they were to entice to take a bait. Inspired by some forgotten source, I called them 'margin walkers', since, irritated by parasitic sea lice, which attach to their tails and gills, they could be seen leaping clear of the waves or dancing between air and water, like their cousins the salmon.

As a lure, my father and I would cast strips of mackerel belly, presented on barbless hooks to imitate sand eels; and buoyed along the outer edges of the weed beds by inconspicuous, translucent plastic floats, threaded along delicate monofilament lines. It was no doubt a fitting coincidence that my mother loved the easy-to-catch mackerel, grilled or smoked, because delicious though the sea trout were, I would have found the killing of *one* creature merely to facilitate the capture of *another*, to have been wholly unpalatable. Absolute truth to tell: I never really cared much for fishing *at all*: particularly not the *killing* part. Even by my fourth year of life, I would frequently down rod and wander as far as I could get away with, towards the large boulders behind the shore, or (best of all!) in the direction of the low cliffs up at Loch Tuath, on the Isle of Mull; and I would pick out what seemed to present themselves as the most 'interesting' routes to the top. The exhilaration of the ascent and the alternate perspective on one's surroundings that the view from the summit would provide: *those* were the drivers for this growing inclination to climb. "Get him *down*, Donnie!" my mother would demand anxiously of my father, concerned as she often was throughout my early years, about her little 'rock monkey'.

The partial misnomer was both understandable and easy to forgive.

Whereas my mother was an intelligent and reserved figure, always quietly *there* with considered, sensible advice, my father was a man of whom I was often in awe. Unlike some fathers and their sons, we shared little in the way of common interests, but I was more-often-than-not sure that he loved me. Aside from such a fundamental, however, our relationship was almost paradoxical. He had – just like *his* father – been a fisherman (and hunter): as much to survive in a harsh environment as anything else. But *I* had come into the world in the post-Tony Curtis era of the *teenager*, when sons no longer had to be only slight modifications of their fathers: and heaven knows, I was *very* little like mine.

26

"When my information changes, I alter my conclusions.
What do you do, sir?"

— John Maynard Keynes

In conveying how it was between us, I might best refer again to two of the classical elements. He seemed to me to be solid and still, almost like a creature rooted in the earth. Possessed of a bull-like physical strength and great determination, he was wise to matters that, as a youngster, I might often overlook; and notwithstanding the modesty of his formal education, he provided me early on with sound and ongoing introduction to this or that dialectic and apposite fields of logic and espousal. In growing up under his auspices, I thereby developed the discipline of approaching issues from as many angles as my imagination and intellect might afford me, before adopting a particular (loose) stance: I sensed intuitively that *opinions*, once arrived at, might as easily become *burdens* as benefits.

I sometimes wonder why he never went forward for officer training, but I never asked him about it. Most likely, he just liked being a fire engine driver.

In contrast to my perception of my father, I must have appeared to him like some fleet, airborne creature: constantly full of questions and inclined as much to tangential, mental gymnastics as I was to completing dull household chores at dizzying speed.

Seldom had a bad word passed between us, but it was not until many years later, as *he* walked another 'margin' – between this life and whatever comes after it – that we shared a more complete understanding.

It was an evening in the early spring of 1993 and, for periods throughout the day, I had been sitting beside his bed, where he was dying slowly of cancer.

Some months before, my mother had reached the retirement age of sixty-five, in her job of looking after elderly tenants at Jedworth Court, a sheltered housing complex in Bearsden, near Glasgow. We had first moved there as a family in the mid-seventies, when I was twelve; and both my sister and I had attended Bearsden Academy, the local secondary school.

Part of my mother's agreement with her employers, the social work department of Strathclyde Regional Council, was that she and my father would be rehoused in suitable accommodation upon her retirement. Instead, they were offered a flat situated directly above a pub, and which could be accessed only via a flight of thirty-two steps. Notwithstanding the restrictions imposed by an artificial hip joint, my father's ability to walk was, by then, diminished by cancer to the most pathetic order.

Understandably, my parents declined the proffered lodgings. The council were nonetheless merciless in their insistence that no alternative offer would be made.

During the morning of that spring day, again while sitting with my father in the downstairs dining room, which we had adapted as a bedroom when he could no longer manage the stairs, I listened through the thin adjoining wall as an eviction order was served on my mother. Given the circumstance of my father's impending death – something of which her erstwhile employers were well aware – this was a barbaric imposition, which served most effectively to compound her agitation at that time.

Less than a year before, my father's progressed oesophageal carcinoma had been 'overlooked' by the pathology department at Glasgow's Western Infirmary. He was sent home with medication formulated to assuage the effects of indigestion, and my mother told to 'stop worrying'. One week later, at my mother's insistence, my father was admitted to Gartnavel General Hospital and his cancer was diagnosed. Following an exploratory operation, it was discerned that secondary malignancy was widespread and a prognosis of three months' survival time was made. He was fitted with a bypass tube to facilitate the passage of food to his stomach, and then sent home, where he survived for almost a further year.

Knowing my father as she did, and finding the consultant surgeon empathetic, my mother was able to secure an agreement that my father would not be told, point-blank, of his bleak prospects. As it was, he probably suspected the extent of the gravity of his situation anyway, but my mother's long and varied nursing experience had made her well aware of the importance of a positive outlook in particular cases.

In the hope of setting a seal on this accord, my mother telephoned the local surgery. The GP with whom she spoke, however, was in no way disposed to accede to any such received wisdom. He insisted that any direct enquiry from my father would be met with a complete and forthright appraisal of his condition. By 1993, however, the tendency in certain areas of Scottish medicine to substitute inflexible administrative policy for basic human decency no longer came as a surprise to me.

In the silence of that early spring evening, I turned these conspicuous events of the day – and of the preceding year – over and over in my mind.

"I never lost confidence, you know ..." It was my father's voice. Deep in contemplation, I had been oblivious to the gradual quickening of his suppressed breathing. He trailed off for a moment and then became lucid again.

"… Except once. It was at Cheapside. I came on duty the next morning and discovered the bodies of a couple of my friends: men I *worked* with."

Cheapside was a street on Glasgow's south side, where a number of adjacent whisky-bonded warehouses had exploded, to devastating effect, one evening a few years before I was born. A number of firemen lost their lives in the course of that night. Back then, during the first twelve years or so of his career, before he had trained to be a driver, my dad had also been a fire fighter.

My father's outburst was so completely unexpected that, for a moment, I struggled for any words of response. Then, selfishly, I began to want to hold his attention, there in the material plane, for just a little while longer. In first experiencing a sense of foreboding that this conversation would be our last, there had come to my mind something that I needed to share with him. It was just that I was not yet sure of how to broach the matter.

Firstly, and more importantly, however, was this notion of 'confidence' that he had raised. I wanted to reassure him about God, and Christ's mission of redemption for fallen souls, but instead I found myself launching into a footballing metaphor.

"You know," I blurted out, "In a game that I was hardly 'cut out' for, but throughout much of my youth found difficult to *escape*, I was never the most dedicated *passer* of the ball. More often than not, I would choose to ignore that football is a *team* game; but I daresay that ever since I can remember, I must have emerged with possession in over ninety-five per cent of the *tackles* I've been involved in. Even *so*, that's not something I've ever become cocky about. You see, neither confidence nor that ridiculous piety called 'Team Spirit', with which it is forever bound up, have ever really *figured* with me. I mean, I could *define* confidence for you: that's to say I well understand its denotation and connotations, but I've never really had any *use* for it."

I was talking quick-fire now, as I used to on our walks together: up hills or between the car and our regular fishing spots.

"I would be uncomfortable in deciding how to tackle a problem much in advance of my stepping right up to it. And the thing *is*, I wouldn't have it *any* other way. Somehow, *purposefulness*, almost *independent* of the conscious mind, lends a poetic aspect to *any* game: and maybe to much *else* in life. Some folk might say that's nothing other than improvisation, but what I'm talking about is more like *meditation*, wherein the intended outcome can be generated almost *independently* of time, without recourse to elaborate process or dependence on self-confidence: a bit like Shaw's assertion that the *unconscious* self is the true genius, I suppose. Come to think of it, I would be hard-pressed to distinguish between some of the sensations I experience in reading, say, *Keats's* poetry, from those induced by old footage of George Best in his heyday."

I looked up, having suddenly realised that my rambling discourse might well have been sending him back to sleep, but he was still very much awake, his smiling eyes brighter that I had seen them in a long time. He had the look of being way ahead of me: waiting up at some point that I had yet to reach.

"You just be *careful*, lad! That little outer island devil won't let up. You need to be especially on your guard – for yourself *and* your mother – from *here on in*."

Unbeknown to my dying father, I had, towards the end of the previous year (1992), extended and completed an investigation of the aforementioned 'devil', which *he* had begun in the early part of 1988. His interest in MacSween's background and extracurricular pursuits had been piqued by the revelations of an elderly 'well-to-do' couple, who had befriended my father throughout the course of a series of conversations while, in his retirement years, he had worked as a Children's Patrol Crossing Officer (aka 'Lollipop Man') in Milngavie. I do not imagine that this work had been by choice, but rather that he had taken it up simply because the exigencies of the family economy had demanded it.

MacSween had formerly been an occasional dinner guest at the elderly couple's home, but having gotten wind of some of his more detestable activities, they had abruptly cut all ties with him. To my father's astonishment, they had particular knowledge of MacSween's involvement in my gross mistreatment (and wrongful exclusion) while I was a medical student – a few years before that time – and laid low by what developed into a life-threatening (viral) illness, from which I eventually made a full recovery. The couple were, by my father's account to me, explicitly forthcoming with all that they knew about the matter.

Apparently, I had been an 'early adopter' of language, both in its spoken and written forms, and my parents had passed to my godmother copies of both a jotter of my early scrawling and an old reel-to-reel audio tape of my spoken thoughts and musings on whatever was preoccupying me at aged one-and-a-quarter: the quality of my most recent 'Farley's' rusk, my views on the recently (2015) vilified (by its original broadcaster, the BBC) 'Watch with Mother', and other such matters of great import, I now imagine.

My godmother was Mary Stewart (né MacSween, and a second cousin of the aforementioned 'Roddy'). Unbeknown (at that time) to my parents, Mary took it upon herself to present my recorded output to this burgeoning psychopath, for his consideration. *This*, she would probably have done with some accompanying 'highland' epithet of the manner of: 'such a *clever* wee boy'.

Soon afterwards, a long-running dispute developed between them. I have never been able to discern its nature, but I cannot quite imagine how *anyone* could have arrived at the condition of enmity with a soul as gentle and kind as 'Aunt' Mary. I would later discover, to my abject horror, that MacSween's interest – and the interest of more than one of

32

his 'superiors' – in my progress *pre-dated* those events. All that befell, came about *not* merely – as I had speculated in the early summer of 1988 – in consequence of one mentally ill individual's determination to 'prove' a *confirmation bias*, which had been sparked by (his) familial hatred, but by something *much* more sinister.

When in 1980, MacSween was apprised of my choice of higher educational pathway, he moved decisively and all but unchallenged against me, using the tremendous leverage that he had amassed over certain colleagues at the (by then) much-diminished Faculty of Medicine at The University of Glasgow. Following my decision not to graduate in a BSc. – undertaken, naïvely in an attempt to gain readmission to Medicine – from G.U. in 1990, after I had been manoeuvred (in the third year) into the 'chokepoint' of his *Experimental Pathology* course, MacSween had rained down, like boiling water on rice, all the (considerable) resources that he could command to inflict a manner of *living hell* on my parents' lives: 'raids' on their finances; anonymous threatening phone calls; regularly repeated vandalizing of their property, including: the wrecking of my study-cum-workshop-cum-laboratory at their place in Bearsden, plus several break-ins at their cottage, located in an area where such events were – *back then* at least – largely unheard of; an assault and robbery on my mother, one evening while she was walking near Bearsden Cross, with another break-in having taken place during our subsequent attendance at A&E; and the discovery, upon our return, of a family photograph that had been removed from its frame, the image of my mother's head excised from the print, and the picture then replaced in the frame; plus a host of other 'inexplicable' impediments to the smooth running of daily domestic living, each of which, in *isolation*, would have amounted to little more than a temporary irritation. *Cumulatively*, however, they constituted nothing less than unerring torment.

33

I have little doubt that even certain 'persons of interest' to the *Staatssicherheitsdienst* of the former GDR would have had to endure less in the way of iniquitous vicissitudes.

Somewhere in the course of *his* investigations in 1988, my father had slipped up and been 'punished' with an attempt on his life, in the form of slivers of glass delivered in the substance of a west end restaurant meal. He had almost 'bled out' over the course of the following twenty-four hours: something that might have been a mercy, in view of the prolonged atrocious suffering and death that that episode subsequently brought him to.

In taking up the baton of his endeavours (in late 1992), I did things that pushed the limits of my abilities – at that time – *way* beyond anything that I would come to undertake throughout the year that followed. As for detailed description of the techniques and methods that I employed, I would – writing even *today* (2015) – have considerable difficulty in finding a meaningful common frame of reference for conveying same to just about *anybody*. What is more-or-less *certain* is that the *methods* that I used in applying my very limited *physical* resources would have been deemed illegal; and what is *suggestive* is that when, in remaining credulous hope of due process, I eventually presented my dossier of written, photographic and recorded audio and video evidence against MacSween, at Milngavie Police Station in early 1993, I was *not* arrested.

After a very long wait, that day – for the arrival of a superintendent from Pitt Street, in Glasgow, and a 'plain clothes' individual, who was neither introduced to me nor, I suspect, a *policeman* – I was, following an incongruously *brief* interview, *threatened* with arrest; but when I challenged them to do just *that*, with blithe expression of my delight that these very serious matters might at last come under public scrutiny in open court, they backed off. I never saw them (or the dossier) again, and I received no further contact on the matter.

In his short 'prose poem', *The Generous Gambler*, Charles Baudelaire wrote that 'the greatest trick the devil ever pulled was convincing the world that he doesn't exist'. Nowhere better is this exemplified than in reference to Freemasonry. The mere mention of it summons up, for many, the image of a portentous 'jobs for the boys' club of silly men, with its weird rituals, secret handshakes and rolled-up trouser legs.

'I do conscientiously and sincerely believe that the Order of Freemasonry, if not the greatest, is one of the greatest moral and political evils under which the Union is now labouring ... a conspiracy of the few against the equal rights of the many ... Masonry ought forever to be abolished. It is wrong – essentially wrong – a seed of evil, which can never produce any good.'

US President John Quincy Adams, *Letters on Freemasonry*, 1833.

Note the date of this written statement by the last *non-Freemason* president of the United States of America! And they have been slipping into the world unannounced, and strangling most of their perceived opponents in the crib – and proceeding to go about other wicked business, effectively unchallenged – for a *lot* longer than that.

Although almost nobody seems to be paying attention anymore (induced 'Conspiracy Fatigue': *another* good trick), the evidence for Freemasonry having at its core the worship of the fallen 'Light-Bearer'[1], Lucifer is, today, not

---

[1] More accurately: 'Light-*Thief*'

difficult to discern; and even a cursory search through the mutually self-aggrandising web entries of *pia fraus* 'son of the manse' MacSween and his inner circle of criminally over-promoted cronies, reveals a plethora of undisguised masonic connections. Many of these connections are with other individuals involved in *medical* practice.

To be *crystal-clear*: outside of general practice, the great majority of senior medics (in *this* country, at least) are now freemasons.

This is what Scotland, and the UK as a *whole* – although removal of the 'w' would seem to make ever-more sense – has long-since permitted: and *continues* to permit. In this post-MacSween, post-Angiolini, post-Kelly, post-outrage after outrage era, are you really all just resignedly uninterested *humanists* now: clown-sized footprint-leaving, submissively accepting victims of a non-linear war against individuality, which renders each of you mindlessly content to go on pecking away at the touchscreens of your annually updated devices, assembled by Chinese teenagers and incorporating cobalt and rare earth elements, scraped with broken spoons by Congolese pre-adolescents from the walls of near-airless (if not already water-flooded) narrow mineshafts, and delivered across the oceans by direfully polluting cargo ships … just so that you can say that you are using so much less *paper* these days?

In this new age of *extinction* where, amidst the pornographication of almost *everything*, values are disappearing like mist in a stiff morning breeze, will you have to find yourselves in situations worse than even that of today's Libyan, Syrian, and other refugees – risking all to try and escape a veritable hell-on-earth, the creation of which your current, increasingly unreachable leaders (*posing* as so-called humanists) played no small part in – before you collectively demand measures to tackle the *cancer*, constituted and metastasized by the likes of MacSween and his ilk occupying positions in public life? By then, of course, it will be too late.

Anyway, suspending all that for a moment: perhaps … *electronically*, I should, in the interests of balance, point out how much *easier* it has become, over the last couple of decades, to access decent organic coffee, fine biodynamic wine, and even delicious dairy- and lecithin-free chocolate. And where would *any* of us be without any of *those* essentials?

And as for each individual Freemason involved directly in this obscenity: do you have even an *inkling* of what you are letting yourself in for? There come to mind a couple of lines from Upton Sinclair's 1906 novel, *The Jungle*, a study of the hardships endured by Lithuanian immigrants working in Chicago's stock yards: 'Life, for all its cares and terrors is no such great thing after all but merely a bubble upon the surface of a river.' We may all 'have it coming', but *what* exactly – if you do not take the opportunity that life yet affords you to extricate yourself from such vileness – have *you* got coming when *your* bubble bursts?

Both my parents came from the inner Hebridean island of Mull, and we would holiday there, usually once or twice each year. As I continued to sit beside my father's bed on that spring evening, there next came a moment when it was as if he and I really *were*, once again, walking at dusk, up through the hazel wood, above the rocks near Torloisk, on the island's north-west coast.

I spoke into his eyes: "You know, I read somewhere that, in the past – and maybe to some extent *today* – certain doctors train in surgery or pathology because the very nature of those areas of discipline afford a socially-acceptable means of sublimating sadistic and other depraved impulses:

sawing people's legs off in record time, before effective anaesthetics were discovered; 'abusing' cadavers: *those* kinds of things. So, I guess that what I'm trying to say is that although I was heedful of what you told me about MacSween in the summer of '88, I just wish that I had gotten 'off my marks' a little more quickly – in terms of trying to find some sort of effective … workable … *acceptable* defence strategies … *remedies*."

"I'm sorry I let you down, lad."

"Let me *down*? No, you did *not*, Dad. You stuck your *neck* out for me. How many fathers do *that* for their offspring?"

"I just mean that I could have been less discouraging: less *harsh* on you, at times."

"Don't be *daft*: you're *fine*!" I replied, as I found myself thinking about the first of only two occasions on which we had gone to the cinema together: a *double bill* – as still occurred in the mid-seventies – at the local *Rio* film theatre. Fortunately, we had *just* managed to sit through the execrable *Eiger Sanction*. '*Fortunately*', because the second film was Sydney Pollack's *Three Days of the Condor*: a fairly successful distillation of James Grady's novel, *Six Days of the Condor*; and it had given us much fodder for discussion throughout the twenty-minute walk home: particularly Cliff Robertson's CIA deputy director, *Higgins*' speech at the film's end.

'God rest ye merry, gentlemen'

I had not always *liked* my father, but in that moment – sitting beside his deathbed – I knew that I loved him; and realising that he had been waiting patiently for some time, I let go entirely of my self-consciousness and hurled towards the inevitable.

"Old thing, I've been running up against a brick wall for a decade: trying to get back on the path I know I'm meant for. Do you think I'll ever make anything of my life?"

Perhaps I ought to have shut up right there and then and listened for his answer, but I was uncharacteristically fired up and 'on a roll'.

"I mean, I see medicine and the so-called *caring* professions – in *Glasgow* at least – run by a minority of not-so-well-educated degenerates. *You* know the talent that's in me, and I'll be damned if I'm going to fade away or drift into some area of work that I have no love for, because of the uncalled-for attentions of a deranged little sadist, who until less than five years ago, I had never *met* or even *heard of.*"

"I'm not that old, and I do believe you're ranting," came back my father's now fragile voice.

"Well, you're no *spring chicken*, and I *do* believe you're smirking!" I joked. I think he might otherwise have laughed at that, but he was just too tired and hurting to manage anything more than a wry smile.

Then, I made to speak to him of my most pressing concern. *She* was the only person that he had seen me with who I could ever remember him commenting on, and I knew that he liked her.

"Mr MacKinnon?" she had once begun an enquiry, as the three of us drove up to Loch Fyne, in a van hired to transport some furniture to the cottage.

"Call me *Donnie!*" he had insisted, to my amusement: although not to my *surprise*, given how taken he seemed to be with her. And call him 'Donnie' she did: as *ever*, effortlessly and guilelessly beguiling as falling comets.

However, the usually reserved, steady and measured Taurean – even in that wretched state that he had come to, nearly four hard years later – had somehow gotten ahead of me again.

"You still miss her?"

"All the time," I replied, trying to return his smile. "The sight and scent of her, the image of her face, her touch, her very *presence*: the excitement and stillness, contentment … wonderment. I have of late, and on and off, been in the company of others where she has been present, but *all* these things – while I find myself in this more-often-than-not state of unaccustomed … *inflicted* … *numbness* – all of these things that I fear that I'm beginning to not quite … *remember*…

Sometimes now, I move as I imagine the *damned* do. *Then*, in rare moments, I *know* that the true *essence* of her is in my heart and that even with *every day* that she may seem further from me, I've consoled myself with the thought that we will be close *again*. The *thing* is, you see, I *love* her. In some odd sense, I feel as though I have *always* loved her. But if my unexplained and confusing conduct towards her, these past three years and more has had even a *fraction* of the impact on her that it has had on me, then what manner of 'devil' does that now make …?"

With that, I paused and was lost for I don't know how long, in some mindless daze. Then, I noticed my father again: just looking at me, still smiling.

"'Toxic by association': that's the expression, isn't it? What I want most – with the *best* part of me – is for her to be *happy*: for her to have a *good* life; though rendered as I have been, this decade past, I just don't see how I could contribute towards that for her anytime *soon*. And I *will* be damned if I'll risk again her being troubled by the disfavour of that little fiend, just by dint of perceived association with *me*. I would not chance her being further entangled, to even the *slightest degree*, in my predicament. Maybe once she is clear of Glasgow … *who* knows?"

As I had continued to speak, I had become sensible of my composure teetering on the edge of disintegration; and

40

with the sudden recognition of both my lacking any mechanism for maintaining my equilibrium in the face of such raw and unalloyed reflections, plus my selfish self-absorbed monopolising of our conversation, I checked myself: *doubly* embarrassed.

"Forgive me: you must be in need of a rest!"

> I went out to the hazel wood,
> Because a fire was in my head

From: *The Song of Wandering Aengus*, by William Butler Yeats

Momentarily, his fading grin seemed to become almost conspiratorial. Then he said something that I shall never forget: not so much for the form of language that he employed, but rather for his precise intonation in voicing it. He said, "I think that everyone has his day."

In the hazel wood, on the steep slope between the rocks and the sky, our sensibilities came as close as they ever would. I hoped that he meant something profound, such as that, *somehow*, all would be well: that I would get back to Medicine and have a life with her. But as ever it was with my father and me, there was that slightly awkward, perplexing gulf: that imponderable impediment to full mutual understanding.

Shortly afterwards, he drifted back into a diamorphine-induced sleep. Although we never spoke again, we had – *both* of us, in as well-intentioned a manner as ever we each had done – *covered the ground* together.

The next morning, my mother told me that she had spoken briefly with him in the night and that he had said a peculiar but heartening thing: "Don't worry about Brian: he'll make it yet!"

Some days later, my mother would decide to pursue legal action in order to overturn the eviction order. In this she was successful, but by that time my father had died.

In order to preserve my own sense of integrity, I could discern no alternative to a rather more radical form of action; and that sudden – if unfamiliar – sense of 'cold rage' that overtook me at the sight of my father's atrocious and untimely demise, served only to intensify my resolve to project myself along that hasty desperate trajectory.

Chapter Three

23rd June 2015

I appear to be standing in the corridor of one of the old annexes of Bearsden Academy, beside Morven Road. I turn to look towards the classroom on my right. The door is open. Inside, I can see Dr Hunter, the R.E. teacher, sat at his desk. He is an old, tall foreboding-looking man: bespectacled and with lean craggy features and short grey hair. He does not appear to notice me. It strikes me that Dr Hunter, given his advanced age back when I last saw him, would – were he still *alive* – look *much* older now; and I am also aware that Bearsden Academy no longer *exists* beside Morven Road. Although I have not dreamt of that place for years, I realise that I *am* dreaming.

Although I invariably 'did my bit' to contribute towards the activities in those classes – which were compulsory back then (1975 – '77) – I had never enjoyed religious education. I sensed all *manner* of life everywhere around me, and I was drawn to Christian ethical-moral values, but I could not reconcile my sensibilities with the dictate that human intercessors – in the form of churches and their ministers or priests – had any business in what were, essentially, *personal* matters. It was therefore of some surprise to me when, in late 1977, while I was in my third year of secondary school, Dr Hunter, or 'Josh' as the boys almost *inevitably* called him, sent for me to come to his classroom one afternoon. He was keen that I should enter an essay-writing competition, which had been set (for high school entrants throughout Scotland) by Stirling University.

The subject was 'Why do we suffer?' I *liked* the question. It seemed to be one of fundamental importance. As preparation, I read a couple of texts, including 'The Problem of Pain' by C. S. Lewis. However, in the mainly Christian-based tradition that was bound up in the books that I studied, I could discern no satisfactory answer. I was one of two individuals awarded first prize (£50), although I am not sure as to *why*: there was hardly anything revolutionary – or even *revelatory* – in my conclusions. Riled by the inadequacy of what I had gleaned, and prompted by a quickly growing suspicion that I – and, by extension, Christians *generally* – had been 'sold a pup', I deemed the subject worthy of further (and more particular) investigation.

At that time, however, I had no conception of just how long and absorbing that investigative process would become.

'Those who love wisdom must investigate many things'

— Heraclitus

It would be over fourteen years later before I would discover a copy of the 'Pistis Sophia', a Gnostic text in which Jesus is quoted as having said – in connection with the return of a soul from the 'beyond', and into a human body – that the soul drinks from a "cup the drink of forgetfulness."

The belief in the rebirth of a soul is as old as humankind. The law of cause and effect (in the *spiritual* as well as the physical sense) and the idea that a human being can incarnate several times, are entirely 'normal' beliefs for more than 50% of all people. These concepts can be found in *all* cultures: not merely in those of the East, as many people have been led to think.

The concept of reincarnation was part of both Ancient Egyptian and Greek philosophy, and there were – and are – over and over again, great minds, authors and thinkers who approbate that we may live on earth *often*, to 'purify' ourselves. At the time of Jesus, the concept of reincarnation was also found in Jewish popular belief.

The Jewish religion scholar Schalom Ben-Chorin writes: 'Apparently the concept of reincarnation was a popular belief in Judaism at the time of Jesus … So people thought Jesus was one of the old prophets who had come again …' (Luke. 9:8 & 19).

During the time of the Early (or 'Gnostic') Christianity, in numerous scriptures passed from hand to hand, the concept of reincarnation was assumed as a matter of course. The Pistis Sophia stands prominently amongst those scriptures. However, the Pistis Sophia, like many other scriptures, was not included in the official canon of the church Bible. Towards the end of the second century, the developing church of power, which Jesus of Nazareth did not found, first began to favour certain texts over others. This process of purposeful selection ended only towards the end of the fourth century.

In the year 383, Jerome (345-420), received from Pope Damasus I the task of compiling a unified Latin Bible text. What emerged from this assignment is the so-called *Vulgata Bible*, 'sold' right up until the present day to people as the faultless word of God. However, Jerome had anything other than a unified text for a basis. There are presently 4860 known Greek handwritten copies of the New Testament, no two of which are the same. Theologians today count circa 100,000 different versions. Jerome, a seemingly *conflicted* individual, who changed approximately 3500 passages in the gospels during his work, wrote to the pope at that time: "Is there a man …, who will not, when he takes the volume

[Bible] in hand ..., break out immediately into violent language, and call me a forger and a profane person for having the audacity to add anything to the ancient books, or to make any changes or corrections therein?"

What *was* it that Jerome omitted, and *what* did he add? Moreover, what did he *change*?

Above all, this refers to the knowledge of reincarnation and the pre-existence of the soul. Jerome knew very well that reincarnation was part of the Early Christian teachings. In a letter, he wrote about the Early Christian teacher Origen (185-254), stating that according to Origen's teachings, the souls of human beings "change their bodies." In another of his letters, there is the statement: "Since ancient times, the teaching of reincarnation had been ... pronounced as a belief that was passed down."

It is via the teachings of Origen that it can be discerned how active the teaching of reincarnation was in Early Christianity, before it became a victim of a conspiracy of the caste of priests. He was, without doubt, the best-known and most significant scholar of Christian antiquity. His teachings and life seem to have 'spiritually brightened' the entire Mediterranean region for over three centuries. The pre-existence of the soul was also part of the teaching that he promulgated.

However, Origen lived during a time in which the reversal of Early Christianity into an institution of power built on external rituals and customs taken from paganism was already in full swing. He was treated with intense hostility during his lifetime.

Origen's writings were already falsified by the end of the 4th century and were systematically destroyed by representatives of the Church. Only a scarcity of his original writings still exists today. Nevertheless, Origen's teachings were spread over much of Europe by way of Arius (c. 260-336) and Wulfila (313-383). This 'heresy' was something of a thorn in the side of the Church. Emperor Justinian had Origen's teachings, insofar as they were still known, banned in 543 at a synod of the Eastern Church in Constantinople. This was done in nine martial-sounding *anathemas*.

Reincarnation as such, was not expressly mentioned in these anathemas, but they did bring about the proscription of the teachings of the pre-existence of the soul and the '*restoration of all things*': that is, that all people and souls would again be with God and that there is no '*eternal damnation*'.

With this, the Church put an end to the Early Christian teaching of reincarnation, simply because belief in reincarnation releases people from all dogmas and ecclesiastical laws: thus, rendering Churches redundant.

It might seem reasonable to speculate that if Jerome had included this Early Christian knowledge about reincarnation, contained in Origen's writings – as well as in the apocryphal gospels – in the Bible, and thus made it available to western culture, the past 1700 years would have taken a completely different course, with mankind actualizing totally different, *higher* ethical-moral values in daily life: because the acceptance of reincarnation as a reality – and of the law of sowing and reaping – also implies an awareness of responsibility for one's own life and behaviour. However, instead of the teachings of reincarnation and of the love of God for his children, instead of the teaching that God dwells in each one of us and is the life in all things, and that the earth is a place of probation for fallen souls – as Jesus, the Christ, taught to His disciples, and thus to humanity generally – an 'externalising'/worldly doctrine of ceremonies and rites, plus the teaching of eternal damnation and a punishing, cruel God was proclaimed by the Church.

Knowledge is always the ultimate threat to religious superstition. Spiritual knowledge and its corollary, enlightenment, were the ultimate aims/'God' of the Gnostics. Gnostics taught that all spiritual knowledge *could only be experienced directly and immediately by the believer*. No priests were necessary; no pastors, no rabbis. To the Church, built on priesthood, hierarchy and authority, such a teaching was heinous.

Original Christianity has it that the seat of the soul in human beings is close to the anatomical position of the pituitary gland, and that the 'spirit body' is constituted by seven connected consciousness centres, situated along the length of the spinal cord. From bottom to top, they are: Order, Will, Wisdom, Justice or Earnestness, Patience, Love (in the head) and Mercy (top of the head). The centre of Mercy is connected to the 'Divine Wellspring'.

I doubt that their inclusion in standard Anatomy texts will come about anytime soon, but, to me, they 'feel' about right.

Heaven, according to the Gnostics, has *seven* dimensions, far removed from the *time* and *space* experienced in this dense *material* realm.

Interestingly, Jerome is also notable for his prejudice against the activity of dreaming lucidly.

The early gnostic Christians used the metaphor of the lucid dream as one of their central images for unity with God; and in the fifth century, Greek bishops would tell people that while they dream, 'the soul is taken to a superior region where it can come in contact with true things'.

Jerome (later canonized as *Saint* Jerome, thus proving the old adage 'It's not *what* you know …') himself had a dream that had far-reaching consequences. In it he perceived that he had been given a message to desist from studying the pagan literature that so fascinated him. Many of these texts were concerned with lucid (and *active*) dreaming techniques and practices. He therefore interpreted this 'message' to mean that he should turn his back on lucid/active dreaming as a whole. His ensuing prejudice against it was therefore also reflected in his fifth century 'translation' of the Bible into Latin. He selectively mistranslated many passages mentioning witchcraft, as also encompassing lucid dreaming. Suddenly, this Vulgata Bible, full of passages saying that working with dreams was wrong, was inflicted on an unsuspecting and, sadly, all too credulous public; and the history of dreaming within Christian culture was changed for the foreseeable future. When, in the thirteenth century, the influential Christian philosopher, Thomas Aquinas, suggested that 'some dreams come from demons'; and (in the 1500s) Jesuit priests went as far as to claim that 'the devil is almost always implicated in dreams', that seemed to put the kibosh on the whole thing for Christians everywhere.

Back in my own now-lucid dream, I close my eyes and begin:

"When I open my eyes …" But before I can complete, I hear a peculiar noise to my right and, reopening my astral eyes, I observe that another door has appeared on the wall of the annex corridor: a little way along from the opened door of the R.E. classroom. I move towards it, open it and step through. I seem to be in a laboratory of sorts, with marker boards on the wall. I am sensible of a figure, a little way off and behind me, to my left. I somehow know that it is the tall, once silver figure of earlier dreams.

Many years before, in the 'real' waking world, while pursuing a line of enquiry related to the subject matter outlined earlier in this chapter, I had come across a prayer in a short text; and feeling at a very low ebb, as I did on that day, I recited it aloud and with desperate hope that it might help me:

'O Angel of God, my Guardian dear,
To whom His love commits me here,
Ever this day be by my side
To light and guard, to rule and guide'

This verse comes back to me, even before I turn to look at the figure in my lucid dream, and I am again – just as I was when I first had sight of the verse – momentarily disgruntled by the inclusion of 'rule'. On first sight of it, my natural inclination had been to raise objection to it, as a modern-day bride might remonstrate against the inclusion of 'obey' in her marriage vows. However, I had nonetheless simply spoken the verse as written.

As I meet his gaze now, he speaks.

"You have never asked my name."

"What might I call you: Embalmer? ... Benign *Dictator*? Are you even *entirely* benign?" I demand.

He regards me coolly ... impassive.

"You know," I continue, "due consideration of the principle of *Occam's razor* tells me that when I hear the sound of horses' hooves, I should first think of *horses*, not *unicorns*. I further know that there is often a false sense of lucidity that accompanies grief – in *waking* life at least – but I've been doing this a *long* time, and whatever the insistent *debunking* dictates of these days, I *know* that you are *no* part of *me*. It *was* you, wasn't it: that slow *ingress* ... all those years ago: like cold fluidic tendrils around – and into – my heart and other organs ... into the very *blood* that courses through my body?"

"You had a lot to cope with brother. It would have been too much for *anyone*: even *you*."

"And now: the *murderous* fallout of these past months, since you let go of me. What *now*, as I find myself lost and still without her, or anything else that once seemed to promise to be my *life*: just as though it were the day after that awful day twenty-two years ago, when I expressed to her my heartfelt desire that she should have a *great life*? I have been accused of obsessing over a stolen education. Lest my accusers might lay claim to having anything resembling a *point*, I should not like to add *lost love* to that."

"You do not *summon* these lasting feelings for her, do you?"

"No, they just … *well up*. They just keep welling up in me."

"And have they changed over all those years?"

"No. But you have … *lenified* …"

"And would you have it so that you had never been with her, had never even *met* her?"

"*No*, I would *never* wish that! But what of *free will*? Is it just a *lie*? Is it, one way or another, all just determinism, as so many of the current crop of researchers and theorists would have everyone believe?"

The question had the seed of my next question in it.

"Is it that no one and nothing matters *after all*? Daniel Dennett's assertion that 'we are determined to be masters of our own fate, to a surprising and gratifying degree' seems to me, these days like little more than a sop to a burgeoning baying majority."

"You just came under fierce and sustained attack brother, and entreating me as you did, it fell to me to aid you. And *what* do you think made you 'imagine' that the speed of *thought* may exceed that of *light*. Where might the 'proving' of *that* leave the spurious claims of this 'current crop'?

51

Where would that leave their experimental designs? And if you would seek truth in the bandying of quotes, then why not Bertrand Russell: 'The fact that an opinion has been widely held is no evidence whatever that it is not utterly absurd.'?"

"Well," I ponder, my mind readjusting: once more *reaching*, "it is argute to maintain an open mind, but not one *so* open that your *brain* falls out!"

"When you think about it, thinking about thinking is the hardest sort of thinking there is, which makes you think ..."

— Philomena Cunk (Diane Morgan)

"*Quantum entanglement*:" I muse, as much to myself as to him, "as regards the speed of *thought*?"

"And a wholly overlooked, fundamental error concerning response latency," he adds.

I am lost in contemplation for some moments.

"Does it fall to me to *thank* you?" I ask at last. "Because, you see, I just cannot *feel* that gratitude yet."

"In your own time," he smiles. "It seems you *do* have heart *after all* brother; and I sense that it is full of *song*." And as he speaks, there is new abundance of that sparkling light in his eyes.

"Aye ... and these past months, since you finally let go of me, I sing it out to her: *that's* what I do. Right or wrong, I can do no otherwise. Am I just *weak* after all?"

"No, quite the contrary."

"I don't think I *quite* understand. What I *do* apprehend though, is that love is sempiternal, and all that I can hope for now is that, before long, I will be enabled to transcend *entirely*, all human feelings and wanting; thinking and striving."

As there is no further response offered to me, I pause, reflectively, and finally I ask him why it was only *then*, after so many years, that he let me go. Again, however, he makes no reply. There is only his persisting compassionate smile; and as it moves now, towards me, expanding and engulfing, the dream quickly fades and I am suddenly awake.

My first thought, on awakening, was of the final lines of a version – a direct translation from the early Gnostic Christian Aramaic – of the Lord's Prayer. In contrast with the pompous-sounding, imperialism of '... the glory, For ever and ever', in The King James Bible version, it comes out as '... *the song for everlasting ages*.' Strangely, in view of the impact of the barely-gone dream on my yet lowly spirit, I was not sure which version I found to be the most unnerving.

Chapter Four

At the beginning of my first complete school day as Brandon Lee, in the waking world of 1993, Mrs Holmes escorted me along the circuitous corridor leading to the rear of the main building. Our destination was another of the annexes, where I was to register each morning and afternoon.

In between short episodes of polite conversation, as we made our way along the stark featureless hallway, I glanced repeatedly at the timetable that had been constructed for me. All five requested subjects were there and I was to be placed in registration class 5C.

Crossing the yard to the annex, I considered the system that I was taking advantage of here. I saw immediately and clearly that an abstraction like 'the system' becomes nothing other than a meaningless *dis*traction, when one is in the thick of things. For a moment, I felt vaguely guilty about not feeling guilty. These were, after all, human beings assisting me here and I could not help but be touched by that. However, this was their paid work, not altruism, and I had my own long-term work aim to pursue. I *knew* that, in the great scheme of things, I *mattered*: so, I *had* to matter to *myself.*

Even in view of this somewhat iconoclastic line of pursuit, my ultimate aim still felt worthwhile and – in the sense that it remained morally justifiable – *legitimate.*

Bull Terrier-like, however, I would not let it go at that. I knew that if I were not caught out, my purpose in all this (regaining a medical school place) would be effected easily, and that it might be argued that such an eventuality would deprive someone else of that place. This was all ground that I had covered before, but I had to be *quite* certain that what I was doing was justifiable, as my plan began to be actualised. I had never been a competitor. The widely esteemed *competitive spirit* had never conveyed any sense of nobility to me. Whatever I did in life stemmed from a gut feeling for what was right and what I knew that I could do well and elegantly: whether that was climbing or medical studies and practice. I had *earned* my place on the MBChB course at Glasgow University, and I had done *nothing* that had justified that place having been taken from me. Once, some years before, when through no fault of my own I had fallen ill, I had been immediately, falsely and criminally characterized as a 'could not'. As surely as I was and am still in the world, I would – and shall *yet* – remedy that vile infliction.

As we mounted the short flight of wooden steps into the annex, all such considerations were overridden by a suddenly – and perplexingly – emerging dread that my time at Bearsden, as Brandon Lee, would be as short-lived as that of one of those unfortunate engineering ensigns on a Star Trek landing party.

As it turned out, I need not have entertained any such fear. Mrs Lightbody, the Modern Studies teacher, who also took the register for 5C, extended to me the same cordial welcome as had Mrs Holmes.

I mean no slight against any of the teachers then at Bearsden Academy. I found the majority of them to be thoughtful and agreeable individuals, but it may well be a truism that the *vast* majority of adults are all too readily accepting of the rubber stamp of officialdom. One might reasonably further suppose that this must be particularly true in a profession as preoccupying and stressful as that of teaching in schools.

For my own part, the striking of a peculiar dual balance between naïve boyishness and maturity; aloofness and reserve, seemed to come easily to me: aided as I was by my light frame and a clear, wrinkle-free complexion.

Whatever the underlying reason(s) for it, I was relieved at my having been so readily accepted. I had been given the initial stamp of approval, and my contrived persona remained unchallenged throughout the year.

Of course, institutions and their servants can, likewise, be damning in their use of stamps and seals: particularly as more and more of those created bodies are moulded into becoming – in terms of their primary function and, increasingly often, with all other functions temporarily or otherwise rescinded – supportive 'limbs' for what Noam Chomsky and others identified as the 'Power Infrastructure'[2]: *not* the 'faces' that you vote into (perceived) power every four or five years. For many in the mid-nineties, this would no doubt have been a startling concept, but in today's (2015) world of intelligence agencies' 'Crisis Actor' groups and major world events being driven via deep occultism … maybe *not* so much so: 'Divide, bind and rule'.

When the 'story' of my endeavour was first brought to light on September 18th, 1995, it was claimed by Alan Douglas and Leslie Anderson, in their 'exclusive' on the BBC's *Reporting Scotland*, that I had been involved in a 'rumpus' in a Tenerife bar. They went on to say that I had

---

[2] The Global 1% – Exposing the Transnational Ruling Class. By Professor Peter Phillips and Kimberly Soeiro. Article available at: http://tinyurl.com/97dsxvh.

subsequently been arrested and found, by local police, to have had two passports, one of which showed me to be a 17-year-old. None of those claims were true. Nevertheless, when that quickly became clear, BBC Scotland broadcast neither a refutation nor an apology: such was their self-assured hubris, even as far back as 1995.

Shortly thereafter, and in between 'correcting the public record' and holding press conferences, the respective deans of Medicine at Glasgow and Dundee Universities saw fit to malign my motives and cast doubt on my integrity. Prior to their little-heralded occurrences, I was not made aware of those press conferences, but over time thereafter, I *did* become aware that they involved the presentation as *bona fide*, of three letters *attributed* to me, although never *written* by me, and not in any handwriting even *vaguely* resembling my own; plus examination essay papers: similarly not mine.

Such a tremendous expenditure of public money to mount a sophistic exercise designed to lend weight and credence to a set of sordid lies; and all to conceal the identity and misdeeds of one of their *own*: a depraved little pimp to (and blackmailer of) the perverted, connected 'powerful', spinelessly craving indulgence in recherché forms of turpitude. Where is the 'integrity' in *that*?

Almost as sickening (for me) has been the discovery (actually, as the result of a tip-off from my one 'source' inside the University of Glasgow) that there was added (in 2009) to their records an indication that I graduated *in absentia*, in science (a BSc.) some nineteen years after the course ended. This is something that I did *not* do, and – for reasons to be disclosed anon – would *never* do.

Transfer into essentially administrative roles by qualified medics is of course necessary and commendable, under a variety of circumstances; but surely these are men whom it behoves to be very cautious about perpetrating *real* fraud, in addition to passing quick and damaging judgement on one who is trying to pursue a similar manner of work to that which they have decided to abandon, either wholly or in part.

A man is *generally* what he feels himself to be. I would hope that these hollow, perverted habitués of the despicable procurer-cum-blackmailer and killer, Mac-Sween, might each read what I write here. Better yet that they might meet me in some open forum to debate the soundness of their reasoning in undertaking these actions and making such assertions. Perhaps I am in no great position to adopt a high moral tone, but I could still show them where integrity grows aplenty: and not only of the *moral* variety, but also the *academic* integrity, that at Glasgow they distinctively – and disgracefully – lack.

As I entered the annex classroom, one glance towards those implacable faces forcefully reminded me of something that I already knew: *youth* is a colossus possessed of tremendous intuitive powers, which are invariably (and sadly) discarded in later life. In most humans, it is in late adolescence that these powers are at their height. As I looked for the briefest aeon into that sea of sixteen year old eyes, I realised that they could not be fooled: not by *me*, anyway.

Maybe it was the rhythm of the time – a couple of years into the rave era, with its harsh, repetitive beats and insistent drones – that saved me, by commanding their comprehensive acquiescence. More likely, they just felt that someone who was obviously over twenty and masochistic enough to go back to school, wasn't worth the bother of a pointed finger of accusation. *Or*, maybe it was the case that I had more of the talent of the *Varou* in me than I gave myself credit for.

I sat alone at a table near the front of the class. There, out on my own, was as a good a place as any to begin each morning and afternoon: after all, there is nothing quite as *enabling* as being out in the open and 'in plain sight' when it comes to hiding successfully. I had my back to the others.

They could see *me*, whereas I couldn't see *them*. I suppose that only served further to keep me 'on my toes'.

One of the girls in 5C was assigned to look after me until I was comfortable with finding my own way around. A quick glance and exchanged disdainful smirks were enough for us to establish our mutual disaffection with this instruction. I intimated that the school map that I had been provided with seemed straightforward enough, and we parted company amicably.

The day did not, however, pass by without a few more worrying moments.

The ability-graded maths classes had already been set in place and I was directed to see the principal of that department, Mr Blair. I remembered Mr Blair well. He had been my maths teacher during my first year at Bearsden Academy, between 1975 and '76.

It was, to say the least, a *tricky* situation in which to find oneself, but with time running out between the inception of my plan and the beginning of the school academic year, I had been unable to find another school (within commutable distance) which: (i) operated a policy of accepting students from outside its catchment area; and (ii) was geared, in any sense, towards fifth (as an acceptable alternative to sixth) year exit.

"So, your father has seen fit to send you up here for the benefit of a Scottish education. *Well* son, you could do a lot *worse*." He was preoccupied with some paperwork on his desk, as he sat in front of a class from the lower school. In the intervening years, he had gained a few more pounds than I had lost, and his mop of red curly hair had turned a little grey. Otherwise, he was the same old Mr Blair: good-humoured, but authoritative; and still calling me 'son'! Mr Blair called all the boys 'son'. It was just part of his way of talking. He looked up only once during our short exchange, and if our eyes met *at all*, it was for a shorter interval than I could usefully register. With guardedly bowed head, I answered his questions about what level of studies I had reached.

Beyond adopting a West Canadian accent – which, somehow, came just about 'naturally' to me anyway – to fit in with my professed background, my one concession to the art of physical disguise had been to perm my normally straight hair. If he did not recognise in me a kindred spirit, then at least he saw before him a not wholly dissimilar phenotype. His voice mellowed a little. "I think we'll put you into the second section son: Mrs Jaffray's class. See how you get *on*, okay?"

"Yes sir."

As far as I knew, mathematics classes were the only ones designated according to past academic record. With university application reports to be written and submitted well before the end of the year, I reasoned that I had little longer than until the end of the *month* to impress my way into section one. As things turned out, that did not prove too difficult.

Later, in the afternoon, all fifth-year pupils taking higher chemistry were herded into one of the ground-floor science labs, and yet another register was called. As a late addition to the school roll, my assumed name had been tagged on at the end of the list; so, with the passing of the 'L' surnames, I relaxed … only to be shocked back into that state called *dread*, the merest discernible moment later.

"Brian McKinnon?" boomed the physics principal's voice. My arm twitched, as my brain busied itself with retrieving any vocal reflex before it manifested itself as sound. I managed to stay silent: *just*!

"Here!" came my near-namesake's voice from the other side of the lab, as a massive surge of adrenaline wreaked havoc throughout my immobilized body.

In rare moments of great stress, I have found it beneficial to concentrate upon my breathing without consciously trying to alter my respiratory rate. The effect is to reduce gradually the sensations of unease and discomfort experienced at such times. I spent the next few minutes *entirely* focused upon my breathing.

"And finally, Brandon Lee?" sounded the department head's voice, one last time.

"Here," I replied, no doubt sounding rattled.

"Brandon *Lee*?" It was a girl's voice from the back of the lab and she followed her startled query with a short burst of giggling.

During the afternoon break, she approached me and asked, with barely concealed incredulity, about my proffered name.

I remember thinking: "What on *earth* is going to go wrong *now*?"

For my edification, she informed me that Brandon Lee was also the name of a martial arts movie star of some note (the son of Bruce Lee). Apparently, he had died a short time before, following an accidental shooting on a film set. Martial arts movies had never been my 'bag', but ironically, I had sourced the name Brandon Lee from film and television. My full name is Brian Lachlan MacKinnon, and mindful that I would have had to reveal my true identity upon graduating from medical school, I wanted in the meantime to retain at least the 'B' and 'L' of my initials. I was determined that *this* much would not change. I was also looking for something short and punchy: in contrast to my cumbersome moniker.

I first heard of the name 'Brandon' on a television show called *Beverly Hills 90210*, and it stuck in my mind. Even after everything that has happened in my adult life, I retain sufficient ego to add that I would never actually have sat down with the intention of *watching* this programme. I just happened to be visiting a friend one evening when the TV was switched on. Anyway, I liked the name and I later found out that, like 'Brian', it is of *Irish* origin. It also has much the same meaning as my own name, insofar as a name can *really* 'mean' anything: something about a meadow or a clearing in a wood. That seems to me an odd denotation for a name, but I am glad to have found it out; and at the risk of being politically incorrect, I *daresay* that I could have done worse: I might have been unwittingly drawn to a name of, say, North American Indian origin, and not found out until too late that it meant 'he who lurks behind the tepee', or 'pissing dog' or some suchlike. 'Lee', I purloined from 'Christopher' of that ilk, because it was short and he was an actor of whom I *was* a fan. As a child, his menacing Count Dracula at once used to terrify and fascinate me.

As the initially amused girl, whose name I cannot now remember, seemed thereafter to be satisfied on this point of nomenclature, I considered briefly the rather cumbersome possibility of 'fiction being stranger than truth being stranger than fiction'. However, that was just too exhausting a notion to dwell upon.

A more appropriate concept for me to have considered back then might have been what the psychoanalyst Carl Jung, together with the quantum physicist Wolfgang Pauli, dubbed 'synchronicity'. This is the idea that events, coincidental in time, are somehow linked by a deeper motivation. Although, in terms of peer pressure, it would have been intellectual suicide for Jung to have made overt indication of such scientific heresy – in as much as psychology is a *science* – I rather suppose that he was talking about God. I would surmise that, even today, an individual pursuing the possibility of studying conventional medicine at an accredited institution would be unwise to expound upon any, as yet *arcane* spiritual law, such as that of *correspondence*. I shall therefore merely indicate whatever rational sense I can of two particular experiences.

The girl with the tale of the actor Brandon Lee would come across to chat with me during a number of the break times, in the few weeks before the summer recess. Whatever influenced her to do so, I cannot imagine.

She looked like the original Wild Child: pink lipstick, blonde hair, minimum length skirt (had it been any shorter, it would have been a belt), maximally uncomfortable shoes and attitude aplenty. All she wanted was to be 'well *shot* of the whole school thing'. Still, she seemed sane enough: even 'cool' – her most oft-employed descriptive – in her own juvenile fashion. I, on the other hand, *bereft* of cool and appearing like some quaint cross between Tim Buckley and 'man at C&A', wanted nothing more than to return to *medical* school and continue my studies there. I was therefore determined to make the best possible impression, academically, during the months ahead.

Our nonchalant conversations were, I suppose, a blessing in that her proximity seemed to deflect approaches from other, possibly hostile, quarters. She most often spoke of Spain and of her boyfriend there.

In August, with the recommencement of school and the beginning of the fifth year proper, she was nowhere to be seen. Someone told me that she had gone to Spain to travel around with the boyfriend. I thought, 'Good on her!', and synchronicity or not, I reasserted my firmest intention never again to be pummelled into giving up what was right for *me* either.

The second striking event occurred two years later, at the end of September 1995.

I had been strongly advised by a journalist called Ron Mackenna, from the Glasgow-based *Herald* newspaper, to take part in a televised 'explanation' of my actions. He was adamant that I take up one of the offers from the BBC. I had

63

not watched any of the television news reports from the previous week, and it was not until some two weeks later that I managed to see someone's videotape of most of them.

My reasoning in approaching a newspaper had been straightforward enough: going out onto the lawn, at 11 Whitehurst – following the several days of preparation that MacSween and his well- and *widely*-placed cronies had had, while I had been zigzagging my way back to Scotland – could, I had reasoned, have been a fatal move ... *literally*!

Since 1991, I have maintained a single contact/source at Glasgow University. For the purposes of this account, I shall refer to him as 'Tom', although that is not his name. We are not exactly *friends*: he seems to derive Schadenfreude from occasionally giving me the 'heads up' on whatever 'challenge(s)' that I am likely to have to cope with next. I have tolerated his sporadic contacts over the years because his information has proven to be consistently reliable. I have also gradually come to accept that the hatred of MacSween that he has, from near the outset of our association, professed to harbour, is genuine. Hours before embarking upon my anfractuous return journey to Glasgow, in September 1995, I called him from Michelrieth in Bavaria. His assessment was, to say the least, *bleak*. Particularly worrying was his sign-off paraenesis that I should 'watch out for myself'.

Whatever the exposure afforded by the varied topography of the expansive backdrop beyond the main road in front of my mother's Whitehurst flat, the placement of a sniper may well, at that juncture, have been *too* bold and dramatic, even for MacSween. Had it not been for Tom's uncharacteristically empathetic exhortation, I might have wished *him* there instead of me: 'Tom', with his inordinately large cranium. *He* would have been a sniper's *gift*.

I still wondered, though, if I could say what I then knew *loudly* enough (*quickly* enough had by then already dissipated as an opportunity) to make them all afraid enough to complete – with the 'short order' murders of both myself and my mother – what MacSween had started. *That* done, the manipulation – in terms of all-important public perception – of the genuinely obscene and outrageous into what Americans term the *penny ante*, would have presented them with few further difficulties: applied *hypodermic needle theory*. From the moment that I had dropped the receiver at the end of Tom's telephone discourse, I had had to accept that keeping my mother alive, in the face of what would be MacSween's redoubled determination to have us killed, would thereafter become a matter of straightforward day-in-day-out pragmatism. As it would turn out, I would cheat him of that goal for only another twelve years.

There must have been a crowd of well over one hundred and thirty out in front of the flat, when I got back; and I would certainly have been very closely surrounded had I gone out there to make my statement. Even with the element of surprise on my side, the few yards from taxi to door had been nerve-wracking enough. I absolutely did *not* wish to walk out into a situation where a stealthily-delivered hypodermic, full of aconitine – or any other of a group of lethal toxins easily 'overlooked' at autopsy – could have been the death of me; with the subsequent coroner's report *inevitably* citing cause of death as some unfortunate (but 'natural') cardiovascular event brought on by stress. It was not so much that I was *afraid* of dying then: I just did not want my mother to have to cope with any more *on her own*. I had only left her *at all* for that week, in capitulation to her chivvying insistences that I 'needed a proper break', and her assurances that my sister would be checking in on her at least twice during my absence.

We had, I think, *both* been much relieved at my return.

The conflation of exhaustion and naïveté was the determinant of my permitting the representatives of *The Herald* to enter the flat. 'If there is a doubt, then there's *no* doubt', a circumspect individual once advised me. My *first* moment of doubt came when, having telephoned their editor, with the offer for publication – without payment – of my written account of my experiences, he had said, "*That's* not how it *works*." At that point, I should of course have told him that I would have been happy to go to another publication, but even by 1995, I still wrongly believed that the West of Scotland's most *respected* newspaper would have had to be respect*able*. With the subsequent redaction of all mention of MacSween in the published 'version' of what I submitted to them (plus various other alterations to- and truncations of my handwritten account), I realised that matters were every bit as grim as I had anticipated that they could conceivably be. Not then fully realising the remarkable extent of the interconnectedness of the various media organisations – although I was about to embark on a very steep learning curve – I still avidly wished to take up the opportunity to put my case via television.

Cave quid optes.

Interviewed on camera by BBC Scotland's Jackie Bird, our discussion filled four twenty-minute tapes. The ensuing half-hour programme, entitled 'The Lives of Brian' – as was revealed to me only just prior to broadcast – contained less than nine minutes of edited extracts from that eighty minutes: far from what I would have considered ideal, but as much, time-wise, as I might realistically have hoped for within a thirty-minute format.

Nevertheless, there was *nothing* else about the programme that might have been considered *balanced*. An expert film and video editor later conveyed to me his amazement at how (and how *crudely*) the continuity of my answers had been tampered with.

The programme was originally broadcast on BBC Scotland *only*, around the first week of October 1995. Later, on 23rd November – and not merely in response to maintained and widespread public interest – it was re-broadcast nationwide in more or less its original form, as part of BBC2's *Public Eye* series. Divorced, as it was, from all three Reithian principles (entertain, educate, inform), it might at least have proven useful for anyone in need of tutting and eye-rolling practice.

At one stage, Bird questioned me about the name 'Brandon Lee', which I explained as I have herein. She then proceeded to follow with "And what about 'Marsha Hunt': the fictitious science tutor, whose name appeared on the progress report which you presented to the school? Marsha Hunt is a former girlfriend of Mick Jagger." This latter question and my response to it were not included in the programme. I still cannot decide whether this was a good or a bad thing for me.

Immediately upon hearing what was put to me, I must have betrayed the sort of surprised expression otherwise seen only in someone who has just had an ill-fitting object inserted vigorously per rectum. I had never even heard of *the* Marsha Hunt; and, in any case, I was certain that I had signed the fictive tutor's letter 'Martha', not 'Marsha'?

"Oh well," I remember thinking, "there it *is*: the *beast* in action. 'Do whatever it takes to obfuscate along the lines stipulated.'"

This manner of *invention of trivia*, as I was already discovering, was the *least* of the means, of *all* branches of the media, which could be unceremoniously – and partisanly – deployed to achieve such aim.

Neo-Gestalt

One evening, when I was four years old and my parents were due to attend a social function in Glasgow, I was left at home with my father's sister, Mhairi, and her husband, John: with both presumed to be fulfilling the roles of babysitters. John Beattie, a crafty, hulking, disconcerting character, who had been a commando in the Second World War, was possessed of both a generally unpleasant disposition and a very short temper. I was sent to bed before my usual time and, having *none* of that, I soon snuck back out into the hallway to resume my involvement in matters of prime 'waking world' importance, such as playing with my toys.

I cannot remember seeing the figure of the hundred-and-ninety pounds of male ex-commando fury as it descended upon me, nor the ensuing beating; but what I *do* remember – once the involuntary sobbing had begun to subside and I stared, bewildered, at one of the developing defensive haematomas on my right arm – was my sense of vexation at not having seen it *coming*. Soon after that, I began 'instinctively' – or so it at first *seemed* – rather than after any consciously systematic process of acquisition, to 'read' faces: not in terms of the 'broad stroke' expressions, which may-or-may-not be revealing of underlying motives; and certainly not in terms of trying to correlate those expressions with what was being said (I had long-since worked out that words, as spoken by a great many human beings, of all ages and both genders, are often 'unreliable' signifiers of the truth), but rather by watching out for those fleeting surface flickers around the eyes and mouth, arising as a result of involuntary contractions of underlying muscles. Those are the 'tells' which, as higher primates, most humans cannot avoid, and which a good poker player will ruthlessly exploit. As my newly-acquired skill quickly began to change my life for the better, in what was not always the most agreeable environment to grow up in (outside of domestic life), it began to dawn on me that this unusual means of procurement of new knowledge had something to do with the way that I would – oftentimes, and from as early as I can remember – *dream*, i.e. first recognizing that my dreams were something *inside* myself and that they had no reality within the everyday world (while still being very real to *me*). There quickly followed from *that* the awareness and acceptance that it was my own mind that was producing the images, that they were 'only dreams', and that the inner world was separate from the outer world. Beyond this, there came the ability to recognise 'within' the dream that I was dreaming (lucid dreaming).

'The universe Richard Dawkins imagines couldn't last for five seconds.'

— Robert Newman

Progressing from Lucid Dreamer to Active Dreamer need be little more than an act of will, coupled to possession of an undamaged right dorsolateral prefrontal cortex and frontopolar regions of the brain. Cautious and chary as I was often disposed to be in early life, it also took years of sedulous research into the subject – borne ostensibly as an offshoot of looking into 'The Problem of Pain' – for me to coax myself as far as I have yet reached into those phases of reality: 'sedulous research' *and* the experience of the manner and magnitude of challenges associated with current theories of *speciation*.

'New species originate only from tiny, isolated, unstable populations of struggling misfits at the ecological fringes.'

[Mayr, 1964; Eldridge, Gould, 1976].

It seems at least promising that this submission is now stimulating thinking along lines at variance with the

69

determinedly blear, specious, obstreperous, capitalism-inspired tripe which arose from a pervasive flourishing of impetuously-circumscribed thinking – intimately bound up with its hubristically-presumed fundamental that *any* religious belief can only be 'wrong-headed' – that preceded Ayn Rand and culminated in Richard Dawkins.

Robert Newman has dubbed it '*Misfit Theory*', and although there are yet more 'dots' awaiting human recognition – with 'joining up' to ensue – it is heartening to note its overdue emergence.

Immediately after the BBC Scotland interview was recorded, Ms Bird made great play of assuring me that my puzzled expression had confirmed my unfamiliarity with the real Marsha Hunt. It was an excellent opportunity to obtain a clear 'reading' of her character. I could discern only an idiotically rapacious, but otherwise indifferent narcissist: nothing I had not seen countless times before, but sufficient to have made me ashamed at my mistake of having had anything to do with her or, indeed, her colleague: the even more odious Tim Luckhurst – or their anti-journalistic grief vampirism – *at all*.

Under Blair, Luckhurst was given the position of Professor of Journalism at one of the late-established (1965) 'plate glass' universities (Kent), although 'Journalism Professor', in a *British* context at least, nowadays denotes little else of worth than a prime example of an oxymoron. In June of 2014, Bird was presented with an honorary degree from the University of Glasgow. As an astute friend of mine is in the habit of saying, "*Of course* she was!"

Whatever Jung's synchronicity might have had to tell me in terms of those experiences: I would not care to speculate here.

On the subjects of showbiz references and dreams, no less than David Duchovny's character, Fox Mulder, in that (sometimes) diverting Power Infrastructure propagandist entertainment, *The X Files*, said in one episode, "I've often felt that dreams are answers to questions we haven't yet figured out how to ask." I agree. They *can* be. The process of dreaming can also serve as a gateway to much else.

The Jackie Bird interview was conducted in a hotel at a remote location on the west coast of Scotland, in order to avoid the rest of the media. The BBC had arranged for both my mother and I to stay on at the hotel for a further week.

Early on, during the afternoon, my mother overheard the proprietress object strongly to a request from the camera operator to film me walking along the hotel's private beach. She was insistent that her establishment should not be recognised as the location. She was also concerned that my mother should confine herself to her bedroom for the rest of the day.

Uncomfortable with staying on in a place where she was made to feel like a social pariah, my mother asked me if, after the interview, I would just take her home. I readily agreed. I had, well before that point, been experiencing an increasingly 'bad vibe' about the place, and the whole 'set-up' (in both senses of that term), anyway.

That night, for the first time during the three weeks since the headmaster of Bearsden Academy had written to me about a 'discrepancy in school records', I slept for more than an hour at a stretch. I slept and I dreamt once again of another interview that I had felt obliged to attend at Glasgow University, many years before.

In this instance, I use the term, 'interview' somewhat euphemistically: if not, indeed, *wrongly*. It was more like an *assault*. At its end, however, and in common with the end of the BBC Scotland interview, I compromised. I agreed, on both occasions, to take time out and reassess my outlook. There was no rationale. I was just tired: sick and tired of all the pernicious bunkum.

What I found both times is that my vocation is part of what I am, and that it remains appropriate.

I think that for the many who choose to subscribe to it, there still exists in this country a tendency towards meek capitulation, should success entail any loss of social grace or standing. It is the feudalistic subordinate's cap doffing to established authority, regardless of how reprehensible the behaviour of that authority may be. This proclivity is often as deep-rooted as any recurring dream.

Our North American cousins are characteristically free from – and disapproving of – such inclination. They seem to me to embrace a more courageous dream.

Whether because of being weaned on American television culture, or for other reasons – questions that I 'haven't yet figured out how to ask' – I *too* do not take kindly to being put down, or kicked when I am down either.

Chapter Five

"I hear you're interested in studying medicine."

"*Huh?* Oh ... *yes*," I replied. It was Sarah Cobb, one of the 5C girls, in whose physics class I had also been placed.

It was during registration on a cold autumn morning in 1993, and she had just walked up to where I was sitting. She had previously said 'hello' a couple of times, as we had stood outside the annex waiting to go in of a morning or afternoon, but we had not spoken to one another beyond that.

"My dad's professor of cardiology at Glasgow University," she proceeded to announce. "So, you might want to talk to him sometime. Are you going up to the Dundee open day?"

"No, I looked for their stall at the Careers Fair last week, in order to get a prospectus, but I gathered that they didn't make it down to Glasgow that morning."

"I could pick one up for you, when I'm in Dundee," she offered, maintaining her distinctively impersonal tone. She had a sort of matter-of-fact, unsmiling quality about her. No bad thing in itself, I suppose, but I had felt, perhaps mistakenly, that her letting it be known what her dad did for a living may have had something to do with her coming over.

"Thanks, that's good of you," I said, and without another word, she turned on her heels and was off, back to her seat.

It was bad enough that circumstances had precluded all the other nearby schools except Bearsden Academy. There was, however, *no way* that I wanted to return to Glasgow University. I therefore thought no more about it.

Of course, it is invariably the little, seemingly insignificant occurrences which you dismiss without so much as an afterthought, that submerge, run latent and re-emerge in passive dreams.

During that night, I dreamt for the first time in years of a long-gone experience at Glasgow University. I dreamt of Professor Jennett, the then dean of Medicine, and of Dr Holmes, the advisor of studies, who sat with him in the faculty office. The dream, like the reality from which it stemmed, was a nightmare.

"If you are seeking readmission to medicine at a future date, you are required to sign this document indicating your voluntary withdrawal from the medical course." Jennett demanded again, for the fourth time that morning, with each demand having been delivered with increased pitch and urgency by this creepy, cadaverous little sadist, whose otherwise constant scowl would – oddly as it at first struck me – betray momentary signs of *guilt*. I surmised that this was guilt over something more immediate than his having appropriated, over a decade before, the work of an American researcher, to create – along with two discrete partners – his plagiarized 'legacy', in the forms of what, *to date*, are termed 'The *Glasgow* Coma Scale' and 'The *Glasgow* Outcome Scale'. I was surprised that the Americans had let them get away with it.

"Am I guaranteed readmission when I get well again?"

"No," piped up Holmes.

"Then no, I'm not signing it."

In my nightmare, they may well have been wearing the ceremonial garments of sixteenth century Spanish inquisitors, but the dialogue is precisely as it was on that morning back in 1982. They kept insisting and I kept *re*sisting.

With this stand-off, the interview was almost over. By comparison with some of what had gone before, they were now adopting a *less* severe attitude. However, that was as light-hearted as it ever got with them. For the past half hour, they had been angrily pressing me to give up entirely.

On Wednesday 27th September 1995, the day before Dundee University officially withdrew their offer of a place to me for the '95/'96 academic session, one Alison Spurway – an administrative assistant who would subsequently enjoy a series of promotions out of all proportion to her qualifications, but who on *that* day was appearing in the role of '*ad hoc* media whore mouthpiece' for men too craven to speak their own lies in public – told the BBC's *Reporting Scotland*: "Brian MacKinnon provided us with no medical certificates. He proceeded to sit in both the June and September exams and on both occasions he failed to reach the academic standard required to obtain a pass, and for that reason he was excluded."

She was then asked by the reporter, Colin MacKinnon, "But *after* the exams, he told you that he had been feeling unwell. Is that not enough?"

I had in fact told them well *in advance* of my *one* time of sitting the examinations (the September 1983 'resit' diet): examinations in subjects that I had been too unwell to attend any but the first ten days of the courses for.

Ms Spurway's follow-up scurrilous lie was, "Yeah, I'm afraid it's *not* enough, because we must have that evidence prior to the exams and then, in fact, he would have been advised not to sit the exams. So by sitting, in fact, he was declaring that he was sufficiently fit to do so."

Throughout that near-fatal viral illness – from which, no thanks to anyone at the University of Glasgow, I eventually made a full recovery – I provided the University with medical certificates from my GP; and after I had become too unwell to do that *myself*, my parents did it for me.

Later in the same collusive 'report', Professor Brian Whiting, the dean of Medicine – swathed in moral rectitude and determinedly disregarding of the fact that every individual is better than his worst act, and that we have all (doctors included) lied – appeared on camera and said, "I wouldn't like to give any advice to the dean at Dundee, but I think anybody who's indulged in this particular behaviour does not give the sort of feel that that's a good basis for a career in medicine or a good career as a medical student."

Even setting aside his employment of a somewhat *binary* moral compass, plus the fact that it was the morally bereft actions of unscrupulous *medics* who had left me with no further option *other than* to indulge 'in this particular behaviour': if one considers the word 'but' as the central/pivotal point of Whiting's declaration, it ought to be apparent that what he said is sufficiently self-damning to warrant no further response from me.

What were far more interesting than Whiting's *words*, however, were his 'tells'. In contrast to 'the dean at Dundee' (Dennis McDevitt), who – when he was later commanded to appear on camera to deliver a final damning denouncement of me – presented distinctly as one under the influence of a benzodiazepine tranquilizer, Whiting's untrammelled micro-expressions spoke of a vicious, unscrupulous character whose *primary* instincts were to dissemble and lie.

The following constitutes the remainder of my account of my difficulties, while at Glasgow University, during 1981/'83.

I had been called to this interview with Professor Jennett and Dr Holmes soon after the beginning of my second year as a medical student (1981). In advance of the interview, either my mother or my father made an appointment for me to see my GP, Doctor Mathieson. Because of the sorry physical state that I was in at the time, I was unsure of my ability to cover even the hundred yards from the family home to the surgery on nearby Drymen Road. My mother walked with me to the surgery and sat in during the consultation. Like any normal eighteen year old, I would ordinarily have been offended and embarrassed by such 'kid glove' treatment, but on *that* day I was glad of it.

I had already seen the alcoholic, incompetent Mathieson on a number of occasions over the preceding spring and summer. At first, he said that he suspected that I was suffering from infectious mononucleosis (glandular fever). Later, other possible viral agents were mentioned, but I do not recollect any blood test having been taken back then. It would take a difficult and painful trip to Germany, the following year, to obtain a definitive diagnosis.

Dr Mathieson wrote a note, which I took with me to the faculty interview. That is something that ought to be documented in my medical records and on file at Glasgow University medical faculty. As I ascended the stairway to the Dean's office in the old quadrangle, I had to pause a few times to regain my breath, and I recall trying to hold the envelope by its edges, because my palms seemed to be sweating continuously.

77

I had felt sure that my appearance and the GP's line would lead to their granting me a reasonable leave of absence. I was, however, mistaken.

Empathy did not appear to be their métier.

In the course of their barrage, the Dean's one other oft-repeated expression was "You are failing!". It registered more like a *command* than his opinion. Like policemen engaged in some 'good cop, bad cop' pantomime to try and break down a difficult suspect, they had contrived their own game of 'bad administrator, bad administrator': just two new, nasty, uncalled-for and, patently, *physical symptoms* that I had to contend with.

My primary concern that day was that I might fail to *live* much longer. Professor Jennett was, of course, referring to my studies; although if I *had* died, I do not suppose that either of them would have been moved one iota.

I had begun to feel unwell about a year before. One Saturday afternoon, off the Ayrshire coast, I had been testing out a new design of 'sailboard' (for windsurfing) of my own inception and styling, when, having fallen into the water for only the third time that day, I found myself surfacing in what was quickly revealed to be a patch of untreated sewage. Once ashore, I suddenly felt very unwell, and I vomited a couple of times; but it seemed to pass after that.

Around two weeks later, I began to feel as though I was coming down with the flu. In common with most teenagers, I had experienced influenza a couple of times previously. On those occasions, I had taken a couple of Disprin and sweated it out overnight. This time, though, the symptoms progressed differently. I seemed to be always thirsty and I drank copious volumes of water and fruit juice. I began to lose weight – almost forty pounds in the course of about fifteen months – and I only ever regained about two thirds of that.

I may not be the world's *greatest* athlete, but until then (and since my recovery), I was – and remain – blessed with considerable powers of assimilation and analysis. Perhaps more alarming than the realisation of my *physical* decline, was that although those powers remained intact, I had come, over the course of less than a year, to a state where, increasingly, I could barely summon the stamina (or interest) to conduct myself adequately in simple conversation.

All that I seemed inclined to do was to sleep and drink water.

Because of what ailed me, I had failed my professional exams at the end of the second and third terms in the first year, although I had managed to gain high marks in the class exams earlier in the winter. Perhaps ironically, I believe that above all other positive influences, it was my interview with the then outgoing dean, Professor McGirr, in the early summer of 1981, which inspired me to press on towards success in the resits.

By the end of that summer, I slowly began to come to terms with the fact that I was seriously ill and, increasingly, I was certain that I would die. Indeed, on a couple of occasions – and it shames me now to admit it – I even wished for it. I had only recently turned eighteen and I had never before *imagined*, never mind experienced, such suffering. Sure, like everybody else, I had seen gruesome images, both from real life and art, but such objective forms had not really prepared me for what it was to endure an apparently unstoppable decline in one's own overall health. Eventually, I just ran out of fight and, consciously at least, I let go. I became zombie-like, enervated. I would sleep for much of any given day and my weight continued to drop.

With perhaps some residual hope that the worst was over, I dragged myself to classes for a few days in October, at the beginning of the second year. By then, however, I was experiencing frequent headaches and often felt nauseated.

Years of football, running and climbing had made my legs strong and I had always reckoned that if my *legs* could hold out, then *I* could.

One morning, towards the end of the first week of term, I arrived very early for the day's first lecture: in anatomy. As I entered the lecture theatre and headed towards the third or fourth row of old wooden benches, my legs suddenly gave way below me. I was the only person in the auditorium that early on and, for all I *knew*, in the whole department. Nonetheless, I was determined not to panic. I managed to pull myself up onto one of the benches and there I sat, waiting for another face – *anyone* – to show.

D'ye ken John Peel

Title of (and lyric from) a nineteenth century song
about an English huntsman

From around the end of my high school years, I used to round off my evenings of study – followed by walking/running – with immersion in that exercise in anticipation that was 'listening to the John Peel Show'. 'Anticipation' because the rewards were often scanty, but when they *did* come … *what rewards*! After I had become ill, I tried to maintain this practice because I would sometimes find that this or that track would bolster me in the face of the dread of a (more often than not) rough night to come, with its bad dreams in which often – and disturbingly – I could not achieve lucidity, but would instead experience sudden, jolting transitions into wakefulness, with attendant delirium and night sweats.

One such track was called *Insight*, and it emerges with a peculiar sound, like the steel doors of a prison cell opening at the far end of a corridor. The very *liberating* nature of that resonance brought with it a reassuring infusion of a commodity that I was in dire need of: *hope* – perhaps not a quality that is often associated with *Joy Division*. Still, I always try to be magnanimous / neutral whenever I employ the expression, 'there's no accounting for taste' in relation to *others*, so why shouldn't I be as generous to *myself*?

From some distant corner of the anatomy department came the very same sound, and the song was thus triggered in my head. To my surprise, it seemed somehow to buoy up my spirits. After a minute or so, I managed to get back on my feet. Slowly and shakily, I walked out of the department and onto University Avenue. From there, I telephoned my father, and he came in the car to take me home.

My first vivid recollection after that time is of another interview that I was called to attend with the Dean and the faculty secretary. The Dean said that he was arranging, via my GP, to have me sent for examination by Dr Brebner, a consultant clinician at Gartnavel General Hospital.

Brebner was a kindly, good-humoured man. I told him of how it had been with me, for well over a year, and his expression indicated genuine concern. I recall him telling me that I had unusually high muscle tone and his taking a sample of my blood.

Sometime afterwards, the Dean wanted to see me again. This was during the early summer of 1982 and, on that occasion, it was again Dr Holmes who accompanied him. I was ordered to see a Dr Cheynne, the university psychiatrist.

I had been happy to see Brebner, because I wanted to know what was wrong with me – something that my GP seemed at a loss to uncover – and to receive effective treatment for it. Brebner had, I was told, discerned no causative organism (bacterial, viral or otherwise) for whatever was ailing me. I suddenly feared that they had decided to eject me through the hatch marked 'Mental Health Problems', or, more brutally – it having been, after all, eighties Glasgow – '*Loony*'.

With the perspective afforded by hindsight, I see that my fear was well founded. I tried to refuse the appointment, but again it was made clear to me that this was no *suggestion*. Either I went to see Cheynne or I was *out*. They seemed unimpressed by (and uninterested in) the German diagnosis of Coxsackievirus plus discovered fragments of an apparent Lyssavirus: but one of unknown serotype.

"*What*? You can't be suggesting that my son has *rabies*?" my mother had – with uncharacteristic expression of apprehension – impeached the German specialist clinician.

It had been near the beginning of a consultation that took place towards the end of an arduous sojourn that the two of us had undertaken in Frankfurt am Main during the hot European late spring of 1982: back when there was permitted general acknowledgement of *weather*, as opposed to today's inculcated *dismay* at the (also engendered) perception of periods of *nothing in particular* punctuated by named catastrophic climatic events.

A thunderstorm had begun as we had sat waiting to go into the consulting room, and heavy rain had quickly followed the first thunderclap.

"*No*, I am not of that view, Mrs MacKinnon," he had (sort of) reassured, before continuing: "*Serovar*: you understand this meaning?"

My mother shot a sideways glance at me.

"Same as serotype," I put in.

"*Yes*," he continued. "The sero*type* is not *known* to us."

Feeling ghastly and just a little 'removed' from proceedings as I then did, *that* had nonetheless gotten my full attention.

"Would you feel comfortable with *speculating* as to its specific variety, then?" I had then asked him, bringing to bear full, sustained eye contact.

He had returned my fixed gaze for fully five seconds before answering me: this big-framed, circumspect Teuton.

With experience, over the foregoing months, of the hyena-like Jennett and Holmes uppermost in my mind, the psychological 'blast doors' were, by then, primed to close at an instant's notice; and as he stated – with initially darkening demeanour – that he was of the view that it could serve no good reason to speculate, I was already hovering over the button.

However, as he completed, there emanated from him a smile: warm, non-patronizing and full of mercy and goodwill. Then, after barely noticeable further caesura, he spoke again, addressing me in German.

"Ich denke dass Sie ein ungewöhnlicher Kerl sind: unbeugsamen. Und ich denke auch, dass man noch durchsetzen könnten." Then, following more discernible pause: "Wir haben vor ein anderes bekannt ist, habe wir uns nicht?"

Immediately thereafter, and before I could quite marshal my thoughts regarding his comments – never mind put together a form of words that might have constituted an adequate response – he had stood up, turned a little in the direction of my mother and, reverting again to English, advised her that the best thing would be for me to have plenty of rest over the following months; and, insofar as was possible, in a peaceful, stress-free environment.

Finally, he had redirected his attention to me and, in English, said: "A chance to *dream*, yes?"

My mother had struck me as having become a little prickly shortly before that point. Indeed, she had been that way, off and on, during much of the trip. It was, on at least a couple of levels, understandable: she had not received any manner of categorical assurance about my prospects, one way or another; she did not speak German; and, with her having had lived through the second world war – during which she had worked as a Land Girl – there was that residual unease around anything or anyone connected with Germany. Nonetheless, there remained, to *my* mind, a certain incongruity in relation to her established outlook. I knew that during her time as a nursing sister at Glasgow's Western Infirmary, she had formed a friendship with a German doctor named Ratzer, who also worked there. This was at a time (the late fifties and early sixties) when there remained lingering prejudice against Germans in Britain. I had seen a picture of them together and Ratzer could easily have passed for this Bavarian virologist's sister.

As we left his consulting room, I offered the German doctor my hand, and as he shook it, clasping his other hand around the back of it, he gave me that affecting smile again. It was just a *smile*, but it helped.

Outside, my mother asked me what he had said to me when he had spoken in German. I told her that he had let me know that the prognosis was not as bad as we might have feared and that he had thought that he and I had met before.

"You've met him *be ... fore*?" she asked, with initial puzzlement giving way to dawning realisation, and contemplation, before she had finished uttering the last word of her question.

My mother knew well that the door to the dwelling place at the front of my head was always open to her. And why *shouldn't* it have been? She was, after all, the only incarnate with whom I was then familiar, who was *equipped* to enter and peruse as she might feel inclined. There had therefore been no need for a further spoken reply.

By that summer, some eighteen months after I had first become unwell, I seemed to have hit 'rock bottom' and I was, *physically* at least, beginning to re-establish some sort of equilibrium. I was not sleeping quite so much, but I felt light and fragile. Even the duvet on my bed felt heavy on top of me. Whereas previously I had relinquished all concern for matters worldly, I again began to worry about my future and about what these merciless savages in the faculty office had in store for me next. Some might deem that 'paranoia', but I knew that I had due cause to be thus concerned. My certainty in that regard had arisen from a first-hand experience of what it was to be brutalised while effectively paralysed.

Cheynne seemed to be cast from a different mould than Jennett and Holmes. He lacked their unremitting, insistent aggression. However, it took less than a couple of minutes of reading his facial micro-expressions to realise that I could not trust him.

He asked how I was feeling. I told him that I had lost a good deal of weight and although I still slept a lot of the time, I no longer constantly craved water. I added that although I now wanted more than anything else to be well again, I still often feared that I might die. He said little, but made copious notes.

At the end of our first or second meeting (and I was instructed to see him on a number of occasions), he prescribed me one of the tricyclic antidepressant drugs, amitriptyline. Back then, it was one of the 'wonder drugs' for the treatment of clinical depression. Nowadays, it is recognised as having a number of undesirable side effects and has been superseded by a new generation of 'wonder drugs'. No doubt, they too will have to forego that particular label, as tomorrow's trends and perspectives kick in.

I never took it. My reasoning was akin to that which you might employ if someone offered to upgrade your personal computer using a Stone Age flint tool: you only get *one* brain per lifetime. It possesses self-regulatory, repair and preservation mechanisms, which are as yet well beyond the comprehension of the greatest neurologists.

In view of my awareness of that extraordinary organ's status, plus the then still-lingering hope that I was on the way to recovery, I therefore decided not to surrender responsibility for what I considered to be my greatest asset.

My next summons to Jennett's office – after the first enforced appointment with Cheynne – was on an afternoon when I found myself experiencing what was, by then, a rare (if very slight and short-lived) resurgence in my general vitality. I focussed in on Jennett's often near-inscrutable countenance for that particular combination of micro-expressions that betrayed anything atypical or anomalous. On having entered his office, I had immediately discerned that he was already in a foul mood, which he proceeded to manifest without pause, and *with* all the mercy of a subterranean *Sonnenmensch*.

It was fully five minutes in before I *caught* it: a revealing of *guilt*.

Mindful of how 'background information-poor' I then was, I realised that I could at best hope only for something *approaching* accuracy. In that moment, I went for my best Holmesian (after 'Sherlock', rather than Jennett's usually-present sidekick, 'Dr') deductive leap; and, confronting him with his awareness of his own culpability, I demanded to know *why* – and on *whose behalf* – he was causing me, and my parents, such unwarranted and inhumane harm. Then, and for the life of me, in an attempt to *temper* (with a little de-escalating *compassion*) what one such as he could only have construed as an *attack*, I asked him if he was being *blackmailed* into what he was doing. For a *moment*, it may also have – to some lesser extent – *felt* like a clever and deserved catharsis; but on reflection, it certainly was not my smartest ever move. Instantly jettisoning his customary icy calm, he became *Rumpelstiltskin* incandescent with rage. As he started shrieking at me, with his voice suddenly elevated to a castrato pitch, he sprung out from his familiar position – seated behind his huge antique desk – only to retreat moments later: stung by some perception of exposure … *nakedness*. At the sight of that outlandish development, the note-taking female PhD student, who on that one occasion had replaced Dr Holmes, shuffled uneasily on her chair, which had been carefully positioned to the one side of- and a little behind mine.

Whatever the wisdom of my reactive behaviour that day, part of me still does not regret having just *once* put that insufferable little prig's nose out of joint.

On the subject of labels, I was perplexed and somewhat upset by Cheyenne's sudden suggestion that I was depressed. My immune system may well have been *sup*pressed – and I was certainly far from happy – but all I wanted to do was get better and get on again. Indeed, for the first time in about a year and a half, I was daring to hope that I might eventually do *both*.

At Cheyenne's mention of depression, I was reminded of a pertinent sketch from the comedy show, *Not the Nine O'Clock News*, which I had seen shortly before on the television. Rowan Atkinson was dressed in a gorilla suit and sat beside Mel Smith: *himself* done up as some manner of Desmond Morris/David Attenborough, anthropologist-type. Atkinson's ape character had been captured from the wild and had (absurdly) learned to speak English while in captivity/cohabitation with Smith's safari-suited academic.

"When I caught Gerald [the gorilla], in '68, he was completely wild," intoned Smith's character.

"Wild?" piped up the gorilla. "I was absolutely livid!"

With Jennett's psychiatric card in play, I was thereafter bounced between the faculty office and Cheynne. I protested repeatedly that I still felt unwell, and continued to ask for some more time to recover. Jennett's consistent response to anything that I tried to say was to shout me down with his own repeated demand that I either reapply for admission in the 1982/'83 year, or accept that medicine was not for me.

'Thanks' to lazy, cowardly callous doctors like Jennett, Holmes and Cheynne, I surmise that a UK student *today*, finding themselves in a position similar to the one that *I* did, could, conceivably, be subject to even more damaging abuse. If you find that difficult to countenance, then a reading of Martin J. Walker's *Skewed: Psychiatric hegemony and the manufacture of mental illness in multiple chemical sensitivity, Gulf War syndrome, myalgic encephalomyelitis and chronic fatigue syndrome*, or James Davies's *Cracked: Why Psychiatry is Doing More Harm Than Good* certainly could not do *you* any harm, reader. And if either of those should leave you with a sour taste, then I would be inclined to recommend Ben Goldacre's *Bad Pharma* as a 'chaser'.

During the last two months of the summer recess, I heard nothing. When I contacted the faculty office on a couple of occasions, I was told that the Dean was unavailable. Intensely worried about what was to happen, my health began to deteriorate again.

At the end of the summer of '82, Jennett finally called me to see him, in order to reissue his Neronian and (long since and irrevocably) established command: 'Reapply for readmission *now*, or you're out!'

Inexperience is the curse of the young. I signed his form, under protest.

To my mind, there is undoubtedly a relationship between what you *think* and what you *become*. Had I not been subjected to such torment by Professor Jennett, in all instances of contact with him, I might well have recovered sooner – 'psychoneuroimmunology' and all that.

In the course of living, I have found a fair proportion of the people whom I have encountered to be worthwhile acquaintances. It has been only very occasionally that I have met up with the likes of Jennett. Maybe I ought to be glad.

I was not able to attend classes during that year, and in late March of 1983, while on a ventilator for about a week, I was 'sick reported', i.e. the doctors who examined me judged that I would not survive longer than twenty-four to forty-eight hours. It was only (and eventually) with the occurrence of that *crisis*, that I finally shed the virus and began to make a slow, steady recovery.

With that, I renewed my determination that, at nineteen, I was not going to have the most important thing in my life taken away from me by that horrible little man on the Gilmorehill, with his penetrating laser-blue eyes and his voice like something from the bottom of a crypt.

I did not *then* fully comprehend that Jennett was merely acting as a stooge, subservient to the will of another.

Contrary to the claims made by Ms Spurway, at Glasgow University in September 1995, I continued to visit my GP throughout 1982/'83; and I complained, at every opportunity, to both him and the Dean about the position I had been forced into. My complaints, both verbal and written, seemed, in all instances, to fall upon deaf ears.

I sat only the September 1983 ('resit diet') second professional examinations: *not* 'both the June and September', as was falsely announced by Ms Spurway via an all too collusive BBC Scotland.

It is the US linguist and social critic, Noam Chomsky, who is widely accredited with having identified the media as extensions and supportive limbs of the Power Infrastructure (aka The Establishment). I needed neither the insight of the great Professor Chomsky nor a second viewing of the above-mentioned BBC Scotland sound bites to realise how readily the Scottish Establishment limb of 'Auntie' had fulfilled its primary function on that occasion.

In September 1983, I was passed in only one of the four subjects examined. One always knows whether one has passed or failed an examination as soon as one has finished writing. I knew that unless the recommended (and other) textbooks that I had studied from throughout that summer were pathological liars, then I had absorbed more than enough to pass all four; and that *in particular* I had done very well in Anatomy, Physiology and Biochemistry. Bafflingly, it was only in Pharmacology that I was granted a pass.

I am minded also to add here that at the compulsory oral exam component of the Physiology professional, my examiner was Professor Jennett's wife: herself a physiologist at Glasgow University.

Chapter Six

On the day after my first, short conversation with Sarah Cobb, I was having another chat. This time it was with 'Monty', one of the lads in chemistry class. He too was intent upon going on to study medicine, but only after an extended period of grind in the sixth year; and he expressed the view that I was deluded if I imagined that I could get in *anywhere* straight from the fifth year.

On my UCAS application form, I had, for appearances' sake, selected four Scottish medical schools (Glasgow, Edinburgh, Aberdeen and Dundee), plus Newcastle in England. I had also applied separately to Cambridge, because I reasoned that an early (fifth year) application to either Cambridge or Oxford would, although doomed to failure, help to create, in the opinion of my assessors, a helpful image of a serious-minded young man in no doubt about where he wanted to be.

Above all, there was *no way* that I was prepared to countenance the prospect of more than one year of school. I had figured on interviews (also new since the early eighties) from at least the *Scottish* universities, but suddenly my immediate prospects looked decidedly grim.

Sometime after my exclusion from medicine in 1983, my mother confided in me that, angered by how I had been treated, she had gone to see Professor Jennett and asked him to explain why he had acted as he did. Throughout their meeting, he had been his usual arrogant self, until right at the end, when she had put a particular point to him.

When I was ill, my mother had been told by a mutual acquaintance that a Mrs Howatt, the wife of a local GP – and mother of one of the boys with whom I had attended school – had been claiming during ladies' coffee mornings that I had been using drugs. It was assumed that she was not talking about Disprin. I have never taken illicit drugs and it is inconceivable to me why this Howatt woman, whom I had met but once at a barbecue – and spoken with only briefly, but politely – would wish to say such a thing. At the time, I let it go as a piece of fatuous gossip. Much later however, Roddy Menzies, a friend from school, recounted the same information to me: his mother was another member of Mrs Howatt's coffee morning circle.

In any case, her son managed to segue into medicine at Glasgow University after a year in science at Strathclyde. I suppose that such a thing is quite unusual.

Further infuriated by the news of this malicious and false tattle – which could not have done me any good at the time – my mother undertook to find out all that she could.

At the end of her run-in with Jennett, she put it *all* to him. By her report – and I have never known her to lie – his demeanour and attitude changed dramatically and on an instant.

"Doctors' sons fail as well," he blustered.

"I think we *both* know that Brian *didn't* fail, sir. However, I'm not talking about failing, but unfair entry and *dismissal*." Almost reduced to tears, she was by this time making her way towards the door.

"I don't suppose it's going to break the bank if we let Brian back in," conceded the Dean, unexpectedly and in an altogether more humble tone.

"That is exactly how I feel, Professor Jennett," she replied, as she left his office.

When she eventually related this startling tale to me, she concluded with the advice, "Sometimes in this world, the sad truth is that *who* you know often gets you further than *what* you know." At that juncture (late 1983), however, neither of us had even *heard* of MacSween, or of his having had, for many a year, supplied Jennett with – in addition to other 'services' – illegally-harvested human juvenile neural tissue. Equally, neither of us could have known that MacSween was not going to permit indulgence in feelings of guilt to dictate the actions of his diminutive neurologist familiar.

By 1996, desperate and disgraceful measures were being put in place to cover up much of the carnage that MacSween had wrought in the lives of bereaved families over decades. An in-house professor of 'Law & Ethics in Medicine', Sheila McLean – a Chrissie Hynde lookalike, but with more facial piercings – was brought in, so that a change in the law could be effected, in order to deny a multitude of otherwise legitimate compensation pay-outs that would have bankrupted the university. Remarkably – or maybe *not* so remarkably, this being *Scotland* after all – it all went through, swiftly and with nary a whiff of robust challenge – or even any broadcast bromide – from a compliant Media.

The Families of the victims were denied any further hearing in any public forum.

After the not dissimilar Alder Hey scandal, in the same era, the English at least held a public enquiry, which led to the Human Tissue Act of 2004. It is a terrible thing to contemplate, but I surmise that the scurrilous and flagrant cover-up at Glasgow was, at least in part, motivated by the concerns of the guilty – with MacSween foremost amongst those guilty – that crimes *even worse* than the unauthorised removal, retention, and disposal of human tissue (including children's organs) might be held open to public scrutiny.

By way of turning away from remembrance of such horrors, I sought to re-engage Monty in conversation. But even in that attempt, there seemed to be little that I could do to shake off the dreamy, oneiric gloom of that autumn afternoon. As I reached for a new subject to broach with him, something struck me about the shape of his head: the forehead, the eyes … the shape of his nose. Who was it that I knew …? The moment of perplexity had arisen because it was nobody that I 'knew': except in the sense that I had witnessed his *art*.

It was the actor, John Malkovich. Most films that I had found rewarding had – up until then – never proven terribly difficult to watch. The adaptation of Choderlos de Laclos' *Dangerous Liaisons*, in which Malkovich had played the role of the Vicomte de Valmont, had however been an exception. I had first seen it in 1988, and although it was certainly *captivating*, the two leading protagonists were just *so* dissolute and nasty, as to be quite *beyond* identifying with in almost *any* aspect of their respective characters. In particular, any hope of redemption for the eloquent charming Valmont that I may have entertained, as events unfolded early on, dissipated entirely after his repeated protestation of "It's beyond my control!", to the wretched Tourvel. The line 'stuck' with me, though. And it *bothered* me.

A few nights before my conversation with Monty, I had gone alone to see a production of the play in the city, in an effort to discover if the renewed perspective might afford me an 'opening' to shed light on this trepidation: so that I could face it down.

Not so very long before that occasion, I had had audience with my darling Augmenter.

94

As I write, today, there comes back to my mind a song, entitled *Blind Dumb Deaf*, by the Scottish band, Cocteau Twins. I first heard it performed 'live', as part of a John Peel session, in January 1983. The lyric – in which the singer laments that she should 'welt' and 'gash' were she to enact stages of intimate physical contact with her beloved – coupled to its insistent high-pitched guitar and deep bass with delay, moved me deeply. Back then, it seemed, oddly, like something 'for future reference', and I simply tucked it away into the back of my mind. It would be on the day of that audience, over a decade later, when seeing no further option but to remove myself entirely from the human being that I had come to love above all others and all else, that – my gender notwithstanding – I would at last arrive at a full, grim personal appreciation of Elizabeth Fraser's viscerally-sung lyrics.

It was no longer merely fear of harm that might come to her (while she remained in Glasgow), by dint of MacSween getting renewed wind of our being close; but *now*, having succumbed to cold fury at my father's despicable – and criminally ignored – torture and killing, and, as a result, having rushed headlong into this high-risk endeavour, it was hardly for me to do anything but ensure no further interruption to the flow of her life: a life that I surely held more precious than my own.

Unlike Valmont's so-called 'alpha male anti-hero', who could not imagine himself giving power to his potential beloved – because then, he would not have been entirely in control of his own heart – she had had my heart from almost the first moment; and never another would have it thereafter. I loved her unconditionally, and I had later resolved that likely threat to her success and wellbeing, arising from perceived association with me, could not become a condition of our being together. But when, uncharacteristically, I had foolishly permitted a different, rare and unfamiliar 'passion' to propel me into this outlandish undertaking, just as she might have been set to be clear of Glasgow, I had at first failed to see that it would mean my losing her. 'Rock and a hard place': unable either to explain myself or to delay her any longer, I could only express to her my wish for her to have a 'great life', because, by then, matters were indeed *beyond my control*. In effect, I had acted no less despicably towards her than the contemptible Valmont had towards Tourvel.

"No wonder," I thought, "that he impaled himself on Danceny's blade."

Inundated as I was becoming by that worst kind of pain, I felt myself slump a little forwards towards the gas tap of the chemistry lab bench; and I had the sense that I too was beginning to die. Deep inside myself, I reached for the standard admonition: "Come on pilgrim, cowboy the hell up!" However, it was to no avail.

It was then that I could discern his presence ... *just*: my 'Guardian' (though never, even *yet*, quite 'dear'), exerting his prerogative to 'rule'. I do not know exactly what it *was* that he did, or how he did it. I may as well have been an injured domestic animal undergoing a surgical procedure at the vet, for all the understanding that I could glean of his methods; and in the years that followed, *that* would remain the case. It would be the autumn of 1996 before I would even think of him as maybe *being* benign, but I guess that what he did that day, as I sat listlessly on the hard wooden lab bench, qualified as an act of mercy.

Suddenly, I was aware of Monty snapping his fingers in front of my face.

"Earth to *Brandon*! Is anybody there?"

"Who? Oh, yes," I found myself being able to confirm. Then, fully returned to the realm of the living, I attempted to raise an empty smile.

"You alright mate? You look like *crap*!"

"Yeah, I'm *good*," I muttered.

The Augmenter was canny and beautiful; and never in a Titania's breast beat a heart so regal. Who then *could* do aught but love her? '*Life and how to live it*' … I reckoned that if anyone had *that* covered, then it was *her*; so, assuredly, she would soon have contented herself with choice of another consort, and forged new alliance there. In that conclusion, that better part of me brought a moment's equanimity. Then, with creeping, weaselly, selfish ego – armed to the teeth as it was with weaponized hypergolic thoughts of gynocentric economy and the disrelished '*exigency*' – elbowing its way back in to wrest control of my psyche, I was swiftly and mercifully rendered emotionally numb.

Chapter Seven

"I have often wondered at the curious
conceit that would attempt to determine
tastes and ideas by decree."

Colonel von Waldheim (Paul Scofield) in John
Frankenheimer's *The Train*

The theatrical theme re-emerged that year, with my
involvement in a school production of Rodgers and
Hammerstein's *South Pacific*.

Quentin Crisp, the famous wit and social commentator,
who in his later years and until his death lived in New York,
once expressed his disaffection with the inability or
unwillingness of contemporary American youth to embellish
their views on just about anything, beyond saying that
something is either 'cool' or it 'sucks'. While I am inclined
to sympathise with the bewilderment of a 'stranger in a
strange land', there does seem to be an absolute rectitude –
and a vein of sustainable humour – in such an unalloyed
binary system of classification of would-be artistic
endeavours: particularly in an era *so* chock-full of
backhander-shushed, pabulum-pushing, mainstream critics,
that it has become nearly impossible to gain an idea of what
might be worth a visit to even one's local *independent*

cinema, until any film under consideration is well on its way to DVD format.

If that makes little or no sense to you at all, then all that I might suggest in support of my claim is that you attempt to sit through an entire episode of *Beavis and Butthead*, with their similarly limited vocabulary: not always an *easy* watch – and best viewed when not in full possession of your wits: perhaps after a measure of your preferred tipple – but *sometimes* strangely rewarding. On one level, they are just plain morons, yet these idiot savants' meaningless existence is regularly punctuated by their own devastatingly insightful critiques of the television shows that they spend so much of their time watching together. Barely literate their damning commentaries might be, but one cannot help but feel that Samuel Beckett – if certainly not Crisp himself – would have pronounced them 'Cool'.

If having to go back to school 'sucked', then Mrs Ogg seemed 'cool' enough to me.

I attended her English classes throughout 1993/'94. Whereas all the teachers in the various classes that I found myself in were smart people, Mrs Ogg often appeared genuinely *wise*. She could spark interest in the most unconcerned and obdurate pupil.

Her reading one day of Wilfred Owen's *Disabled* moved me sufficiently to look again at the works of some of the war poets.

Soon after the beginning of the autumn term, she asked me if I might be interested in the forthcoming school play: adding loudly, for the benefit of other male members of the class, that there had been little interest from the boys so far that year. I deferentially declined. Sensible of what I gathered to be a degree of disappointment in her reply, I cited the concurrence of the final production and the Higher exams as my excuse. Not long afterwards, she broached the matter with me again and, mindful of academic reports yet to be written, I conceded that I might find the time to do something in a *backstage* capacity.

"Oh, with *that* accent, Brandon, I'm sure we could find a more useful role for you," declared the determined English teacher, with more than a hint of zeal creeping into her voice.

The ball was back in my half and I had to conjure an unexpected way round and forward. In short, I had to find some unanswerable yet acceptable repartee. The sad reality, however, was that it was just one of those sorry moments when even an attempt to discover horse manure in a stable would have proven about as productive as the hunting of the Snark.

If the sagacious Mrs Ogg was also wise to my overall deception, no sign of pantomime, that *I* could detect, ever flickered up into – or around – those clear and alert eyes.

I do not believe that I am blotting anything out, but I simply cannot remember how things thereafter got to the point where I was required to attend an upper music room audition for the singing – *dancing*, I would not have minded so much – role of Lieutenant Joe Cable, in the 'Bearsden Academy Production of South Pacific'.

Stage fright is an easy enough concept to grasp. The clue is in the term itself: a state of fright experienced prior to going on *stage*. However, as I entered the music room and headed towards the end *opposite* the stage (occupied by the small assembled group of teachers), for what was merely an *audition*, stage fright – as described in 1861 by the lauded actress Ellen Terry – was altogether what I encountered.

Gripped that year, as Terry had been by the phenomenon, while she struggled to learn five parts simultaneously, she left a visceral description, which matches my own experience.

"You feel as if a centipede, all of whose feet have been carefully iced, has begun to run about in the roots of your hair. Then it seems as if somebody has cut the muscles at the back of your knees. As your mouth slowly opens, no sound comes out. It was," she went on to say, "torture. Like nothing else in the world."

As one committed to an extended process that primarily depended on maintaining an effective ability to 'hide' in plain sight, inviting the close scrutiny of a defined and designated *audience* struck me as a very counter-productive move indeed. Yet, wanting – as I most definitely *did* – the requisite all-round 'glowing' report necessary for even a *chance* of entry to Medicine directly from the fifth year, I could, in that moment, envisage *no* alternative to extending that invitation.

Maybe it was the preponderance of green in the room that made me think of the Augmenter again, or maybe it was just that I would have thought of her anyway, as I did so many times each day. I thought of the glorious light that shone through the portals of those green eyes, and of how one afternoon, years before, I had without thinking at all, kissed both her eyes, and her forehead, just above the top of the bridge of her nose. Then, those years later, I thought of that *look* she had given me in return. There had been no words to accompany it: none had been needed. It had expressed and inspired more than a lifetime's worth of words.

Instantly, in crossing the music room floor, I again experienced the very *essence* of her: the essence that I knew would somehow always be a part of me. As *ever* it would, it came with the gift of music: an *apparent* auditory perception – more intense and energizing than the music of the 'real' world, and giving rise to inspiration applicable in the material world.

"*That's* interesting!" she had sometimes declared in the course of our conversations. How noble and brave and elegant – as *ever* she was – would it be, I found myself thinking, if in this moment of intense vexation, I could take a step back from the entire mess and regard it with *interest*. A step *back*: *Verschiebung*, or at least something *resembling* displacement; but *how*, exactly? Music ... *musicals*! *The Rocky Horror Picture Show*: that had been her 'kink' back then, but maybe it had also informed her thinking. '*Don't dream it. Be it*!' That was the theme of Richard O'Brien's high-camp musical, wasn't it? With that thought, both the song in my head and the intensity of the anxiety that I was rallying against now with quick-fire thinking, spoke to the notion of *wakeful* lucidity. 'Don't dream it. Be it!' ... Don't *just* dream it. Be it! ... Dream it. *Then* be it!

Still, the question of *how* persisted unanswered. Back to the German: *Von oben nach unten*: Top Down. Up, down, side to side ... Side *by* side: that was how we had sat one evening, waiting in a Chinese takeaway in early 1989. We had exchanged glance after glance, as though the practice was soon set to become outlawed. I just *couldn't* take my eyes off her. Ten minutes in, and I felt that for the sake of decency – or even the retrieval of a modicum of *decorum* – I simply *had* at least to *pretend* to be otherwise occupying my attention. I picked up one of the menus. At its end, there was depicted a set of animals: each corresponding to a year of birth in the twelve-year cycle of the Chinese horoscope. Hers was the Monkey. Two animals, the rabbit and the cat, were associated with my birth year. Curiosity, resourcefulness, adeptness at getting out of trouble ... all in one package: advance and retreat ... backwards and forwards ... side to side ... down and up ... *matricize*; and then – and *only* then – the control afforded by 'von oben nach unten'.

Consider *any* activity: any art or science, discipline or skill. Then, think about pushing it as *far* as it will go: beyond where it has *ever* gone before; beyond the edge of any ill-perceived confining 'envelope'; *becoming* it, as though becoming that *particular* electron, dually primed for the glide, as it floats determinedly upon a Nano circuit of superfluid helium in a quantum system. It is *then* that one avails oneself of the realm of *magick*.

And, *sometimes* – particularly when you have expressed a little *gratitude* for your lot, whatever that 'lot' may be at the time – an outcome which derives from a source immeasurably more powerful than even that of magick can just seem to come about *unbidden*.

For the re-inspired romantic ideopraxist that I had discovered that I could still be, there then came something analogous to a reactive hypoglycaemia ('sugar crash'), which brought me immediately back down to harsh reality: an *unusual* harsh reality, certainly, but harsh *reality* nonetheless. A vestige of the 'inner music' remained, but all those highfalutin propositions, having been noted, had had their moment. I was on my *own*, and I was simply going to have to focus as best as I could, moment in-moment out, and *wing it*: all the way to completion, if I could, while clinging to the unerring hope that *good luck* would turn out to be something more than just the residue of unavoidably extempore design.

Chapter Eight

I had tried and failed to hold to her as, providentially, she had passed me in the flow of The Great Turn of Time once *again*. Instead, I had found myself having to summon my most effective 'inscrutable' face and tell her that I hoped she would have a great life, as I slipped back, at the last, into the confining, deafeningly silent and suffocating gyre that is life without her.

Still, though, I dreamed that I could at least *one* day demonstrate to her that I was far more than a *profane* intelligence: a cynical joker ... a *joke*. Whatever strange territory beyond science or even *art* that I might have had to negotiate my way through to get there, I *was* going to try. Then again, she probably knew as much – that was *true* – as could be known about me anyway. Certainly, other than the 'collectives' that would decide on reports about medical school applicants – and those were groups that I had to dazzle only *temporarily,* and galvanize in the direction of my favour – there was no one else that I felt any need to impress *anything* upon.

Even in crossing the Rubicon, I would not lose sight of one important 'music lesson' that I had taken on board years before: one which might persuade politicians – were they ever to take heed of it – to pursue more worthy work. It was a principle that I first grasped via the lyrics of a song entitled *Convincing People*, by the English music and visual arts group, Throbbing Gristle.

Music may once have suffused a part of my existence; and inside my own head, I may have a faultless singing voice: but it is when that singing voice emerges into the material world that things can start to go very badly wrong. It has been demonstrated 'scientifically' on the television comedy programme, *8 Out of 10 Cats Does Countdown* that the saxophone solo from Gerry Rafferty's 'Baker Street' can be dovetailed seamlessly into the chorus section of just about *any* song. When, however, Dead Can Dance's 'Summoning Of The Muse' – the music which that morning's remembrance of her had set off in me – is playing in your head, then no matter at *which* point you choose to switch to singing (out loud) 'Younger Than Springtime', there is *no* dovetail possible. It just *does not* work. So, inadvertently, and without even having given the *appearance* of wilfully perpetrating acoustic torture, I managed to screw up the audition *big time*.

As the last shaky note escaped my lips to pollute the chamber, I sighed contentedly inward and smiled across to Mrs Thomson, Mrs Montgomery and the student music teacher whose name I now forget. They were sat together in a judicial huddle in the opposite corner of the room. There was *no way* anybody in their right mind was now going to let me near a microphone. *That* much was inescapable.

In physics, certain 'laws', previously deemed to be incontrovertible are, increasingly, turned on their heads as new perceptions come into the world. The same, it would seem, is also happening in the realm of common sense.

They *loved* me!

Had I been looking for horseshit on *that* particular occasion, it would have been easy enough to find. It seemed to be raining down by the bucketful, with neither an umbrella nor even a wide-brimmed hat in sight.

On the subject of *madness*: Cheyne was not the *only* psychiatrist whom I saw back in the early-to-mid-eighties. I arranged to see one other of my own choosing, on a single occasion, after my peremptory exclusion from Glasgow University.

The day that they excluded me, I had been told to present myself at some big chamber in the old (quadrangle) part of the campus.

Inside, there was a long, oval table. At the middle of one side sat Jennett, flanked right and left by various other faculty staff members. I was directed to sit down at the midpoint of the opposite side, facing the Dean.

He reiterated the same old fiction about my failing. I remonstrated again about his treatment of me, including: my not having been given the uninterrupted and unpressured time that I had needed for my recovery from life-threatening illness; my not having been afforded the opportunity to undertake the courses; and my having been permitted to sit only *one* diet (September 1983) of Second Professional examinations – a *single* sitting that I had undertaken only under protest. This time, however, he added that, as an individual prone to depressive illness, I was unsuited to a career in medicine.

This was to be the closing lesson in Jennett's 'master class': how to piss in someone's ear, tell them it's raining and then – given that you have the necessary power and autonomy to abuse – get *clean away* with it.

Franz Kafka would have found a real hotbed of material in there that day.

The psychiatrist whom I later saw wrote me a favourable report, repudiating Professor Jennett's claim. Copies of it ought to be on my medical records and, equally, on record at

Glasgow University medical faculty, as it was sent there as part of my subsequent appeal.

I tried a couple of other avenues throughout the period 1983/'85, in attempts to redress my situation. These included petitioning local politicians (Michael Hirst and Sam Galbraith, to name but two) to plead my case for me, but they always ended in the same government 'White Paper' quote: 'Universities in the United Kingdom are autonomous bodies, entirely responsible for their own internal administration.'

Having exhausted these end-stage approaches, I tried to put my case to the European Court of Human Rights, only to find that attempt thwarted by a six-month statute of limitations on the presentation of *any* case.

Shortly before receiving a definitive diagnosis (in Germany) of the viral illnesses which had afflicted me, I visited a Glasgow-based neuropathologist called Peter Behan. By then, a condition characterised by symptoms similar to those that I had suffered was being talked about. It had been dubbed myalgic encephalomyelitis, or 'M.E.', and an Oxford team had developed a test to detect the presence of (what was then thought to be) a causative agent. Behan was not forthcoming with any more enlightening detail. My assessment was that either he did not *have* those details or, if he *did*, he did not fully comprehend their meaning.

Unfortunately, the moment that I started reading Behan's micro-expressions, I had a powerful sense that he was not a man who had the *slightest* interest in helping me.

He asked me about my symptoms, and I began to tell him how, for a long time, I had felt almost constantly sleepy and had lost nearly three stone in weight.

He appeared indifferent, and quickly interrupted with an enthusiastic, waffle-rich – but particulars-poor – discourse on the new Oxford test. Suddenly he pulled up and said:

"You know, sufferers tend invariably to be oftentimes thirsty and prone to drinking large quantities of water."

"Well, that's what I was going to say before, about my experience …"

"Yes, but you didn't tell me that when you were describing your symptoms."

"But you interrupted with all that logorrhoea about the new test."

"Ah, but you didn't *tell* me, and I certainly can't justify the considerable expense of recommending you for this test, when your symptoms are just not ...," he trailed off, moving his hand out and away from below his lower lip and widening his eyes in unmistakable glee.

My unspoken reply was none too polite.

"It seems to me that the individual today stands at a crossroads, faced with the choice of whether to pursue the existence of blind consumer, subject to the implacable march of new technology and the endless multiplication of material goods, or to seek out a way that will lead to spiritual responsibility, a way that ultimately might mean not only his personal salvation but also the saving of society at large; in other words, to turn to God."

— Andrei Arsenyevich Tarkovsky

Like his counterpart, Jennett, Behan's bent also extended outwith neurology, and well into the field of bovine scatology. I suspected that the 'bliss' of ignorance might well have long-delayed this tribune of the foolish from having to face Tarkovsky's posited dilemma.

It would later strike me that the difference between the service that I received in Germany and that which I had to endure in my native Scotland, was broadly comparable to the difference that might have been experienced between running an Audi and being burdened with ownership of an Austin Allegro. Whereas there would have been the sense that the former had been constructed by artisans who took *pride* in their work, it would quickly have become apparent to any unfortunate purchaser that the latter had been thrown together – and with scant attention to detail or quality control – by individuals either unacquainted- or wholly *disaffected* with the very *notion* of diligence.

I nevertheless forced as polite a smile as I could muster, thanked the unpleasant Behan – though God only knows what for – and left his office.

Years later, on the BBC's *Newsnight* programme, Behan would breach patient confidentiality over what he claimed to be a case of atypical Creutzfeldt-Jakob's disease. The unfortunate subject of his incompetence and gross insensitivity was a young girl from Bearsden. On the same day that he appeared on television, he told the girl's parents that she had just "months to live" after contracting CJD. This enabled the press to track down the girl – who was unaware of the diagnosis – and her 'case' was subsequently splashed across the front pages of the following days' newspapers. Behan attributed her condition to an addiction to hamburgers. It later transpired that she was a vegetarian, and she subsequently returned to school.

His next contribution to the neurology canon – again revealed via a further unabashed attempt at self-promotion by means of television – was to fudge the results of an experiment: those same results having generated a paper, which he had managed to get published by not divulging that he had selected his experimental group in a non-random manner.

There were some rumblings about his facing investigation by The General Medical Council, but when certain connections were made amongst the ranks of the aforementioned 'unseen', the media quietly desisted from any manner of follow up.

My understanding is that this dangerously ignorant individual – one of many similarly *un*learned professors then at Glasgow – was effectively 'suspended' from his position, only to be quietly reinstated by another of that ilk, Dean Bryan Whiting, less than a year later: 'jobs for the boys', as the English have it.

In the course of a tirade lamenting the disappearance of any discernible standards in Scottish public life, a climbing companion – let's call him 'Jerry', although that is not his real name: but it goes with 'Tom' – who, for a *solicitor*, is prodigiously prone to 'colourful' language, once felt the need to lay it all out in 'black and white' for me. His precise words were "Some of those guys are worse than *politicians*! I mean, what the fuck do they have to do in order to be *answerable*: shag a *zebra* … in *public*, for *fuck's* sake?"

Impolite phraseology again sprang to mind – but, again, no *further* – during a rehearsal for *South Pacific*. I had just accidentally stabbed myself with a pen, in the middle finger of my left hand.

The role of Joe Cable, which, incredibly, had been foisted upon me, had turned out to be one of the two male romantic leads.

At some stage in the proceedings, myself and a girl called Val, who played the character of Liat, had to kiss. For reasons hopefully obvious to anyone reading this, I was disinclined to perform the actual osculation during rehearsals (or, for that matter, even during the eventual performances of the production). Mrs Thomson, the teacher in overall charge of the play, was, however, becoming increasingly suspicious of my ability to come up with the goods *at all*.

It was an afternoon in May 1994, and Val and I had been summoned by Mrs Thomson to attend a 'special rehearsal' in one of the common rooms in the main building.

The Higher exams were already in full swing and I had bought some of those stiffened felt-nibbed 'fine liner' pens, as I found them smooth and fluid for speedwriting. They did tend to wear down very quickly though. I had brought one of them with me to the rehearsal, along with a notepad.

My far from inspired plan of action was to break off at propitious moments, just before – and thereby *instead of* – the kiss, in order to feign making notes about stage directions or whatever.

"Aren't you going to try the *kiss* now?" enquired Mrs Thomson, in an overblown, cutesy kind of tone, as Val and I gazed forlornly into one another's eyes at the end of our big musical number.

"*Nah*, we'll save that for the big night, Mrs Thomson," I answered as casually as my state of near desperation would allow, while I simultaneously shot a pleading, sideways glance at Val.

Luckily, I could not have wished for a more 'together' associate under such way-out circumstances. She appeared to be completely calm and more than self-assured enough not to be bothered one jot about my ongoing unwillingness to kiss her. For all I knew, she was *relieved* about it.

Val nodded her agreement towards our director.

Although apparently not overjoyed by this state of affairs, Mrs Thomson let it go at that.

I heaved a sigh as quietly as I could, and my gaze fell. I saw the front of my white school shirt. However, it was *not* entirely white. It was speckled with blood – my *own* blood – as was my left hand.

In remonstrating, pen in hand, over the avoided kiss, I had stabbed myself in the finger with the aforementioned stylus. It was *permanent* ink, to boot, and as a memento of the occasion, I still have a single-point 'tattoo' just below the nail of my middle left finger.

Val was standing to my left and slightly ahead of me. I thought, "Oh blast!" or words to that effect. "As if my embarrassing the poor girl hasn't been enough, surely I haven't *bled* on her, as well?"

I looked her over as discreetly as I could, but thankfully, my hand and shirt were as far as the blood had reached – a moment of relief, to round off a hellish afternoon.

Chapter Nine

"What happened to your finger, Brian?"

"Oh, I caught it on the edge of one of those new shelves in the periodicals extension."

I had been bleeding again; or rather, *before*.

It was the summer of 1986 and I had been talking to Gordon.

Gordon was one of the highest-ranking academic staff members at Glasgow University library. I liked him. He was an unusually tall, genial chap and his overall demeanour reminded me somewhat of one of those stoic, engineering genius-types from movies like *The Dam Busters*: except that I never saw him smoking a pipe. His total lack of self-aggrandisement made him an easy person to chat to informally.

"Hi Brian!" he would say, and before I knew it, we would be off on some meandering discussion.

Although it was the just return onto the path towards my *purpose* that I needed – and not another time-wasting aimless job – I had secured work as a library assistant, around March of '86; and at the end of one working day during that summer, I told Gordon about my unsuccessful attempts to gain readmission to medical school, and my then forming intention to explore possibilities abroad.

"That seems a pity, Brian. Did you lodge an appeal at Senate level?"

"Yes, but although I gather that there are *many* Senate members, my case was considered by only a small group of them, and I wasn't allowed to appear before them in person. I noticed too, from the letter of rejection, that one of them was a Church of Scotland minister. That *really* cheesed me off! I remember sitting in church one time as a teenager, and thinking to myself, 'If all this is supposed to bring us closer to the consciousness of God, then why all the *ceremony* and *outer splendour*? Surely the point should be to encourage folk to look *within* themselves, in an attempt to connect with that *greater* consciousness, rather than to confine and bind them by instilling dedication to endlessly-repeating, material world, rituals and dogmas'? A touch of the 'Philip Larkins' you might say, but my complete disillusionment with that particular convention helped me to achieve escape velocity that day, and I stopped attending church thereafter. God's just fine with me, but I guess that my perceived image of my future being decided by some 'conman in drag' just stuck in my craw."

"No, it's a worthwhile point, Brian. Did you know that *I'm* a Senate member?"

I was a little startled by his reply.

When I snapped to, a moment later, I frantically checked back over what I had said to him. I would not have liked to have had offended the man, even inadvertently, but I saw that he was still smiling and that it was okay.

He had a 'way with the words' did old Gordon, and intentionally or otherwise, he had just provided me with an idea.

Gordon was a reasonable human being, *and* he was a Senate member. Maybe there were at least a *few* others like him in the Senate.

That night, I reformatted my original letter of appeal to the Senate. The next morning, I went up to the reference section in the university library and found the then current listing of Senate members. Armed as I was with a bag full of ten pence coins almost large enough to warrant having 'SWAG' printed on it, the only other required effort was a marathon photocopying session and a further two hours spent labelling and stamping envelopes.

With the exception of Gordon, I sent copies of my letter to every Senate member.

At their press conference, 'to correct the public record', in September '95, the medical faculty at Glasgow, aided and abetted by the media, painted a picture of me as a frantic obsessive who bombarded the university with over three hundred letters.

The vast majority of these letters were compiled and sent over two days in the summer of 1986. There was no great effort, either on my part or, it would seem, on the behalf of any Senate member: I did not receive a single reply. In 1986, I assumed that it was another example of reasonable adults acquiescing under the rubber stamp of officialdom. I knew that I had just cause to complain.

"Surely," I recall reassuring myself in a moment of ill-advised credulity, "they could not *all* be thoroughgoing bastards?

It would not be until late 1992, with my own follow-up investigation of MacSween, that I would come to the fullest understanding of how *un*reasonably compliant a body of (largely) men could become, when so many of them – having been indulged in some of the *foulest* practices imaginable – found themselves subject to the tightening screws of a master blackmailer.

The Headmaster Ritual

"Who's *that* fat bastard?"

"His face looks as though it should come with free garlic bread!"

"What a pure and utter *tool*!"

These, and other choice remarks, emanated from a group of fourth and fifth-year lads standing not far from me, outside the entrance to the science department of Bearsden Academy. Their target was an overweight youth from maybe the second or third year. He had just kicked one of the girls – presumably of around his own age – as she stood talking with her friends in the yard. She, however, was having none of his bullying and was now proceeding to beat the hell out of him.

"*Y-e-s!*" exclaimed another of the assembled fourth and fifth years, as the intolerant damsel caught her now frazzled former assailant with yet another well-aimed left hook: this time to the jaw.

As the sorry hunter-turned-prey backed off with all available haste and a now *doubly* inflamed face, I suddenly noticed his *hair*. It looked as if it had been cut using a kitchen bowl as an edging guide: in the manner of Mo from *The Three Stooges*. And as if that was not *enough*, the poor soul also had a grey – or, more probably, *bleached* – streak, Mallen-style, down one side.

With that halting of hostilities, the head teacher emerged from behind the swing doors and onto the concrete; and his belated appearance marked an unequivocal end to that morning interval's 'entertainment'.

All of this had occurred during a morning break in January 1994. The prospect of the play had recently been putting something of a damper on my spirits, but seeing this wretched creature reminded me that there is always someone worse off than *you* are, and that despair is therefore *usually* self-indulgence.

With the short-lived spectacle of the fight over, I again surveyed the sweeping schoolyard vista, and a particular artist's depiction of hell came to mind.

As the bell rang and I began to make my way through the riotous heaving masses in the corridor, and towards physics class, I wondered if Hieronymus Bosch had ever gone back to school at thirty.

Chapter Ten

Around late September of 1986, there appeared newspaper and television reports concerning the ongoing decline in applications to colleges and universities for places on science-based courses. I checked around, and found out that the same dearth had applied at Glasgow that year.

Mindful of my own academic potential, and of the Howatt lad's sidestep from science at Strathclyde into medicine at Glasgow, I reasoned that one or even *two* years of hard graft and good results in a BSc course might bring an offer from somewhere.

I asked for – and received – a favourable report from Mr Wale, the head librarian, and I proceeded to see the adviser of studies in the science faculty, a Dr Redmond as I recall.

Two weeks later, I started in science.

It was not in itself what I wanted, and I realised then that, were I able to get back to studying medicine via this route, there would – in all likelihood – be no accompanying vindication of my efforts over the previous three years to gain redress.

This understanding did not come to me as any logical progression. Instead, it struck me hard and out of the blue as I was climbing the stairs to make my initial appointment with Dr Redmond, in the university's Boyd-Orr building.

Suddenly, an unfamiliar sense of loathing descended upon me: *self*-loathing. I had to make my way quickly into the men's washroom, where I was actively sick.

It was, however, only the contents of my stomach that I was successful in purging. The dilemma inflicted by my new course of action *remained*, and almost everything that I *was* told me to walk away. Somehow, though – and with no imaginable alternative in sight – my ego took up the challenge and I pushed on towards Redmond's first floor office.

Not a great way of life, *whoring*; but after your first little sell-out, you reason that you can live with it for a while.

Today, I will not live with it any longer.

Back then, however, I turned my tricks well enough.

In the first year, I applied myself diligently. I gained exemptions in all subjects, first-class certificates of merit in those subjects where they were available (biology and chemistry), and I was awarded the second-top mark in psychology. Disappointingly, however, there came neither interviews nor offers, from either Glasgow or any of the other medical schools to which I had applied at the start of that academic year.

In the second year, I did well again, even jointly winning an essay competition set by Spillers Foods, and open to all undergraduates then studying science subjects at British universities. It was the first of two national essay competitions for which I was awarded first prize – and published – throughout those four years.

The subject was 'Additives in Foods', and my essay was published in the June '88 edition of that 'esteemed' journal, *Food Science & Technology Today*. Spillers Foods invited me down to Crufts Dog Show, at London's Earls Court, to collect my prize of £500.

On the medical school application front, however, the picture remained as desolate as before.

At one compulsory end-of-term visit to Dr Redmond, he expressed amazement that Glasgow had not at least given me an interview, since my academic record up until that time had been 'quite outstanding'.

'Write something, even if it's just a suicide note.'

— Gore Vidal

I can imagine that there must be *many* reasons why people write books, and although I am not disposed towards suicide, the advice of the late patrician and epigrammatic wit strikes me as good counsel now. Given that I have come to expect no just resolution from any British authority, with regard to the few individuals who have sought to deflect the course of my life, I *had* thought that my motivation in writing would be singular. Namely, a little more whoring, in the hope that I might use the complete story as a final, successful application to a (non-British) medical school, where common sense and humanity take precedence over expedience and decorum. Maybe that piece of 'white paper' legislation about UK universities being 'autonomous bodies' might be applied more widely: and in my *favour* for once.

As my writing has progressed, a second – although admittedly *lesser* – impulse, which initially surprised me, has arisen. It is the requirement to communicate my tale, in its apposite entirety, to anyone who might be interested: a sort of end-abreaction in the face of overwhelming odds, and in the hope that some useful advancement(s) in the way that Scotland's universities are run might come about, in order to prevent what happened to me ever happening again to someone else in a similar situation.

In any case – and in accordance with my original drive – I reproduce below my published essay, notwithstanding the fact that I no longer agree with my own conclusions in relation to the subject.

At the risk of seeming to offend or patronise any reader who is not a medical school dean, interested (even vaguely) in me as a prospective student, I would advise you to skip the next few pages. The business of food additives is excruciatingly dull – *believe* me! I spent almost a month in libraries and company laboratories researching this unappetising subject.

As a useful alternative, however, I am inclined at this point to provide you, dear reader, with two things: (i) a quote from none other than Nikola Tesla: 'The truly extraordinary is not permitted in Science and Industry.' Sadly, that observation of the late (1856-1943), great Serbian American inventor and futurist has applied, for well over half a century now, to Medicine as well; and (ii) a recommendation to read *Science For Sale*, by David L. Lewis. And if that work strikes you as having merit, then why not just go for broke and prise your mind fully open with *Einstein Wrong: The Miracle Year*, by David de Hilster.

When is an additive not an additive?

At the opening of the 1983 joint Food and Agriculture Organisation (FAO)/World Health Organisation (WHO) Expert Committee on Food Additives, it was indicated that consumers in both developing and developed countries were demanding firm assurance that food additives were safe. This called for their appropriate and thorough testing, followed by sound and balanced evaluation. In addition, technological, nutritional and other public health considerations made it necessary to ensure the identity and purity of food additives.

The limits and restrictions ensuing from such undertakings are manifest as the main technical problems facing food manufacturers.

Initially, many candidate substances are, in view of their undesirable properties, deemed unacceptable. For example, certain additives may support microbiological growth. Others, such as calcium benzoate and calcium metabisulfite, are members of groups of food additives for which there are reports of a relatively high incidence of adverse reactions in susceptible individuals. It is not clear to what extent these reactions are manifestations of immunological hypersensitivity or of idiosyncratic hyper-reactivity. However, both types of reaction can be regarded as forms of intolerance. For example, excessive consumption of hydrogenated carbohydrates, such as mannitol, can produce a laxative effect, and animal studies have demonstrated that some other additives, at concentrations above certain low levels, are carcinogenic. Faced with such findings, food manufacturers are pressured, on the one hand, to search continuously for new, safer additives yielding high qualities of the desired properties, e.g. preservative, flavouring or colouring; and on the other, to rigorously control the levels of pre-established additives, which they introduce into foodstuffs.

Further problems arise for the manufacturer regarding intentional and unintentional food additives. Depletion of sources of raw materials, in particular certain minerals used to manufacture additives, might result in increases in the levels of contaminants, such as arsenic and fluoride in phosphates, thus necessitating new investment of company resources into more efficient and stringent separation processes.

Finally, certain substances are used as chemical reagents in the preparation of food additives and processing aids (mutually distinct definitions for which are difficult to develop) and therefore only come into contact with food in association with the additive or processing aid (e.g. glutaraldehyde in the preparation of immobilised enzyme preparations, acetic anhydride, adipic anhydride, and vinyl acetate in the manufacture of modified starches). Although it is usually unnecessary to elaborate specifications for such reagents, their carry-over, together with impurities they contain, into a food additive, and thus possibly into the final food, must be taken into account during the evaluation of that additive. Residues of the reagent and of any relevant impurities must therefore be controlled in the specifications, for the purity of the additive. Here, as in other areas of food processing, the chemistry and physics involved are exact sciences, which are both time-consuming and costly to achieve and maintain.

As late as the seventies, those same sciences and the technology to which they gave rise were still seen by consumer and manufacturer alike as unique and noble means for raising the standard of living of people, everywhere. There could surely be little justifiable regret if their sudden intrusion disturbed a society where, in the words of Hobbes, the life of man was 'solitary, poor, nasty, brutish and short'. To the communities of those times past, condensed milk was to be welcomed for children as a substitute for the traditional contaminated gruel, and margarine was quickly accepted as a healthy replacement for butter; although for many, its taste (or lack of it) belied its wholesome benefits.

In food, as with so many other things, the technological revolution has been relatively sudden and wholly unprecedented. It continues still, but, like all other events in human history, it is spending its force and dwindling into the perspectives of the past.

Of late, science has lost some of its former status and respect. Nowadays, physicists may be people who create disasters like Chernobyl, and chemists, those who discharge toxic waste into river and sea.

In this new climate, many individuals have again embraced raw nature, unfettered, and untampered with by man. Terms like wholemeal, organic, biogenic and additive-free have become the order of the day. For instance, it is interesting to note that, despite the lack of cosmetic presentation for many organically grown fruits and vegetables, there exists a growing body of consumers willing to pay the premium for them – a fact that more and more supermarket chains are taking advantage of. On the other hand, the shelves of those same supermarkets still bear testament to a continuing demand for neatly packaged, frozen, tinned and dried convenience foods, many now without, but some still with, preservatives.

From such observations, it would appear that there have emerged ranges of priorities for both consumers and food manufacturers, which are limiting for both groups.

One must not forget, however, that like any other human activity, the marketing and buying of food is a dynamic process, which is constantly evolving. Therefore, the closeness (or otherwise) of priorities on either side of the food business fence, is something which is subject to human influence. Food manufacturers attempt to guide consumer priorities, while certain consumer groups, such as FACT (Food Additives Campaign Team), in the UK, argue that food additives are a political issue and advocate Government incentives to make the business of producing additive-free 'health foods' flourish, and new laws to raise standards of all foods.

In order to offset adverse trends in public opinion and combat the threat of Governmental imposition, both consumer and food manufacturers must not lose sight of the 'fundamental' difference in their respective priorities - financial reward for the food manufacturer, and high quality food for the consumer. The importance of such a difference is axiomatic in any human activity involving the successful exchange of values. It is that it invites the joint application of selfishness and intelligence, driven by goodwill, to generate all-round growth and development. Cynics (lazy rather than blind by nature) might argue that an ideal business environment for such does not exist in the real world. I would argue that it does: indeed, it occurs spontaneously wherever producers and consumers meet – it is the competitive market place; and nowadays the market researcher (or perhaps better, market 'interpreter') ought to have a very useful role at this interface.

Indeed, any viable form for communication between consumer and producer can only help to continuously assess whether, for example, substance 'x' qualifies as an additive or an ingredient; and thereby assist towards the fulfilment of priorities on both sides of the counter.

I am inclined to reveal here – and by way of a coda to the above essay – that I, for one, always endeavour to think carefully about *any* foodstuff that has been processed *in any manner*, before deciding whether or not to consume it.

If you consume dairy products, then you would be wise to think carefully about your best option(s) as regards *milk*.

Milk is a species-specific drink for young mammals. However, if you simply *must* have *cows'* milk, with its growth hormones 'designed' by Mother Nature to put a few hundred pounds on a baby calf within a few months, and tending to stimulate the growth of hormone-sensitive tumours – such as those of the prostate – in adult human males, then (i) make sure it is organic, and (ii) drink *whole* milk only: otherwise you will be consuming a once 'natural' product that has had its balance of fats and sugars altered. And that imbalance can go some way (progressively, and cumulatively, with all the other tempting, refined sugar-laden 'treats'[3] out there) towards pushing many individuals

---

[3] See: *Pure, White and Deadly*, a book by John Yudkin

in the direction of Type II diabetes, and associated conditions of 'metabolic syndrome'.

Don't be fooled by the propaganda about skimmed- and semi-skimmed milk!

Chapter Eleven

I read somewhere that music, while having its effect within the realm of the aesthetic senses, can arouse and inspire us in a manner, which transcends the aura conjured up by aesthetic considerations. In my experience this claim is, for the most part, true.

Until one day around the middle of the autumn term, each of my days at the school, during 1993/'94, was made bearable by two music-filled return journeys between my mother's house and the academy. At the end of those fifteen-minute walks lay situations which were, at best, *challenging*; and the inevitable strain imposed by the situation that I had immersed myself in was, initially, ameliorated by those quarter-hour musical interludes.

Plugged into my Walkman, I would be charged forward by sources as diverse – yet as *close* – as Maurice Ravel and Smashing Pumpkins; Michael Nyman and Pixies; Claude Debussy and Dead Can Dance; and once in a while – when I felt that I needed reminding that I was still a spiritually-developed being and not some lowly caged animal – a little mitigating, mollifying Mozart. At first, I felt that without those sonic 'sources', I could not have tolerated the coming year's experience.

In the mornings, I would leave the house five minutes earlier than necessary, as that would afford me the dual luxury of avoiding the throng of instreaming students, and of having a few minutes sitting on a low wall near Morven Road, in order to 'psych myself up' for whatever the day might bring. 'Sufficient unto the day is the evil thereof', my grandfather used to quote occasionally. I guess that, mostly, I tried to hold to that. It seemed wise.

It was on one such morning in late September, while perched on that wall, and suddenly gripped by renewed despair at the loss of the young woman I loved, that my 'visitor' – my 'Guardian' – moved again to *rule*, rendering that part of me which led to such self-indulgence, *inoperative*. It simply went to sleep: the deep 'cryosleep' of science fiction books and films – a sui generis torpor that, for all but a few brief, desperate and hard-won bursts of renewedly incorporated sentience, would be imposed for well over a further twenty-one years.

My relationship with music changed too after that day. Occasionally thereafter, music would, in some sense, find *me*, but I somehow lost the urge to look for *it* any more: except amongst the canon of old Wolfgang Amadeus, which, in *my* book, is not music in the conventional sense anyway. It seems to occupy a unique category that overlaps with 'brain food' supplements, like Omega (3) EPA & DHA, Vitamins D and B12, Vinpocetine, Alpha GPC, and Bacopa Monnieri.

On the subject of continuity, I surmise that I may safely tell the rest of my story in (something *approaching*) chronological order … *kind* of:

"You've got to tell the punters about the school thing, Brian – let them in on the day-to-day mechanics of how you pulled it off! Otherwise they just won't be interested." This was another pearl of wisdom spouted, in late 1995, by *The Herald* newspaper's chain-smoking, junket-loving 'reporter' Ron Mackenna, who would express a purportedly strong interest in writing a book about my experiences.

I think that his outlook must have been rather jaundiced. My return to school seemed – and seems – to me to warrant only a lesser part of my account, and whatever resulted in my having 'pulled it off' is certainly not a quality of any great consequence. I would merely state that if it was something *acquired*, it may well have come about as a result of my having seen every episode of the first season – the *only* one that mattered, really – of Mission: Impossible, before the age of twelve.

Anyway, back to chronology (after a fashion).

By the late summer of 1988, I found myself in something of a quandary. I had progressed successfully through two years of the BSc course at Glasgow without an offer – or even an interview – from any medical school.

I had entered the Spiller's Foods' essay competition via the Chemistry department where, mysteriously, in the spring term of my second year, I was failed in the minor subject, 'Half Higher Ordinary Chemistry'; although I passed the September resit, 'with flying colours', according to my adviser of studies.

"Once you label me you negate me."

— Søren Kierkegaard

Something of an oversensitive reaction by the existentialist Dane, maybe, but being *falsely* labelled *can* be a particularly unpleasant experience, especially when those doing the damnable deed are 'respected' individuals who ought to know better.

At the late September afternoon conclusion of that chemistry examination, I felt rather good: *quickened*. Then, just a few short steps outside of the hall, and before that quickening waned, there began to enter into me a palpable perception that first moved me to take a seat on a nearby wall and, thereafter, to put on hold my plan to treat myself to half a pint of an unpasteurised Munich Helles draught lager called Fürstenberg, at *The Ubiquitous Chip* bar in Ashton Lane. Instead, I gave the appearance of setting out on a walk back towards Bearsden.

To state in as plain and straightforward language as seems to me to be appropriate here, I had just been provided with explicit foresight of what would await me at the lower end of Observatory Road. Ten minutes later, and once I had reached its junction with Byres Road, I turned hesitantly onto that long, quickly steepening avenue. I had walked Observatory several times before, but on *that* early evening, anticipation of the events to follow re-established it as *terra incognita*.

> "I mean, that things are so in spite of us; we can't always help it that our gain is another's loss."

> — Gwendolen Harleth, from: George Eliot's *Daniel Deronda*

Maybe it becomes a gamble of sorts for me, even *now*, to relate what happened next; but as Eliot's wilful, troubled heroine averred …

By the age of twenty-five, I was, for close to five years, successfully returned to the practice of Lucid/Active Dreaming, the benefits of which were not limited to the hours of sleep. I had, lucidly, forged and secured links between my own conscious and subconscious, and to 'near realms' beyond both, via the maintenance of a state not far removed from what has been described as 'Theta state' (or Theta-wave) consciousness. This continuance had gradually yielded the added benefit of near-effortless waking-life access to those realms.

In more spiritually attuned cultures, the 'hazard' associated with stating the above might be no more than to risk the label 'shaman'. In *this* culture, however, the prefix 'sha' can *so* offhandedly be replaced by 'mad'.

The unco gleaming eidolon, although then more than twenty-six years short of removing himself from me, had never by then moved to torpefy; and he would seldom impose. Outside that exam hall, however, he *had* – and with good reason – undertaken to do the latter.

I was no more than six or seven yards along Observatory, when the transit sized Police van rounded the corner from behind and halted abruptly in front of me, with the front nearside wheel ending up jammed hard, and slightly deformed, against the kerb. As the rear doors opened and two uniformed officers dismounted, the salty-looking thirtysomething male – dressed in jeans and a short-sleeved powder blue shirt; and with a prominent 'Latin-inscribed ribbon wound around dagger' tattoo on his right forearm – who had followed me from outside the examination hall, closed swiftly in and grabbed my arms. While the younger of the two uniforms slipped closely past my right side, with a set of handcuffs in his left hand, his colleague advised me: "It's for *your* safety *and* ours, Brian."

131

With that, I was swiftly and unceremoniously bundled into the back of the van; and the doors were closed by the driver, who had alighted as I was being handcuffed.

Her overall appearance was redolent of a nuclear family kitchen scene: home baking and Sunday dinners … pronounced embonpoint. Dali or Ernst might have had her contrived as an over-padded oven glove made flesh and imbued with life. However, those unruly primate facial muscles, sequentially and indecorously quivering their irrepressibly recalcitrant argot behind the topmost of her homely upholstery, immediately began to betray a quite different constitution.

Nomenclature: give it a name! '*Animal magnetism*': that's what Franz Anton Mesmer dubbed it; and as I began to settle into my physically restricted – and, by dint of same, human will-*inciting* – position across from her, I did not long hesitate to use that animal magnetism to carve my way, unimpeded, into her psyche.

As I commenced, I urged silently to one unseen:

> "At once, upon all
> Given *me* to see,
> Let her *too* recall.
> So mote it be!"

I need not, however, have bothered with such cheapjack mischief. I sensed strongly that *he* would have prompted her to recollect as required, anyway.

Seemingly discomfited by something unfamiliar, and struggling to maintain the air of 'professional' distance that she had undoubtedly been sure of up until only a moment before, she spoke up at once.

"Hello Brian. Do you know, I have it, on some authority that you're not quite a *proper* boy … uh, I mean a *real* boy?"

The faint, quickly disappearing smile that accompanied her remark was merely one of the lips.

> I will never apologize for being me. You should apologize for asking me to be anything else.
>
> — Eusebius

"Misquoting *Pinocchio*?" I asked, distractedly. "It would seem that the compounded impropriety is *yours*."

I had hoped – *credibly*, as it turned out – that the riposte would quieten her for the few seconds that I required to find some jemmy or other that would lend validity to what was certainly an *inferior* distraction.

"Why," I wondered, "another *alienist*?" If the intention was indeed to *kill* me, then this frumpy fat 'trick cyclist' was, surely, inappropriately qualified for the task.

Cleaving deeper, there soon became apparent to me two points of particular interest and crucial importance. Firstly, her general sense of disappointment at the all but vanished hope of *consultant* status; then, images of 'partners' – a whole *string* of them – glasses of wine in hand, in that homely kitchen of hers: and *all* of them women.

I have never given a hoot about the sexual preferences of others (none of my business), but on *that* occasion it was the first useful 'button' that I had been able to access. And I knew that, time-sensitive as this rapidly developing situation was, *insensitivity* was what I had veritable need of. Had there appeared a succession of 'elephantine' buttons beside her in the aforementioned room, I would have pressed any *one* of them just as insistently and forcefully; although in such a near-impossible eventuality, *I* might have been hard-pressed to have come up with a more workable metaphor than the one which had just come to mind.

"Apples or *pears*," I ventured. "Which do *you* prefer? Now, *me*: I'm inclined to look out for that *one*, moist, rare-variety, autumn-ripening pear … *whenever* and *wherever* such a singular fruit might be had: *soft* and melt-in-the mouth *buttery* at first; *then*, in the aftertaste, something of the *musk* of the boudoir … *don't* you think? *Apples*, on the other hand: *they're* just too much *work*: all that hard unyielding flesh. *And* they all taste just the *same*! Wouldn't you *agree*?"

She began to frown.

"*I* think that you *do* agree! I think that you're a *pears* kind of a gal. In fact, I think you can't get enough of those pears: *every* variety you come across."

Then, after the briefest pause, I harried: "It's *terrible*, isn't it, what some women still have to do to get ahead, *even* in the eighties? If you don't mind me saying, you are *very* short-term as serial monogamists go. But this *MacSween* character must have *more* on you than that. How has he managed to set you to *such* a grave task? And what has he offered you? Advancement? *Money*? I mean, shameless *toadying* is *one* thing, but … *this*?"

She glared at me, askance; but there was the beginning of *fear* in her lour as well. Then, in rapid succession, I was given to see, first, my lifeless body being tipped, in the dead of night, from a motor boat, into the murky waters of the Firth of Clyde; followed by a scene of her indulgence in an activity – especially shocking, for its *extreme* rarity as a *female* predilection – with the *equally* dead. And although it lay outwith my comprehension of what could constitute sexuality, the perception of *that* pursuit *certainly* engendered in me senses of revulsion and detestation.

With *that*, I had discovered as much as I cared to know about her, and I chose the final moments to heighten in her the feeling of disquietude that would remain with her long after the temporary incapacitation that she was shortly thereafter to experience.

I took next to no pleasure in it. It seemed like little other than pragmatism. If the ordeal were to have lead her first to introspection, and thereafter to self-improvement, then *she* at least – and, *possibly*, one-or-other of her associates, then present or otherwise – might have posed no further threat to me.

"*Neither*!" I rammed. "He didn't *have* to, did he? Oh, that's *very* bad! That's *cold*: *way* beyond *impropriety*! What *conceivable* appeal could *that* hold for you?" I quizzed, still feeling a little bewildered. Then, as another burst of adrenaline brought renewed focus: "Couldn't you just have been satisfied with all those fresh juicy ..."

"*Shut up*! Shut *your mouth*!" she squawked.

"Oh, *you've c*hanged!" I rounded again. "It seems like mere *moments* ago that you were just *oozing* that delightful faltering charm of yours. You *know*, now that I *think* on it, it *was* only moments ago! And suddenly, *here* you *are*: a time-ravaged, grim-faced, near-hysteric. But you're absolutely *right*. What *is* the use of talking to a mad person?"

"*I'll* shut him the fuck up if you like," asserted the tattooed rent-a-thug clamping me in a tightening headlock.

"*No*!" she countermanded peremptorily. "I want to look into his eyes as he realises that it's the end.

What I *did* realise, thereupon, was that, for *me* at least, she may have been a lost cause; but I kept hard at her for reasons that, by *then*, may very well have been straying outside the territory of the impersonal.

"Oh, you really *are* a warped little *boule de suif*, aren't you? I'd bet you could eat ice cream with a *corkscrew*. Ever *tried*? No, I reckon you just *lap it up* straight out of the carton? Ice cream with *pears*: *mmm, yummy*!"

By then, her composure certainly appeared to be under noticeable strain, as she reached into the little black, zippered, toiletries-type bag, to her left on the bench, and withdrew one (of two visible to me) small-sized near-full hypodermics, each of which had a long, pale green plastic cap covering the needle. Then, holding the syringe at about sixty degrees above the horizontal, she proceeded to remove its cap; and with revealing tremor developing in *both* hands, she began to push the plunger in as careful and measured a fashion as she could still manage, until a tiny droplet of the transparent tube's deadly content appeared, *shining*, near the tip of the needle.

"Now, let me get this *straight* … if you'll *pardon* the expression," I harrowed. "What *is* the official stamp to be: misadventure or suicide? Oh, it would really *have* to be suicide, *wouldn't* it? Is that *perspiration* on your upper lip?"

"Hold him *still*!" she barked. "And remove his right shoe and sock!"

"Look, I'm not so *sure* about this!" protested the youngest of her three accomplices, who was positioned on my right; his faltering voice betraying some loss of nerve.

"He digs it the *most*, you know," I put in, staring intently at her. "Here it *is*, then: moment of *truth*. You are about to take a *life*." Then, grinning broadly: "How does that make you *feel*?"

"*Do* as I *say*!" she insisted overbearingly in the direction of the despairing stooge; but now there were indications of desperation in her own timbre, and palpable signs of tension in all three of her male confederates.

"Look, be a *poppet* will you, and take these cuffs off me?" I piped up again, still addressing my entreaty to the bestial syringe-flaunting medic.

There appeared, for the briefest interval, a look of derision in her returned glance; and then, as she proceeded first, and *unknowingly*, to lay down the primed-but-unused equipage – and immediately thereafter, to move forwards to fulfil my requested task – there *wasn't*.

The other three had just let go of me and were each sat quietly, as though in a trance. When she had unlocked the steel cuffs that had bound my hands behind my body, she moved slowly, and – as was discernible to me – abstractedly, back to her seated position on the opposite bench.

And there she sat: a little stooped, staring ahead, expressionless and seemingly vacant.

I had already been informed that they would all be nonresponsive for some time: so it was to one incorporeal, rather than corpulent, that I addressed my question about what it was that was in the syringe.

I was informed that it was the alkaloid cardio- and neurotoxin, aconitine.

As I stood up, stretched my slightly numbed legs and considered the instrument of intended death, my thoughts returned to an event that had occurred one afternoon nearly eight years previously (1980).

It had been during a 'Human Biology' lab in the nearby Boyd Orr building, only days after my unfortunate wipe out off the Ayrshire coast, and when I had been little more than a month into my first year as a medical student.

A young, male medical doctor had entered the lab and, on his behalf, the lecturer had asked for at least ten volunteers from that section to give a sample of blood for a research project that the junior medic was undertaking. There had been little-to-no enthusiasm from *any* quarter, in response to the request; so, ostensibly, it had fallen to the lecturer to go about the laboratory making one-to-one appeals.

The young medic had moved to a position squarely behind where I sat and, at first, while the lecturer had gone about petitioning on his behalf, he had just *stood* there. Once the requisite posse of reluctant donors had been dragooned into service, the junior medic had leant forward, tapped me lightly on the shoulder and, blunderingly, had entreated me to furnish him with dispensable small portion of *my* blood. I had agreed without complaint, even though he had immediately struck me as being a little strange: *creepy*.

I had been last in the queue to donate, and when it had become my turn, I had found myself alone with him in the side room across the corridor.

He had been fidgety as he had set about selecting his equipment, and before having proceeded with taking the sample, he had asked me if the sight of blood bothered me. It had seemed to me an odd first question to put to someone who had chosen to read *Medicine* at university, and *particularly* because I had not up until then been experiencing or displaying any signs of distress; although *his* general demeanour up to that point had not, in *any* sense, lent itself to setting *anyone* at their ease.

I had replied that the sight of none but my *own* blood ever distressed me, and he had quickly intimated that, being similarly disposed, he had found that *looking away* had always helped him to maintain his composure. I had been content to take his advice. However, it had been *he* – and not the prospect of having a needle inserted into an arm vein – that had marginally unsettled me.

There had followed, in slow succession, two instances of what felt like botched attempts to harvest a sample of my mortal ichor. Each had been accompanied by some (mounting) ire on *his* part, in conjunction with his repeated insistence that I had 'wobbly' veins.

Throughout the years since, I have invariably made a point of asking practitioners – whenever I have found myself in the position of giving a blood sample, or receiving an injection – if, in their professional opinion, I exhibit this condition. The given answers have unfailingly been in the *negative*.

I recalled that when the unexpected ordeal had come to an end, and I had prepared to leave his makeshift 'torture chamber', sporting two more sticking plaster-covered, blood-soaked cotton pads on my forearms than I had anticipated, I had, on observation of his dour woebegone expression, tried to cheer him by making a light-hearted remark about *his* having been 'bowed, but at least *unbloodied*' by the afternoon's experience. In his minimal acknowledgement of the remark, he had not turned his face quite towards me, but whether by momentary scrutiny of his profile alone, or simply by dint of the sheer oppressiveness of the undertone that had by then developed between us, I had felt – and only at that *conclusion* – quite unsettled.

As I moved away from the Police Van and its insensible occupants, and back towards Ashton Lane, on that September evening in 1988, I sought to discover as much more information as I could cope with from 'my Guardian dear'.

"The young medic, in late 1980: he *introduced* something into my bloodstream, didn't he?"

139

"Yes."

"A *virus*. But not the Coxsackie. I would have shrugged that off relatively quickly, right?"

"Yes. Correct. Right."

"It was the *other* one: the one that the Germans found fragments of, *wasn't* it?" I continued, as I began to anticipate his seemingly inevitable response, as I would have a past-avoidable punch to the midriff.

"Yes."

"*Oh*!" I winced. "I thought that there was an internationally agreed moratorium in place, prohibiting even the *development* – never mind the *use* – of those agents. In *particular*, I would have thought it reasonable to assume that bumping off one's own countrymen with them was *strictly* forbidden!"

Luckily, the section of pavement that I was passing along in those seconds was empty of passers-by, as, in my mounting anger, I had unnecessarily spat out the words derisively.

With no reply to that, I stopped dead in my tracks for a moment or two, as I began to contemplate the overall gravity of my situation. *How*, I wondered, could MacSween have been granted access to even an *attenuated* – and, presumably, *non-transmissible* – agent of *that* nature? This *certainly* was not what my parents had paid their taxes for all those years.

Then I returned to that process which lay somewhere between interrogation and supplication.

"How do *I* gain from what just went down in that van? This whole emerging rotten set-up merely causes me to be minded that I *have* to bug out and try another route. I mean, let's assume that word of what just happened gets back to MacSween. Is one seemingly anomalous event going to deflect him, *or* whoever he is in thrall to, *one little bit*?

140

Moreover, I'm not keen on being party to what appear to me to be *non-causal* events. Beyond the Ten Commandments – if there *is* more to it than that – I'm not familiar with Divine Law, but I do know that I am in *this* world and that there *is* causality …"

"You are *in* the world: *active* in the world. But you need not be *of* the world, brother. You should *hold on*!"

"Yes, but I don't yet know if I'm wholly *inclined* to be little other than an *instrument*. I mean, I know that I can be a bit of a *tool* sometimes, but I refuse to be a nonentity: some *nothing man*, whatever the worldly restraints on my progress to date. I *know*, at my very *core*, of one great reason why I entered this world, and I need to be able to *hold my own*: to make my *own* way. So, why should I stay on at a purportedly *academic* institution where, contrary to what *ought* to be the case, *merit* can be so readily and casually *defecated* upon?"

At the time, I could for the life of me make neither head nor tail of his response, which was to deliver to my mind the theme music and lyric of a silly, dubbed-into-English, childrens' television programme, which I had been *little* drawn to as a youngster. Entitled 'The Flashing Blade', it went, '… for life and love and happiness are well worth fighting for…'

Despite the best efforts of others that day, I at least still had my *life*.

"'*Love* and *happiness*'," I mused. If this was some long-awaited revelation of a sense of *humour* on his part, then it was not quite hitting home.

Then, from somewhere deep inside of me there came an impulse, which inspired a sharp, shallow intake of breath, accompanied by a sensation of *such* elation that it brought tears to my eyes. It almost overwhelmed me, but halting for a second time, I quickly smoothed it out as best as I could. I had not felt anything even *closely* resembling it since a

141

morning in the late summer of 1980, when I had received my letter of acceptance to medical school.

Via the most highly vibrating conduit, I had been given a powerful sense of *another*: incarnate, and distant from me neither spiritually nor in years.

I was only twenty-five. Another year's pause did not seem so *much* back then: a pause from struggle: for life and – although I had not consciously been seeking it – for *love*?

On the instant, I decided that I would go back: I would go back and wait, and *see*.

With that matter both promptly and unexpectedly resolved, I was minded to 'speak' to him again.

Ours was not exactly *lingual* dialogue, although I did comprehend some of the minutiae of his responses in terms of my first language. It was a far less restricted exchange: like an intangible, two-lane, mutually customised (and accommodating) information supraconduit, with – when it was in operation – the vast majority of the traffic travelling in *my* direction. I employ the prefix 'supra', here because it was transcendent in two senses: firstly, in the context of the great likelihood that even *today's* most open-minded readers may regard any claim of *any* form of telepathy as a strictly *purported* phenomenon; and secondly – and for one for whom telepathy is as much an aspect of reality as anything else – this 'supraconduit' was on a more highly vibrating level of reality than the one which I had, up until then, shared with only one other (corporeal) being: my mother.

I had been able to gain (and sustain) access to the former manner of channel *at all*, only because I had very occasionally been granted briefly-sustained, lucid access to one even higher: one which I suspect that *all* of us have had access to at one time or another. And it was in relation to *that* that I addressed my Guardian again.

"I have become, these past six or seven years – and with good reason – an occasionally *recusant* fellow; and that recently adopted characteristic of my humanity no doubt impinges on my spirit. Earlier, you exhorted me to 'hold on'. Should I ever come to a point when I feel in *need* of a master, it would only ever be *Christ*; and *no other*. It is through *his* auspices alone that I *know* why I am upon this earth: my necessary path and purpose here. Perhaps in some sense I have *always* regarded him as my master. It's just that when one is still young …" I trailed off.

"Anyway," I eventually continued, picking up my line of thought again, "I know that you are no jinn: you are bright *without* the scorch, and I sense no guile in you. I also apprehend that you are far *above* the base vibration of this dense material realm; and as you must now be *fully* aware, I trust you with my life. *So*, do our outlooks *accord* on this?"

"Yes."

With that assurance – and for the umpteenth time since our first acquaintance – I saw fit to impetrate from him the radix reason for my being subject to these uncalled-for torments.

His long-awaited response followed expeditiously: a huge 'download' of information (fardels, petabytes: feel free, reader, to jargonize according to your sense of generational association), both diverse and interrelated — God's first-born, first-seen son, Christ, given one third part-power of the Primordial Power for his redemptive act for humanity; the defeat – with that act – of Lucifer's long-running plan to dissolve God's created reality, and to replace it with another of his own design; the still possible entrenchment of some of Lucifer's followers/recruiters upon the dense material earth, and the chaos and suffering that they continue to bring to humanity; the wilful dissolution, by a guileful intransigent race, of their long-established covenant with God, and the emergence of a new covenant with a new people; the disappearance of old morphogenetic

143

grids (fixed above and below the earth), as corresponding species disappear; and the appearance of a new grid, boding the emergence of a new type of human bio-system (with two additional autosomes), into which only spiritually-evolved and largely unburdened souls can incarnate; mounting conflicts; cataclysm: all well within a human span, hence. Then, profound darkness and a shaking earth which yields no growth: a difficult era for expectant mothers. And at the conclusion of this purging phase, the emergence of a 'finer' material earth, perfused with light so bright and investing that only the new type of human being (in a much-reduced population, relative to the end times of this epoch) is able to adapt to living upon it: a *raised* earth, finally and firmly-established as part of God's Kingdom.

I have never been an individual prone to mood swings, and moodiness is something that I am not disposed to tolerate well in others; but, for once, as I rounded the corner into Ashton Lane, I found myself in what a Kentish girl who I had been seeing those past two years would have called a 'strop'. Still some years from my maturity, I had discovered an aspect of my personality that caused me to little-appreciate having my senses strained and my heartstrings tugged hither and thither in the course of such a brief period. Intellectual and emotional stability were traits that I both valued and depended upon, and I cared little for their being rocked so violently that it became a challenge to maintain either. I nonetheless suspected that the entire episode had been a necessary strengthening ordeal: a preparatory exercise in the face of uncertain future events.

Rock 'n' roll wild man that I was, I downed not a *half*, but a full *pint* of the aforementioned, funky, unpasteurised, German brew, in *The Ubiquitous Chip*, before taking a bus back to the premises in Bearsden where, at twenty-five, I still lodged with my parents.

Chapter Twelve

The representative of the Immunology department, who I went to see for a second time some days later, cited my failure in the first diet of the Chemistry Half Higher Ordinary exam for their refusal to admit me to their honours course.

With third year about to begin, I faced the unexpected prospect of having no classes to attend.

Then – and again unexpectedly – I received a call from Dr Lackie. He had been my Cell Biology lecturer during the second year.

"If you can understand how a car engine works, then you can understand cytology," he had said during the first day of his course of lectures. Until then, I had long since been of the Donald Sutherland (in the role of the character, 'Oddball', in the film, *Kelly's Heroes*) school of motoring philosophy: 'Man, I just ride 'em; I don't know what makes 'em go!'

Well, that wasn't *exactly* true: as a seven year old, I had, against all expectation, managed to convince my father to allow me to disassemble the 'dying' air-cooled engine of the family car – a Volkswagen Beetle – in order to identify the worn part that had been causing the problem. Maybe it had been the tedium of my insisted-upon (by my father) close involvement in the further process of *re*assembly that had caused me to lose interest in car engines thereafter.

As it turned out though, Dr Lackie's lectures were not to be the dry exercises in nanoscopic biomechanics that he might initially have led one to expect. Instead, they had the mesmerising quality of a good animated cartoon, and were thereby instantly memorable. Mind you, nowadays, with car engines increasingly resembling products from the electronics industry – even after opening the bonnet, one is presented with another cover, like the back of an iPad – I take my car to a qualified mechanic when I need it repaired or serviced.

I could not help but like a fellow with so much up-front, no-nonsense nervous energy as Dr Lackie. The only time that I ever saw him dour was that afternoon, a few days before the beginning of the third year.

"That's not *on*!" he declared. "You're certainly a *very* capable student. And I don't understand why you didn't get 1/2 HO Chemistry: especially with your winning this essay prize. How did you feel the exam *went*?"

"I was sure that I had *aced* it."

What I decided *not* to mention to Lackie was that I had gone to see the Chemistry professor about it, and that he had been unable (or unwilling) to look me in the eye during our short meeting.

According to Dr Lackie, there was a pathology professor named Whaley, who had recently been coordinating a BSc course entitled 'Experimental Pathology'. Normally, pathology degrees were designed for intercalating and postgraduate medical students *only*, but the addition of this 'Experimental' prefix allowed a few science students to be admitted. As I was intent upon regaining a place at medical school, he suggested that I go across to Pathology and speak to Whaley.

As soon as I had heard him utter 'pathology', my heart had sunk. If pawns could ever have feelings, then I suddenly felt like one that an absentee landlord of a God had just sacrificed in a game of chess with the Devil; although, in all seriousness, I would have to doubt that *God* – in the seemingly impossible event that He had *need* to sharpen His wits – would incline to indulgence in a board game that is to connate racism and studied, multiplex, tactical, ethnic cleansing, as monopoly is to rampant capitalism.

I countered the discomfiting sensation with the thought: "*Nah*, it can't be *that* bad. Maybe it's *entirely* this *Whaley* guy's show. Maybe MacSween doesn't concern himself in undergraduate matters."

Fat chance!

When I entered Professor Whaley's office later that morning, he was reading my file.

"Sit down, Brian," he said hastily, and gestured towards the chair in front of his desk. He immediately put me in mind of Joseph Heller's character, Major _____ de Coverley, from the novel, *Catch 22*. The 'blank' came about because the Major looked *so* fierce that no one had ever dared to ask him his Christian name. Whaley too had an aura of fierceness about him: an aura given an almost *comic* twist by the fact that one of the poor soul's thumbs was unnaturally 'flattened out' by what I could only guess to have been an accident where something *very* heavy had landed on it: 'his fucked-up thumb', as I once heard one of the other male students describe it. Thankfully, however – and unlike the formidable major – Whaley had two injury-free and kind eyes hidden behind those thick spectacle lenses, and he betrayed no sign of being anything other than a straightforward individual.

147

"Overall, you've attained an excellent academic standard throughout the past two years, Brian. I can't understand why the immunologists didn't take you. In any case, this degree that we're running *here* would provide a much better foundation for someone like you: intent as you are on going on to study medicine. An immunology degree tends to prepare students for a career in *immunology*, and not much else. I'd be glad to have you on the course." By the time he had finished telling me all of that, Professor Whaley's earlier austere expression had given way to a relaxed smile.

It is an overworn cliché, I know, but if my earlier interview with Lackie had hinted at the frying pan, then, on stepping out of Whaley's office, I was immediately to receive renewed taste of infernal fire. Undoubtedly apprised of my appointment with Whaley, MacSween, this almost dapper and most diminutive of head honchos – with his *ageing European politician-suspiciously* black hair – had come to take a look at me from his vantage point in the shadow of the corner at the far end of the corridor. I was twenty-five at that time, with better than 20:20 vision, but even stood stock-still as he was, peering at me like some upright midget *spotter*, he must either have been *very* long-sighted indeed, or was there simply to demonstrate that I was in *his* dominion now; and that he would be involving himself to a *very great degree* in the 'matter' of *this* undergraduate.

Taking a required moment to tune out out of the world of the visual, there came to me the immediate, visceral and unwelcome sense of being the object of another's bloodlust. To state that, at that *moment*, I felt *myself* de trop, would be to understate. Nonetheless, the quickly ensuing recognition of his contained and controlled rage, left me in no doubt that – distasteful as my enjoined proximity *was* to him – he nonetheless had me just where he *needed* me to be.

148

Even at nearly twenty metres and in poor light, I could reasonably infer that 'a very great degree' was not what I would be getting out of staying on *there*.

I cannot lay claim to the ability to (virtually) *see* the aura of another person, but as I suspect may be the case for *some* other individuals, I invariably and quickly acquire a definite *impression* … an overall sense of what I can best describe as the *vibrational energy* that surrounds them; and I perceive *that* in much the same way as I do colour. That may read as utterly pretentious, but I do not think I am like that: at least, I *hope* that I am not. I rather suspect that, when needed – and where *appropriate* – I can be somewhat synaesthetic: a 'condition' which I have always considered as being a boon – facts, number systems, music, chemistry and other languages, serviceably and commodiously collated with all their possible correlations, like ever-expanding, yet instantly accessible tactile *terrains* – rather than something that could usefully be regarded in terms of any (dare I write it?) 'pathology'.

All that I could perceive around MacSween, though, was *darkness* and shadow, as he stood there glowering at me throughout what became a stand-off of some four minutes. By that point, my youthful bravado dictated that the situation was becoming boring, and I headed for the exit.

Outside, in the much-needed fresh air, bravado quickly turned to anger. '*Unerschütterlich*' – which, in English, is 'imperturbable' – is how a German fellow of my acquaintance once described me. I am not so sure any more if that is a good or a bad character trait to be in possession of in this increasingly chaotic world, but I *do* know that it is one that came close to deserting me outside that inconspicuously bland building at the edge of the Gilmorehill campus.

I stood for a few minutes, trying to compose myself; and concerned as I was that if I had gone back in too *soon*, it might have ended badly, I was certainly going to be sure that I was entirely in control of my emotions when I eventually *did* go back in to confront him. When that point arrived, I could locate neither MacSween nor Whaley, whom I looked for after an initial ten minutes of trying to rediscover the former of the two professors.

As I stepped back out again, I noticed MacSween driving off in his Jaguar.

There was suddenly no doubt in me that this was a *bad* place: and one that I ought to get clear of immediately.

Chapter Thirteen

In *her* aura, there was much of the cool green of her eyes. Tinged with orange and dazzling white, and swirling out into faint but discernible pinks and hues of red, it was big and bright and joyous: an inviting flame that with all that I had to give of my airy element, I would ever rush towards.

Three days after my stand-off with MacSween; two failed attempts to break the news about him to my mother; and one day after I had begun to contemplate the prospect of just 'bugging out' anyway, I was standing near the corner of Byres Road and University Avenue, when she said 'hello': this divine dancing star of a soul who, seemingly out of nowhere, appeared in my firmament – a vessel of order and contentment, and the very best kind of excitement, amidst all of the pervading dreary oppression and hectic horror.

"Remember to leave your keys at *reception* on your way out!" prompted my father one day, as I was about to take the car to visit her. He had accompanied his wisecrack with the manner of wicked grin that I had not seen him exhibit throughout what had been – for him – nearly five months of torment.

"That's very *good*, dad!" I retorted. "But we're just going to donate blood. They've *stopped* rewarding that with tickets for all-night *parties*, you know. All you get these days is a sweetie, and maybe a cup of tea."

Heartened though I was at this sign of my father beginning to rally, there nonetheless started to flicker, in some hitherto dark recess of my psyche, a caution about a degree of increeping laziness associated with my choosing to continue to stay at 'home'.

"_____ the *Great*, she stays out *late*!" my mother chimed in, and the sensation flared just that little bit more irritatingly.

"Uh *huh*! Well, *thank* you for that, *Dorothy Parker*. If it helps any, I can tell you that I should be back well in advance of dinner. Something *iron*-rich, please – if that might be managed – as I shall be exsanguinated to the tune of over a *pint*!"

enbliss

(transitive) To endue or fill with bliss; impart bliss to; make happy.

A dreamy expression of fondness, and finding my head turned shyly away. "May I hold your hand?" A long, toggle-weighted, string Light Pull caught and swung repeatedly … flirtatiously, in the midst of a group of other, less distinct faces, around a trolley supporting matter of enjoined interest: our cards full of one another, as though mutually-immersed in an enchanting Khachaturian waltz.

Substantially, our reciprocated desiderating all at once began.

Past the giddy romantic whirl of inceptive encounters, we each discovered connatural possession of marvellous means to moderate and transform one another's shortcomings: whether it was her (*very* occasional and slight) inclination to imperiousness, or my insouciant cynicism, progressively purged from me by exposure to the lightness of her esse ... her *quiddity*.

I am no wordsmith. My God-given talents lie elsewhere. In addition, I am certainly not a fan of creative prose. It inevitably corrupts the *actualité*. *She* refreshed me on that important point: not via any spoken instruction, but simply by the example of her *being*. Writing about this therefore begins to feel like an *indelicacy*: belittling what it truly *was*. Trying to recapture and set down what was intensely personal, subtle, effortless, and even *ethereal*, in the coarse form of *language* seems to me to be at once *too much* ... yet, now that I have become committed to it, never *enough*. Words are, indeed, no great signifiers of truth. But I cannot wholly omit reference to it: because that rarest and most blissful aspect of life is never just some addendum or side story. Rather, it informs and inspires *all* that was – and *remains* – good and worthwhile. Beyond words, only music – or the odd 'chanced'-upon poem – can even come close to conjuring the merest hint of the wonder of it: ever-more wonder and beauty than that later-to-be-knighted little psychopath could manage to expropriate and choke off, like bindweed choking off a flower garden.

Chapter Fourteen

And once you are awake, you shall remain awake
eternally

From: *Thus Spake Zarathustra – A Book For All And
None,* by Friedrich Nietzsche

Not long after the beginning of the first term, MacSween
turned up for an impromptu 'lecture' in the tutorial room, on
the ground floor of Pathology, where the small group of nine
students would assemble most mornings. He began by
asking who among us 'liked a drink', and then declared that
alcohol was a 'non-predictable hepatotoxin'. "So far, so 'old
hat'," I remember having thought. Next, a single slide
depicting normal hepatocytes – cells of the parenchymal
(main) tissue of the liver – was projected onto the screen on
the wall. And *that* – for a man who proclaimed himself as
being an expert on the liver – was all that he had to say on
anything relating to that major organ, or, indeed, anything
else relating to either medicine or *pathology*: of the
'experimental' variety or otherwise. He devoted the lesser
part of the remaining fifty-five minutes of the designated
hour to stories about the islands of Lewis and Skye, and other
miscellaneous subjects that, at first, seemed to me to be
trivial. However, from about fifteen minutes in, I started to
suspect that there was a *pattern* emerging.

Although he engaged each of the other students individually (with a short series of questions and points directed at each one), over the course of his 'non-lecture', he neither addressed nor even made eye contact with *me*. *Initially*, therefore, there was scant opportunity for me to obtain a reading of his intent or motivation(s). All that I could valuably study was his physiognomy (at best a *crude* guide to character), his general behaviour in that environment, and his 'body language'.

There was the broad square jaw: the remnant of a high-testosterone youth; he was thin-lipped, and I had the strong impression that he was *not* a particularly sensuous individual. As to sensu*al*? Even without eye contact, I could detect something of unmistakable cruelty in the hard-set lines of the face: despite his then affectation of a generous avuncular character, which I for one found less than convincing. 'I for one *of two*' would be more accurate. I noticed that, with *one* exception, each of the other students, after they had had their individual 'audience' with him, within the context of the group, seemed to become calmer and more relaxed and attentive, even though he was surely talking about matters in no way germane to the syllabus: matters which, furthermore, would have made *most* students regret having missed an extra hour's sleep over.

The one exception, who had seemed quite calm *before* his (early) individual discourse with her, had, conversely, appeared a little unsettled – *uncomfortable* even – in the aftermath of their encounter.

'*Audience*' … *That* was *it*! I had been depending too much on seeking the eye contact that I never gained, and thereby had temporarily lost focus on much else that I had been able to register: the nonchalant engaging, *one* at a time, of the students' imaginations … imagining *objects* … *induction*; instruction to re-live memories … relaxation … *trust*: those, and possibly another couple of Neuro-Linguistic

Programming techniques that he was employing, were all methods used by *hypnotists*. Yet, *this* hypnotist had quickly begun to seem as though hypnotised *himself*.

And there was something *else*; something about his jerky upper body movements: clearly repeating, yet abbreviated to near vanishing point. At first, I had dismissed it as involuntary behaviour borne of nervousness: the 'shaking' or pronounced tremor of an ageing, ailing man. But *none* of that fitted in with the other elements of his overall disposition. Again, with no eye contact, I was concerned that I was crossing over from perception to inference. However, there was *something* further that I was getting. Yes, there it *was* … and *again*: momentary, but definite and distinct *tells*, as poker players and other generalists have it. Then it *came* to me: the clear comprehension that something arising from the combination of his displaced attention and those tiny repeated movements was somehow *empowering* his interactions with the individual students. What it amounted to – what I at last appreciated it as manifestly *being* – was a series of escalating deliveries of complex, whole (upper) body *kinemes*, being relayed via a consciousness largely, willingly and distractedly given over to something *else*. And that 'something else' – as revealed by those giveaway 'tells' – was, unmistakably, a *ritual*?

Just at that point, two things came to me, in rapid succession: (i) information that my father had related to me about his (MacSween's) associations and activities; and (ii) something that I had long before witnessed as a 'natural' Lucid Dreamer who would occasionally venture, untutored and unknowing, into Active Dream states.

The process of dreaming can indeed 'also serve as a gateway to much else'. Around the age of twelve, just after we moved to Bearsden, I all but ceased, for a good few years, the practice of those Active forays. Looking back, I cannot recognise it as *abandonment by design*, but rather just an 'unconscious' *drifting away*. *Determinism*: who knows? Around then, I felt myself 'speeding up' in many ways: rushing headlong, and exclusively, into matters of the waking world. There arose a new, bristling and impelling urgency in me to gain ever more ground: to '*catch up*'. And above all, I had that rendezvous to keep with my frabjous friend and glorious love, near the junction of Byres Road and University Avenue.

As for all the other outrageous fortune that I ran into ... *collided with*: I surely could have done without that.

A few of the things that I 'witnessed' (and shied *well away* from) as a preadolescent Active Dreamer, made incomplete sense to me until I came across them again, many years later, in the course of my waking world research. What came back to me towards the close of that Pathology tutorial room encounter was something that may well not be familiar to some who read this: a very old and powerful occult ritual called *The Cabbalistic Cross*.

I made a point of being the last student out of the room. With the others gone, and just as I was reaching the door, he piped up.

"I'm sorry I didn't get round to speaking with *you*, Brian."

It was an obvious lie, but his intonation revealed rapacious curiosity about how I might respond.

I turned slowly through ninety degrees (roughly towards the direction that I perceived to be East), raised my right hand to touch my forehead, and quietly said the word 'Ateh' (pronounced *Ah-tay*). Then I turned rapidly through a further ninety degrees, in order to face him. His eyes were suddenly very wide, as he momentarily betrayed an involuntary rictus of genuine alarm. It did not last, though. This was a creature long-unaccustomed to being startled, and infuriation was quick to follow.

'Foot it featly'

— Ariel, in William Shakespeare's *The Tempest*

It was a good moment to be a Gemini, blessed with considerable short-dash speed. Four '*running away from* ISIS-*swift*[4]' strides along the corridor, just out of earshot – and just as MacSween would have been fully experiencing that inevitable anger – I added "numbskull!" to 'Ateh'.

Much later, in the refectory, I still could not decide whether my having thus separated the component words of my exclamation had been representative of sensible circumspection or of reprehensible faintheartedness.

---

[4] Had Islamic State existed at that time

Chapter Fifteen

Although it was something that I could also have done without, I eventually experienced my first close quarters face-to-face with MacSween eight months later, at a *compulsory* departmental 'get together' of staff and students at Hillhead Rugby Club. I knew that it was compulsory because I had asked one of the staff members beforehand. They were a real *fun bunch*, those pathologists.

He went round the room, insisting that he buy each student a drink. I was with the Augmenter and when eventually he reached us, MacSween made a point of gleefully letting me know of his full awareness of our being together. *That*, and all the rest of the repulsive venality he exuded, barely required a reading of his micro-expressions, but I nonetheless scrutinised him with all the concentration that I could muster.

He had spent the first fifteen minutes, after his early appearance, in discourse with a girl from the final year. She was an intercalating medical student, and she had – as I indicate here, only because of its relevance to what followed – a bust of such prodigious proportions as to make the average Brünnhilde appear like Twiggy.

It would only be fair to indicate here that, growth-stunted as the few trees on the Hebridean island from whence he hailed, MacSween stood no higher than the level of her chin. However, from across the hall, one of the other male students with a keen eye and quit wit for anything ribald, had also caught sight of MacSween's conspicuous and prolonged resistance to eye contact with this girl; and although I had no interest in the matter, I was fairly sure that had '*SPEAK HERE*' been emblazoned across the top part of her tee-shirt, I would have noticed at some earlier point.

Positioned, as he at first thought, in a 'blind spot' to the rear and left of MacSween, this waggish male student made, for my supposed amusement, mischievous mime of (presumably) a *man* concupiscently cupping and squeezing large breasts; and then, with rapid transition to a state of distress, collapsing forward as though in consequence of having been unable to sustain the weight of the lasciviously-grasped organs.

Even under more comfortable circumstances, I doubt that I would have raised as much as a smile at his coarse and overtly offensive antics. On *that* evening, however; at an event that – had it not been for the prospect of my being (and dancing) with the person I loved – I would rather have been able to avoid, I had little capacity for much in the way of mirth: never mind that of the *lewd* variety.

It was at *that* point that I first became aware that MacSween – although he was looking in a direction *away* from his mocker – had become au courant with what was going on behind him. Whether it had been by way of a signal from the girl, who may have *noticed* the exaggerated apery and (quite reasonably) taken offence at it, or because of something happening sub rosa – and to which I had no straightforward access – I knew not. However, my immediate instinct was, *strangely enough*, to try to save the bacon of the moronic mime.

As remains the case today, I was then unaware of any universal signing for 'Give it a *rest*, for *goodness*' sake!', but I did my best with an expression of, firstly, narrowed, then *widened* eyes coupled to slight sideward glances, followed by a tightly-controlled-but-discernible (and *rapid*) side-to-side shaking of the head.

Sadly, however, the self-satisfied, unmasked mummer merely misappropriated my headshaking for further devilment.

And yes, reader, I fully realise that the above *does* constitute an untenably sustained alliteration, but in revisiting the events of that awful and absurd part of the evening, my measured avoidance, here, of more obvious, lazy inclusions is something that I esteem a minor success.

He next simulated the head of the overburdened and forward-collapsed upper body as meeting with startling, side-to-side pummelling by the suddenly, powerfully, and rapidly oscillating giant breasts.

It was just then that MacSween turned around to face him.

The Chinese, in compiling their horoscope, had obviously not predicted the incarnation of my coeval: for *he* was surely *The Cuttlefish*.

Waves of bright rosy red, deathly pale, shilpit grey and – with final and full realisation of his apodictic predicament – valetudinarian green, emerged in sequential pulses from above his shirt collar, then disappeared into his hairline, like a projected video catalogue of wallpaper shades chosen by the non-compos mentis.

I ascribe '*valetudinarian*' because, beyond what must have been his having had to deal with a brief withering stare, he really need not have *bothered* about threat to his *own* wellbeing: because suddenly, MacSween had eyes only for *me*.

When he made his way over to where I was standing with the Augmenter, my immediate reading of him confirmed all – and more – that my father had told me of him a year before; and the sheer force of that realization rendered me too as little more than cuttlefish: but a cuttlefish bereft even of its chromatophores. Had I been dealing with a reasonable human being, I might well have remonstrated about misplaced dudgeon, in view of the only-just-ceased shenanigans of *T.T. Jiggler* over at the other end of the room. But I knew that I was interfacing with someone whose 'reasoning', with regard to *myself*, was long- and *firmly*-established. Deimatic behaviour was therefore out of the question. However, I sensed that, in direct and lawful opposition to the formidable shielding afforded to *him*, I *too* was being protected from useful scrutiny.

That, though, was something that just appeared to infuriate him further. Nor was it doing *me* a whole lot of good either, as I began to feel like some disempowered non-combatant caught in a no man's land between two, powerful, warring cohorts.

I cannot imagine a drink ever having been proffered with less goodwill. I politely refused at first, but with gentle concealed prompting from my companion, I eventually accepted something: although I did not drink it.

After MacSween had finally left us, the music for an old-fashioned waltz started up, and I asked the Augmenter if she wanted to dance.

"*Yeah, yeah, yeah!*" she shot back: animated, eager.

It was something she would sometimes chatter, in staccato bursts of three or four repetitions of the word: an expression of enthusiastic approval. Sometimes when I would look at her, I fancied that I could visualize her at various stages of her life: still young, as she *then* was; very old; and at points in between. When, occasionally, she would pronounce as she just had, I could see the child that she had *been*; and, although her default comportment was most often *super*human, *there* was revelation too of the ordinary human being: the higher primate.

The more I experienced of her – in all her aspects – the more I loved her. However, what had just transpired that evening, had brought home to me the vivid, horrifying realisation that I was in grave danger of losing her.

Whatever the future held though, there was *no way* I was going to miss that *dance* with her!

> Weaving olden dances
> Mingling hands and mingling glances

From: 'The Stolen Child', by W. B. Yeats

She was wearing a blue-green silken dress, and as I write now, there comes back to me something of the sensation of slipping my hand around her narrow waist and towards the small of her back. Quick study that I am in many ways, I was a little slow in realising how sensitive she was to being caressed along the length of her back; but I finally cottoned on to that fact as we glided across the floor.

And as we danced – just as when we would kiss – my eyes began to close.

Whodathunkit: an otherwise low-temperature, self-contained critter like me, all thawed out and in love?

Alas, the time is coming when man will no longer give birth to a star. Alas, the time of the most despicable man is coming, he that is no longer able to despise himself.

From: Thus Spake Zarathustra, by Friedrich Nietzsche

My father was a laconic sort of a fellow, and not someone inclined to bad-mouth others. His consistent characterization of MacSween as a 'devil', however, was something that I could fault neither ontologically nor even on the basis of *morality*; and after the rugby club encounter, that identification struck me as further clear indication of the purposes of: (i) the course project that I had been given: to identify a 'rare' (actually *non-existent*) type of kidney podocyte (cell); and (ii) the near-constant harrying, haranguing and placing – day in, day out – of invariably unnecessary and multifarious impediments to my progress by MacSween's 'attack poodle', Dr Lindop, throughout my time at the department.

The best that I could say about Lindop was that you always knew where you were with him. It was just the lack of a *paddle* that was the worry.

Chapter Sixteen

What matters most is how well you walk through the
fire

— Charles Bukowski

I rather hope that it *still* matters when you opt to *run* through
any given inferno.

Uninformative and slipshod as MacSween's early in-
department seminar was, his extracurricular 'lessons' have
invariably been orchestrated and applied with contrastingly
resolute and brutally-instructive vigour.

One night, around ten thirty, near the middle of
December of 1988, I went out for a quick jog – of around
two miles – commencing from my parents' place at Jedworth
Court, which was located directly off Manse Road, in
Bearsden.

I was approaching the furthest corner of a park area,
surrounded on three sides by Heather Avenue, when two
men whom I had observed sitting on the swings up ahead
and to my right, suddenly sprang up and began to sprint
towards me … *at* me. It hardly required my quick glance at

the frontrunner's grim, determined glare for me to decide that they meant me harm.

Heather Avenue was some three quarters of a mile from my starting point, and I had been pushing hard throughout that distance. So powerful was the ensuing fight-or-flight jolt of adrenaline, that even today, nearly twenty-seven years later, I can – in remembering – still re-register something of its impact.

I went for 'flight', as I rounded the far corner of Heather Avenue, just ahead of them, and accelerated up along its final steep stretch towards the corner of Bailie Drive. That was never my *favourite* part of that route, but under *that* circumstance, with two, fast, apparently very fit, and eerily silent men – each of no more than thirty – in rapid and ill-intentioned pursuit of me, it immediately became not only the usual exercise in pulmonary torture, but also what might nowadays be termed a 'health and safety issue'.

Once I reached the top of the incline and turned left onto Bailie Drive, things started to look up a little . There were *three* reasons for that returning optimism. Firstly, it was the turning point of the run, and every stride from there on in was a stride back towards base; secondly, it was mercifully flat, with some downhill stretches to follow; and thirdly, I was beginning to get my second wind: which meant that I could now inflict something of the lung-burning agony that *I* had just endured, back onto my *pursuers*.

However, there then came a further hormonal jolt, precipitated by the sudden awareness that they were closing on me.

I stepped it up another notch, as I turned left from Bailie Drive onto Edgehill Road, haring hotfoot, street light-to-street light.

As I darted past Edgehill's junction with Morven Road, and set my sights on the intersection with Gartconnell Drive, I heard one of my two pursuers shout something to the other about cutting me off. A rapid glance back revealed something of his intention, as I witnessed him peel off left and down Morven.

That development presented me with two possibilities.

If I turned left down Gartconnell *Drive* – and towards Gartconnell *Road* – then, depending on how fast the detour-maker was, he might have been able to flank me at that corner. If I went right on Gartconnell Drive, and towards the main ('Drymen') road, then I could avoid that flanking manoeuvre. Going for *that* option, however, would have meant: (a) a longer route back to base, and (b) the likelihood of an ambush at or near to Jedworth Court.

I veered right and towards Drymen Road.

Left onto Drymen and heading past the entrance to Ralston Road, I could espy the Bearsden ('Brookwood') Library car park wall on my left. It was low and easy to hurdle, even at an acute angle. However, at its beginning, the drop onto the tarmac on the other side was some five feet: *not* something that would have been readily discernible to anyone unfamiliar with the lay of the land as they approached it at night-time. With this in mind, I slowed a little, allowing my remaining pursuer to gain just a few strides on me before I grew level with the beginning of the wall.

Mid-air, I knew that it would be a good landing, and my plan was to take the next four strides slowly: so that if he made to follow, and then *fell*, I could round on him and end his threat.

As I sprung up from my soft landing, an *entreaty* in the sense of "Do *no* violence! Give me your trust, brother!" arrived faster than speech into my consciousness. I immediately knew who it was.

"You'd better be *sure* about this!" I gave back accelerating away from my alighting. "You'd *better* be!" I repeated, as a scuffing, skidding resonance behind me – which was immediately followed by a shocked indignant declaration of '"*Fucking* cunt!"', with the 'dental' (alveolar ridge) 't' sound of the latter expletive barely audible – indicated that my barrelling chaser had fallen.

At the point where the library car park opened onto Manse Road, I stopped and turned to look at the fellow. He was getting himself upright again and staring irately at me.

At around 6'2", white, a hundred and fifty pounds, and with his Harrington-style jacket, loose-fit slacks and running shoes all in dark colours, his deadliness was purposely cloaked in casual mundanity.

He continued to glare at me balefully for no more than another two seconds, before expectorating the 'C'-word again – *un*sheathed, on that second airing, from dampening adjectival adjunct, and with the 't' fully restored: *striking*, rapier fescennine, then quickly revealed as *silly*, forlorn – and charging once more in my direction. As a physical threat, though, he was – like his bane – near spent.

The impulse from my Guardian was for me to relax. Thereupon, *my* entreaty to *him* was to take what safe control he needed to help *promote* that state in me: as I had just sprinted for the best part of two miles.

I intuited that the flanker would be lurking and waiting somewhere within the square of residential flats that was Jedworth Court. I jogged up past the parked cars and on into the courtyard, which those dwellings surrounded; all the while with constant heightened awareness of my surroundings: in particular, of the diminishing number of paces that the more unswerving of my two pursuers remained behind me.

It was my father's face, behind the kitchen window, that I saw first. He would sometimes wait up and watch out for my return, when I would go out for a late-night run. Immediately thereafter, it was the figure of the second thug that I became aware of, as he was running up the furthermost (from me) path, in order to position himself facing me as I moved diagonally across the central, landscaped seating area and towards the ground-floor door of my parents' flat. He seemed a little taller than the still-pursuing man, and proportionately bulkier; and positioned thus, he had come to be standing with his back to my father, who had a clear view of what happened next.

I had gradually slowed, but not otherwise broken my stride; and I was momentarily aware of the man ahead *running* at me, as I gave up my awareness to all else but what I was being adjured to do.

There appeared a sparkling line in front of me on the grass. I was to regard it as a spring point, and land on it with the balls of both feet, bending my knees as I came to rest.

As I hit my spot, neither of the two men could have been more than two feet from me: one behind and one in front.

In that stretched moment, there came to mind occasions when I had climbed to the top of the old quarry near Furnace, beside Loch Fyne, and then descended in vertical – and near-vertical – drops of up to twelve feet at a time, between rocks: sometimes making use of the rebound potential to spring back up to a higher perch that would better suit the smooth continuation of my overall descent. Those landings, although they might have appeared hazardous to the casual observer, always felt secure and 'soft', especially on certain mild spring or autumn evenings, when I would be most inclined to undertake the exercise. It would often feel as though gravity was, by some elusive means, *assisting* (rather than hindering) me. That is what you encounter *repeatedly* when you are a kid: those fuzzy points of interface at and beyond the meeting place of the *possible*, and what you dream *might* be possible. The ability to complete those formidable gymnastics *at all* though, had – for *me* – some extended link to processes undertaken in Active Dreams.

> "The self in a toroidal Universe can be both separate and connected with everything else."

> — Arthur M. Young: mathematician, cosmologist and inventor of the Bell helicopter.

What followed, as soon as I began to bend my knees and surrender my will, above the fading sparkly line, was an 'assist' certainly quite far beyond those that I had experienced at the quarry. I shot up smoothly and comfortably some eight feet or so into the air; and while I effortlessly ascended, the world around me seemed to slow down.

I looked below me at the figures of the two men. The front-facing flanker's head slowly tracked my ascent, such that when I reached zenith, he was looking into my eyes with a developing look of surprise. Then, the two men collided, with the left temple of my constant pursuer dashing – in what I perceived to be slowed motion – against the left angle of the upturned jaw of his ambush predator accomplice. Even the delayed *thud* of their collision sounded duller and more prolonged than I would have expected.

As both men recoiled – with the erstwhile pursuer remaining upright and raising his hands to the side of his head, and the flanker beginning to fall – the world at once returned to normal speed and I retook my will as gravity reapplied its customary hold on me.

Those practice sessions at the quarry near Furnace appeared to reveal their worth, in the form of a secure landing.

The still-standing attacker was not yet for *giving up* though, and having regained some equanimity, he charged towards me again, telegraphing a right-handed haymaker as he neared. I used both hands, quadrating with fitting body movements to avoid the intended blow, while appropriating his own inertia to move him away from me.

I found that I was able to perform that action as though I had practiced it a thousand times; which, in as real a sense as *any* to me, I *had*.

As he reeled back in the direction of 15 Jedworth Court, I noticed that my father had come hobbling out, and that he and this fellow were at risk of colliding as well. Extending his left arm as the man staggered backwards in his direction, my father halted him with his opened left hand applied against the man's upper back. As the man turned, no doubt surprised, my father smashed his right fist into his face. The blow made a resounding 'whip crack' noise, as at least one of the bones in the man's face lost its integrity. The man collapsed on the spot.

His accomplice had, meanwhile, gotten himself unsteadily to his feet again, and what had previously registered as a look of growing amazement had now been replaced by one of unmistakable – if not easily *explicable* – terror. He thereupon turned on his heels and ran back down the path towards the rear entrance, whence he had gained access to the grounds.

My father turned around, made his way clumsily and uncomfortably towards the first man and knelt across his chest, pinning his arms.

I sensed that it was not required first aid that he was minded to deliver.

My father was as obstinate as *any* man I have ever met, and I had never before even *considered* ordering him to do *anything*. Nevertheless, as he raised his fist a second time, I grabbed his wrist – a wrist at least twice the diameter of my own – and for the first and *only* time, I did just *that*.

"*Enough*!" I instructed firmly, as I lowered my head towards his. "Mind you don't *kill* him!" Then, after a distinct hesitation, and with a forced wry smile, "… *Or* yourself."

It was a shot at tension-diffusing levity. Earlier that year, after the double blow of the attempt on *his* life, and the resulting news that his scheduled hip replacement operation would have to be postponed while he recovered, he had – on one occasion, shortly after I had had to take over the task of chauffeuring my mother here and there – cautioned, "Mind the car!" Then, after an unwarrantably long pause, he had given voice to the (seeming) afterthought "… *And* yourselves."

Although it had given me one of the best laughs that I had had in a while, I had not let him forget about it.

After the best part of a second of concern, throughout which I feared that I might not be strong enough to quell his intent, he – to my momentary astonishment – fell to command; and although he did not turn to look at me, I could discern that *astonishment*, to the point of *bewilderment*, was overtaking him too.

"You were in the *air*," he muttered distractedly, "and there was *some* …"

"*Yeah*, *well*, I'm an air *sign*," I completed breezily, persisting in my attempt at shock-delaying frivolity, as I walked round and behind him to the supine guy, adding: "I'm in my *element* up there, you know."

While getting my first close-up view of the bloodied, broken face of the semi-conscious man, as I turned his head to one side and made sure that his tongue was not blocking his airway, I was moved to make an unguarded and unbecomingly disparaging remark about the level of anger that must have been in my father for him to have hit the fellow quite so *hard*. My comment was doubly disingenuous, as he could not have been certain that doing violence to the man had been unnecessary.

His reply set me straight.

He told me that if *I* ever had a son, I would understand why he had acted as he did. And with the rebuke, he further confounded me with that rare *scowl* of his. It was a scowl that I had been subjected to before.

As I generate this account as a stream of consciousness – which I can *just* about channel and mould into what I hope might be appealing form, only by reason of my being blessed with untrammelled progression of short-to-mid-to-long-term memory – there has just come to mind a quote from the very limited range of music (with *lyrical* content) that I would occasionally listen to all those years ago. It is from the 'post-punk' canon of rock music. Although my thinking of it has been inspired by memories of my father, I reckon I'll skip mention of it, as he probably wouldn't have appreciated it. You see, reader: once, circa 1973 – and as much by way of brash adolescence-cusping provocation, as an attempt at cross-generational sharing – I enthusiastically called him into the family living room, to bring to his attention a performance of the cross-*dressing*, swaggering, snarling *New York Dolls*, on The Old Grey Whistle Test.

Strangely, as it seemed to me, there appeared to be something of the *future* about them, and for a moment I wondered if my father would fathom anything of what I was construing.

They may not have been 'the full *Stooges*', but then, they weren't *trying* to be. Aside from the intermittent appeal of the sound, it was not their most *apparent* motif of *revenge* that fascinated me, but rather the references made to weirdly alien urban street life, lived in obviously 'anti-normative' fashion. *That* much struck a minor chord because it spoke to me of something rather disconcerting that I had observed about several of the married friends and relatives of my parents.

Each individual in those unions seemed, increasingly, to be becoming *less* individual with passing years: conceivably, as though they were fostering – willingly or otherwise – some invisible, mutually-facilitating, 'shadow'-imposing 'structure(s)' between themselves, whereby their once-vibrant *discrete* personalities were being amalgamated into two versions of a new, singular, *deadened* persona: a sort of 'Stepford Wives *and* Husbands'.

I would consider this again in my early twenties, and come to the anticipation that, *lacking* as I was in snarling swagger, whoever *I* might be inclined to spend my days with would have to be someone also so sufficiently self-possessed as to be 'immune' to any correlative decline towards an irrevocable final character *meld*. I affirmed privately that one would surely wish to avoid the inexorable diminution of longed-for, life-long love into little more than mere *tolerance* of a partner who had in many respects become a mirror image of one's own self. As far as I had become concerned, it would *have* to be *amour propre* over ego; and if a great part of life was to be about the *relinquishing* of extant ego, then better to relinquish it to God than to inflict it on one's significant other.

As it turned out, if my father *did* discern anything other than the band members' brazenly glam exteriors – which may as well have had '*ORTHODOX PARENT DETERRENT*' stamped across them – then it was merely the perception of five asylum escapees.

My father's rare scowl was even *more* rarely without effect on me, and after I had had my moment's cheap awkward laugh at the expense of his wasted time, I resolved that it would be decorous and dignified if, thereafter, I were to be more respectful of his boundaries insofar as I could approximate them in a personality *so* different from mine: a psyche, no part of which would find interface with- and access to my own until that night some fifteen years later, when – with his having demonstrably transcended mere biology – he found permanent welcome.

He had been born in 1924, and it occurred to me, while abandoned in front of the television that night, almost half a century after *that* year, that L.P. Hartley had had it just about right: the past certainly *is* a foreign country, and they *do* do things differently there.

In 2007, I saw the documentary, 'New York Doll', about Arthur "Killer" Kane, the band's bass guitarist who died the year before the work featured at the 2005 Sundance Film Festival. It moved me more deeply than the band's *music* ever did; and I think that if my father had still been alive, I would – for only the *best* of reasons – have urged him to watch it.

"Let me help you up!" I offered.

My father did not seem enamoured of that idea, so I stated as flatly and authoritatively as I could: "He'll be unable to move until we're back inside."

"What in *Christ's* name's going on here?" he demanded, raising his voice a notch.

"*Shh*, you'll *wake* someone!" I smiled, before surveying the windows of the surrounding flats. It must have been close to eleven o'clock at night and all of the elderly residents would have been in bed by then. I could see neither a light on nor any figure behind any of the windows. It seemed that we might well have been fortunate in that regard.

"But I don't understand how ..." he demurred, whispering again.

"Aside from a little blood which will have to be washed away from the grass and the path," I offered, deflecting his protest, while scrambling for the best way to meet what was finally emerging, "the situation just went back to *pristine*. I'm sorry that I brought them back here, but I was minded that the only alternative could more easily have worked in *their* favour."

He peered at me dourly, and then in a craftily grudging manner – that was also *probing* – he declared: "That was pretty *smart* of you?"

"Not *that* smart," I countered.

"Then how did you *know*?"

"Oh *dad*," I began, "maybe I just imagined someone *smarter* than me, then thought: 'What would they …?'"

But I was past tired of pussyfooting around in deference to his dogged intransigence, and dropping entirely what remained of my smile, I decided to challenge him further.

"Do you know what I *really* think, dad? I think that you're a *clever* man who occasionally sees more than he makes known to others: a fellow who almost always keeps his own counsel. And I further think that you have long accepted that there *are* more things in Heaven and Earth than are dreamt of in just about *any* philosophy."

Aware that I was in danger of disconcerting him further, I smiled again.

"*I* sometimes get frightened *too*, old thing," I shared jauntily. "It's just the … *human* condition. But when you're doing your *time* here, you sometimes just have to accept what help you *get*: if it feels *right* to do so. And in *any* case, I'm sure *neither* of us has forgotten what you told me about MacSween back in the summer."

At that point, the pinned man began to show signs of coming fully round.

I helped my father up to his feet; and as I did so, I deflected his abiding inarticulate protestation by pointing out that he had not suggested that we call the police.

With my father upright again, I bent down and unzipped the man's jacket. The leather strapping across his chest and left shoulder first suggested a gun holster, but it was a long-bladed, so-called 'combat knife' that hung, inverted and sheathed, against the left side of his ribcage. I withdrew it and looked down at him: this blunted, would-be killer, as he became aware of his surroundings once more.

As he briefly lost control of his bladder, and his lower lip and jaw began to quiver, it seemed to me that the closest term, in English, for his returned look would have been 'piteous' or 'piti*able*'. There is, however, that *deficiency* in either the English language itself, or my command of it. Those terms do not describe what *I* discerned, and I am glad that I do not entertain *pity*: only *mercy* or lack thereof. At *that* point though, I was still finding it a challenge to access my uppermost consciousness centre.

"Not very generous with their commissions, *are* they Detective Sergeant?" I suggested. "First the army, and now the police: doesn't seem *right*, *does* it? In a few minutes – once you feel *able*, and *after* we've left you – get yourself up and *away* from here. Otherwise, it will go very badly indeed for you."

"I can't feel my *body*!" he seethed, literally spitting blood; and with observation of his own gore, his expression turned quickly to one of seeming anguish.

"*Patience,*" I admonished, adding: "And remember: *very* badly!"

"Nothing you want to *ask* me?" he sibilated petulantly, once both my father and I had turned away."

"There's nothing that *you* could tell *either* of us that we don't already know … *pretty boy*!" I replied stonily, as I

177

turned my head to look at him one last time, while I escorted my father back up the path to the door.

In the kitchen, I pulled up a dining chair for my father, while I stood at the window, with one eye on the remaining, recovering marauder.

"I'm going to have to clear out, old thing," I muttered, glancing down at the fearsome, long, serrated-edged blade of the knife, which I had placed on the stainless steel draining board. "You and mum don't need any *more* of this!"

"And where would you go: what would you *do*?" he asked.

"I don't know, dad," I sighed glumly. "Medicine is what's *in* me: so, *same* path, different *location*, I imagine."

"You've done *enough* running for a bit, don't you think?" he riddled. However, it was *he* who was still breathing hard.

"I'm *serious*," I insisted.

"*Please* don't do *that*," he implored. "I'm barely fit to *drive* right now and your mother has more than enough to do without having to take buses and taxis everywhere. We *need* you, Brian: *I* need you to be here! Things will come good again: for *all* of us. We just need to stick together. I'll find a way."

Veritably *Promethean* as his earlier covert efforts on my behalf had been, my father had undoubtedly reached a point where he was no longer capable of further active involvement in such matters. Moreover – and as was then unbeknown to *either* of us – he had, in surviving that summer's attempt on his life, become victim of cruelly slow slaughter. In the midst of the worst of his suffering though, there was at least that merciful, partial, precious remission.

A few minutes after the injured policeman had staggered away, I went outside with a basinful of hot water. On returning to the kitchen, I pulled over another chair; and, a further ten minutes later, over mugs of comforting *Camp Coffee* and cheddar cheese toasties, sprinkled liberally with *Lea & Perrins* Worcestershire sauce, we sat down together and talked long into the night.

Chapter Seventeen

More rewarding (and *seriously* academic) experiences that I remember vividly about the first year of the Experimental Pathology course were the occasional qualitative / quantitative analysis classes that Whaley and Lackie would hold jointly.

Together, they would take a published scientific paper and, in the course of an hour, disassemble it, and examine the underlying methodology, experimental design, and any conclusions that its authors had dared to draw. Often, on cursory examination, many aspects of a given paper would appear reasonable enough, and to have been based on robustly constructed (and rigorously conducted) studies: as well as having been presented in unambiguous fashion. But that seldom stopped these two men from finding at least half a dozen reasons to 'bury it alive'.

The focused intellectual acrobatics of those infrequent tutorials were in marked contrast to the structureless tedium of the weekly departmental meetings. There, the arguments were often petty and circular, rather than scientific or progressive: and the rhythm of these latter tragicomedies invariably akin to that in a box of worms, wherein the concern of each individual extends little beyond the perpetual and all-embracing struggle to maintain a position closest to the lid at the top.

Ours was a small class and we were actively encouraged by Whaley and Lackie to contribute to the proceedings.

It was an important time for me, because a gradual long-term change in my overall make-up was being consolidated. What it all meant became apparent to me during one of those sessions.

I had originally been taught at high school that if you apply yourself constantly and assiduously to your work, with exiguous heed to any 'intruding' distraction, then you will reap the benefits (a vestige of mutating and diminishing Calvinism, I inferred).

Since my complete recovery from life-threatening illness, towards the end of 1983, I had begun to undertake the process of jettisoning such philosophical absolutism.

If, in today's society, you start to talk openly about unseen external influences, then you get 'labelled' on the spot; and you can all-too-soon thereafter find yourself in the defensive position of the mad scientist (over-)trying to make his / her wretched pitch to a panel of pedantic and hidebound logical rationalists: although I acknowledge that I have ventured some way beyond that *safe ground* in this account.

Nonetheless, I will put it as tentatively and in as balanced a fashion as I can.

Once I had returned to full health (towards the latter quarter of 1983), I 'kicked back' and thought of nothing, in order to see what might motivate me. What I came up with was the same vocation, every bit as strong as before. By 'kicking back', I mean giving my human will a rest. I thereby learned that *true* vocation is not entirely selfish.

At that time, it was almost like being a kid again. I had this *tabula rasa* bio system to (re-)educate and use in accordance with best inclination. On the *mind* side of things,

181

I already knew about the so-called 'natural' methods of learning – keen observation, attentiveness, association and classification – so I went on to establish the fullest possible familiarity with 'artificial' methods, like chain/link and hook/peg systems, mind mapping, and various other techniques, such as substitute wording and mnemonic devices (acronyms, creative sentences and rhymes): thus boosting '*near*-eidetic' to eidetic.

I practised those techniques until they seemed to become second nature, and then waited, with my will still largely in check.

"From an evolutionary point of view, higher intelligence seems to be maladaptive rather than adaptive."

— Noam Chomsky, 1998

Professor Whaley and Dr Lackie had been debating some point or other in one of their tutorials when it hit me. Analysis and logic were suddenly revealed as being like artificial 'word categories': offshoots of a single quality that was at once naïve and compelling. Their 'human thinking', as involving as it got, may have been diverting enough, but it had little meaning or worthwhile application beyond the triviality of a game.

Not long into the hour, I suddenly knew what their – and *other* – conclusions might be. It was like seeing a problem anew, almost as if from the inside, and becoming the *sense* of the solution. Again, that may read as pretentious or even preposterous, but it is as best as I can convey it.

I had already reached the point where I could read or see something once and assimilate it for reference and development at any future time. I further realised that whatever wisdom I now found myself possessed of was *received*: *given* to me, rather than acquired through my own will.

All of our talents are given to us. We might only hone and develop them for our time here: at least for those of us who choose – or are *permitted* – to do anything with them *at all*. Back then, I had not yet found my way to the Akashic Records, but the events and processes that would lead to my doing so were already under way.

Current reductionist, 'scientific' wisdom would have us believe that our mental faculties reach a peak between our late teens and early twenties. I believe that in the absence of any pathology, such a state of affairs becomes the case only insofar as the individual concerned chooses to believe it. In general terms, the process of ageing can be similarly considered. A gerontologist will tell you that ageing is a function of *biology*, not *chron*ology. An Active Dreamer possessed of an adventurous and enquiring disposition, will quickly come to realise that ageing – although *not* human death – can be avoided entirely, so long as one chooses not to acquiesce to the expectations of the majority of those around them. It begins with your *dreams*: and with goodwill and firm intent, it can be manifest in your waking life.

After the exams, at the end of the spring term of the third year, the only information on the noticeboard was whether one had passed or failed. One was not told how well – or how badly – one had performed. I was deemed to have passed.

Chapter Eighteen

My run-in with MacSween at the rugby club event had perturbed me greatly; and thereafter, throughout that summer of 1989, I would often fret over my mounting concern that the girl whom I had come to love so deeply might be brought to unjust disadvantage – or worse suffering – for no greater reason than that of perceived association with me. *All* of those ten months when we were together were, in spite of that, the best of times.

Many young men might have been embarrassed about such a thing, but to this day I am as glad as I am about *anything* I have ever done that, once, early on in our propinquity – as we were regarding one another in the upstairs (music) department of *John Smith's* book shop on Byres Road – I managed to blurt out that I loved her. There was nothing *planned* about it: it was just that certain imponderable *way* that she had about her that would sometimes catch me out. At once breathtaking *and* inspiriting, it would remind me that I was *living* as well as being; and that living in the world, in spite of its difficulties, was – with *her* by my side – something that I was very much inclined to *embrace*. If the experience of being with her could have been like *anything* else, then maybe the first mouthful of the first coke float or vanilla milkshake of childhood: but a first mouthful of coke float or vanilla milkshake somehow made numinous. It was, however, *more* than recognition of golden compatibility that had moved me to vent so gloriously on that lunchtime. She had stirred in me a longing that was new and ancient, specific and unique: a *hunger* … a hunger of the heart.

Frequently agonize as I did, I just could not contemplate the idea of separating myself from her, even though I knew that there was *already* in MacSween's mind the conviction that we were an 'item'. Puzzle as often I would, I could find no way of redressing that quandary. I was suffering the horrible conflict of self-reproach and tenacity. *Plus* – and notwithstanding both my remaining cynicism and MacSween's wicked intent – there persisted in me the misbelief that I could, by means of my undeniable (and considerable) academic ability alone, ensure the return to me of a place at a British medical school.

An outing to see an Eddie Murphy film at the cinema had suggested the grimly comic solution of shoving a banana into the tailpipe of the depraved little viper's Jaguar. I was, however, no assassin; and even if I *had* been, my awareness and appreciation of the Hydra myth of ancient Greece may well have proven inhibiting, in view of my (by then) already-established understanding of MacSween's Freemasonry affiliation.

When the Augmenter's 21st birthday came around, in August of '89, I was still awaiting a long-overdue payment from the grant awarding body and I had very little in the way of funds (except for some savings which I could not access): so I ended up giving her a silly little keyboard gizmo with a built-in readout, for the purpose of learning to touch-type. She seemed to be pleased enough with it though, and she took to practising right away. One late afternoon, we were due to go out, and I came to her place with my father's car. As I watched her fast fingers flitting over the keys, it came to me that I could not – *must* not – allow her to be at risk from MacSween, and that that would mean both distancing myself from her, and making him believe that we were no longer together. Initially, I thought to broach with her, at *last*, the full extent and magnitude of my predicament, but there were two things which prevented me from doing so.

Just one of the many qualities that I admired in her was that in an era where the use of coarse/foul language was becoming increasingly commonplace, she was always firmly disinclined to curse. 'Bally' and 'Egads!' were as harsh as it got with her, with the latter of the two usually denoting her strongest disaffection with anything that she considered unsavoury. I had, to the best of my knowledge, *never* provoked an 'Egads!': and I had no intention of 'breaking my duck' in that regard. The other, and far more weighty reason was simply that she was a gifted, beautiful young woman, still full of the joys of life; and, although she knew *something* of my situation, I just felt like there was *no way* that I could bring myself to lay a downer like that on her.

The *worst* of it was that, even though I could appreciate the miracle of our being together *at all*, my every effort – no matter *how* imaginative – to maintain and prolong our harmonious idyll was stymied at every turn.

Human beings sometimes talk – most often pejoratively – of their own (or others') 'demons' as insubstantial and, generally, *self-created* impediments to their progress. Throughout my lifetime to date, I have been mercifully free of any such inherent handicaps. My 'demon' was *incarnate*, well resourced, determinedly intent upon wicked mischief, and (to date) shamefully protected from prosecution or even serious investigation.

One afternoon, a few days later, when I was due to help the Augmenter with the transport of her shopping from a supermarket located somewhat distant from her quarters, I was – as the hour approached – suddenly and unexpectedly denied the use of the family car. On that eerie afternoon of peculiarly sinister energies, which somehow provoked the suspicion that the whole universe had turned against me, there ensued a dissonant plainspoken exchange between myself and my parents, wherein I did my *utmost* to impress upon them the full extent of what she had come to mean to me. Engendering no favourable change in their abruptly-imposed denial, an unfamiliar counterattitudinal incapacitation descended upon me. *Forced compliance* on that, *and* in the broader scale of my experience, was something that was once again irking me greatly. Nonetheless, I had already begun to accept that there was no option other than to acquiesce to the paradigm, in the fragile hope that I might yet secure a happy future for us via a 'long game'.

How *that* might have played out, though, I could not at that point foresee. For the time being, it was a situation where, in being preoccupied with one calamity – my having caused her what must have been escalating bewilderment – I did not heed a consequential trepidation: my heart was breaking. It may well have been all thoroughly distressing and disconcerting, but I was still not so discombobulated as to overlook the necessity of my having to decide whether my just *not turning up* for the last year of the BSc would in itself be enough to convince MacSween that she and I were finished. My quickly predominating view was that it would *not* be. There was no doubt about either 'truly' or 'deeply', but I had to hang onto my *marbles*. Otherwise, I might *never* be of any use to her again. And I just had to figure out the best way – *any* way – for us still to have a chance.

Eventually, late that night, the need to get myself away from my parents' place became overwhelming, and in an effort to settle my *mind* at least, I decided to embark upon a long walk.

Chapter Nineteen

I walked for hours throughout the night: down past Partick and along the banks of the River Clyde. As I walked, I tried repeatedly to convince myself that with *me* gone from the course, she would be fine. As the dawn came and I made my way back out of town again, my earlier sense of conviction had all but dissolved. I began to feel that I was at risk of becoming befuddled: and *not* in the delightful sense that a chocolatier might imply in describing one or other exotic ingredient as being 'befuddled' in the ganache of some irresistibly delicious truffle.

Would I, then, call her once I got back to base, and tell her *something* of my predicament? She was *hardly* some fragile shrinking violet; and it would at least give *her* the option of deciding what *she* felt ought to be done: if there was anything to *be* done that would allow us to remain together.

"*Yes*," I finally resolved. *That* was how I would go about it!

As I made my way beyond the Canniesburn Toll roundabout and up along Drymen Road, a police car pulled up alongside me. There were two uniformed officers in the front. The nearside back door opened. A smirking, conservatively dressed, middle-aged man with unhealthy-looking blue eyes, marked couperose, and short-cropped, Kiwi tan boot polish-coloured, brown hair – that must have been slathered with … *something* to have lent it that damp *straw*-like texture – leant a little out towards the pavement from his seated position. The hair gave me cause to do a double take. 'Coloured' would have had to have been *key* in any description of it, as it looked almost as if it had been *shaded* in place by a child with a wax crayon.

"Hello, Brian! I'd just like to *talk*," he canvassed, revealing the merest hint of Western France in the timbre of his voice. "Would you mind getting *in*?"

Five minutes later, we were facing one another at the far end of the lower car park behind Bearsden Cross. It was a cool, bright, sunny morning. The two 'drones' had, at his spoken instruction, made off on foot and left us alone together. Outside of the car, he at first seemed a little reticent to get too close to me again: positioning himself some six paces distant, and still smirking.

Maybe it was the weariness induced by the uncertainties and vacillation of the foregoing hours that led to my paying heed to a sudden temptation to cast off the carapace of civility and *close* that gap between us as fast as I could, in order to knock him down and thereby wipe that smug leer from his face. But *immediately*, there came massively upon, and *through*, and *deep into* me the admonition "'*No!*'": unheralded as it was, from one whom I had come to consider reliable herald of impending danger.

"*Fulfil* the Laws and continue to *unfold* yourself!" my Guardian elaborated with similar assiduity. He had been *there*, ready to protect me if necessary, all along; but *I*, in my lowly human self-absorption, had been both insensible and *senseless*.

Quickly thereupon, there was remembrance of the third morning after my experience on Observatory Road, eleven months before. Looking in the bathroom mirror I had wondered why it was that, although I felt as though I had lived through five years *overnight*, I had not *aged* accordingly. My demand to my Guardian for *inclusion* ('to hold my own and to make my *own* way') had resulted in a Lucid Dream wherein I was shown how to access (perceptually) extended dream time, for the purpose of gaining knowledge that would take much longer to acquire in waking life. *Improperly* – albeit in an obtruding state of fear for my life – I had first chosen to learn how to defend myself: even in situations where I might be faced by challenges that I would hitherto have considered irresistible. And *this* is what it had gotten me: my coming close to breaking, for the first time in over twelve years, a central tenet of my creed.

The smirking man made to speak.

Cometary fragments and ancient metal cauldrons

In 1990, two British scientists – Victor Clube, an astrophysicist and Bill Napier, an astronomer – warned of a giant unseen comet hurtling in the general direction of the earth. It is concealed within a cloud of cosmic debris called the Taurid meteor stream, and it seems certain that in some 15 years from this time of writing (2015), the earth will once again cross this stream.

Within the thick shell of this comet is a mass of pitch-like tar, which is understood to exist under conditions of increasing heat and pressure. Were the comet to detonate within the earth's solar system, there would arise the compounded danger of this planet being impacted by one or more of the exploded fragments, as well as by some of the largest and most numerous pieces of cosmic debris ('space rocks') which exist around the point of the earth's projected crossing of the Taurid stream.

Some of those rocks are three times the size of the asteroid that collided with the earth 65 million years ago. Fragments from the exploded comet could be more than a mile wide.

As many people realise, though, anything *specific* that gets predicted, *usually* does *not* happen.

In the first half of 2012, a team of Russian scientists undertook an expedition into the ominously named 'Valley of Death' in the Yakutia region of Siberia. Their purpose was to seek out and investigate some 'metal cauldrons', the discovery of which local people had reported.

Interviewed by a Russian newspaper on his return from the expedition (in June 2012), the lead scientist, Michale Visok commented:

"We went out into the Valley of Death to see and investigate the metal cauldrons which people claim exist there, and we actually found five metallic objects buried in marsh-like swamps."

He went on to give the following details about these metal objects:

(i)   They are submerged in small pools of swamp-like water which is anywhere from two to three feet deep.

(ii) They are definitely metallic. The scientists entered each swamp, walked on top of the objects and heard metallic sounds upon striking them

(iii) The tops of the objects are very smooth to the touch, but there are sharp points along the outer edges.

(iv) Two of the team members became ill during the investigation.

(v) The team consisted of three geologists, one astrophysicist, one mechanical engineer and three research assistants.

The team subsequently interviewed four eye witnesses, who claimed to have seen 'at least two' of these 'metal cauldrons' rise up out of the ground only minutes before the explosion over Chelyabinsk in Russia's southern Ural region, which injured up to 1,500 people. It has been estimated that *that* meteor was 17-20 metres in diameter and weighed in excess of 10,000 tonnes: the biggest to enter the earth's atmosphere since the Tunguska event.

The eyewitnesses also claimed to have seen the levitated objects shoot several 'laser-like' beams at the meteor.

Eyewitness accounts – and their presumed unreliability – are of course, and especially *nowadays*, the staple fodder of worthy debunkers; and *I* could *hardly* have claimed detailed knowledge of those matters before the aforementioned reports about them had come into being.

"We have just a little while until they return," began the smirking, bizarrely-thatched man. "Do you *know* what it *was* that *did* for you, Brian?

"Well, I know that it wasn't the length of my recovery time from that nasty little virus that one of your lackeys squirted into my vein."

"You're *right*. It was, in *fact*, your mother's pride."

"I'm guessing you're not referring to that bleached-flour, supermarket, 'dead' bread," I muttered wearily under my breath. Then, snapping back at him, I sighed, "*Do* enlighten me further!"

With that, his head, which he had lowered briefly as he had begun to speak, snapped up and his gaze met mine again: steady and combative.

"It was her *pride*. A pneuma like you would have come with *instructions*. She *must* have known! She really needed to hide you *away* until you came up into the world: kept *quiet* about you until you could strike out on your *own*. But she just *had* to show you off, didn't she? '*Aries-faeries*!' They're just so unpredictable and ebullient; so *forthright*, *aren't* they? I mean, it's just like they say about those fancy shops and wine bars with the high mark-ups: 'we *saw you coming*!'"

"Maybe you've chosen the wrong venue for this," I offered. "Puerile babism like yours seems more suited to the school yard."

"*Really*? *Look* at you, Brian: you're not *one* thing or the other. You've achieved *nothing*; and with your name and face known to us, you *will* achieve nothing."

"Why?"

"*Why*" he appeared to muse archly. "Yes … *why*? I suppose that you must *hate* us."

"I cannot *hate* you," I retorted, "I have nothing in *common* with you; so, nothing *binds* me to you. And even if something *did*, I am not disposed to hate *anyone*."

"You're still strongly inclined to getting that *medical* degree, *aren't* you? But as to that '*why*', it's *simple* really. We don't care for strangers bearing extravagant gifts: the kind that risk *changing* things in unforeseeable … *uncontrollable* ways. We prefer our *own* kind: *not* those who aren't going to toe the line, but *proper* fellows, each with just enough brains and *will* to make a *little* difference: differences that we can *tinker* with as we see fit. Take *medicine* for example: that profession you're so determined to enter. A new 'promising' drug *here* or a design tweak to one or other prosthesis *there*; such things are just *fine* by us. It's the *revolutionary* stuff that causes headaches. They *breed* like flies, you know: the marginally productive, dispossessed *little* people. And as we allow them improvements, by itsy-

bitsy, controllable increments, in *every* field: the *system* …
our system, we require them less and less. We don't want
ever-increasing numbers of them living *longer* lives on our
wonderful little earth, *do* we now?"

With that, he paused again and stared menacingly at me,
as though preparing to deliver a killer blow.

"You know, Brian, if we *really* wanted to, we could
bring down on you a day of reckoning through which you
might live *just* long enough to wish you'd never been *born*."

"Like the day of the chemistry exam, last September?"

"Oh *yes!*" he declared, instantly changing tone from
deathly to animatedly enthusiastic. "You know, you *really*
must tell me sometime how you *did* that. *Here's* an idea:
what if we just keep making life a living hell for you *and*
your parents? And you've a *sister* as well, *haven't* you?"

He had not mentioned the Augmenter, which was *good*;
but I thought it best to call his bluff on the threat to the others.

"None of them have shown much allegiance to *me*. Do
what you *like*. I couldn't care *less*," I declared indifferently.

That plan, however, went '*agley*': to borrow from Robert
Burns.

"Oh, I'm sure there must be *someone* who means
something to you," he inflicted *sotto voce*, while lowering
his head again, so that I could not see his face.

That *tore* it! It was going to have to be the long silent
plan after all.

"Your surety is misplaced. I'm as *free* as a bird," I
insisted.

"*Hmm* …" he considered artfully. "I can, you know,
offer you a *third* option."

"And what might *that* be?" I asked flatly.

"We let you back *in* and you complete your medical degree, *unhindered.*"

Before I could react to that, he pressed ahead again in the same quiet, carefully measured manner: "*And* with the assurance of a consultant's post … *or* a professorship, by your mid-thirties: whichever way you want to *go*," he added with an airy flourish of his hand – as though such a thing was a *trifling* matter – before continuing, "plus money, recognition … in *short*, a comfortable life with some sense of fulfilment and maybe even a little in the way of *legacy* once it's over; *and* …"

As I had begun to process what he was saying, there had arrived an accompanying feeling akin to that which might be experienced by a put-upon clergyman, compelled – due to falling attendance numbers – to start sacrificing goats or chickens, in order to persuade devotees of black magic to attend evensong; or driven to adopt the practice of sticking pins in human effigies in an attempt to reach out to members of the voodoo community.

By way of an attempt to redress this unpleasant sensation, I eventually interrupted him.

"Like you gave the would-be *killer* in the van?"

That gave him further pause for thought before he came back at me anew: intensely *curious* that time.

"Just between you and *me*, Brian, they don't always tell me *everything*. How *did* you manage to get *out* of that?"

"Of *course* they don't tell you everything!" I concurred emphatically, raising my voice a little in exasperation with his self-assured stupidity. "Why *would* they? You're just a barely distinct layer in a very tall *shit sandwich*. You know well enough that, in terms of the foul business that you go about enacting, your only points of 'professional' contact are with those on the layers immediately *above* and *below* you. It's all *secrecy*-based: and not for any *noble* reason! But to answer your question, it was *your* idiotic goons who set the pace. *I* was just trying to keep up."

"Don't attempt to *patronize* me!" he demanded, with both the pitch and volume of *his* voice rising abruptly and unnecessarily. "I want to know how you *overtook* them … *overwhelmed* them, without leaving any marks? None of them could offer any cogent explanation."

"It was the discomfort brought on by a cramped environment and the tension generated by ill-intent that proved more than adequate expedients," I shot back. "With their intention clear enough, I had no qualms about ramping it all up in them until they became near-*hysterical*. After *that*, they were putty in my hands. Had I been so *inclined*, I could even have sent them back to kill whoever had sent them for me."

It was at best a partial truth, but still more than *he* deserved.

He looked a little taken aback, but he persisted:

"It was suggested that you may have had *help*."

Choosing not to *compound* my lie, I did not reply.

Briefly, he took on the sort of expression that I imagined a chimpanzee might adopt on being handed a snow globe. Then, he spoke up again:

"You've more recently been reassessed as too *valuable* to us for anything like that; and we *already* know that you're no *killer*. What we ask is your *allegiance* … *and* details of what you *have*, plus all that you might yet obtain. Perhaps we could start with the matter of the chemical formula that you jotted down on the last page of your exam book. I'm informed that you strayed a little beyond the realm of simple organic chemistry, and into the area of pharmacology. We have a couple of people who want to ask you some questions

about that. And it's been mooted that you may have access
to something called The *Akashic Records*?"

> 'Even a soul submerged in sleep
> is hard at work and helps
> make something of the world.'

> — Heraclitus, Fragments

He peered curiously at me, as he said the name. I had
already realised that he too was a face reader: *of sorts.*

"I know *something* of that … *location*, yes;" I confirmed,
"and as to the formula, it's a modified form of a
sesquiterpene lactone that I isolated from a variety of
wormwood. *And*, given your proclivity for acquisitiveness, I
presented it in *just* the configuration that you might have *use*
for: barely bioavailable, piss-poor pharmacokinetics, but a
nonetheless highly monetizable *commodity* — useful for
maintaining life, but inimical to the restoration of *health*.
Better than nothing *at all* though, I guess. *I* can *just* about get
my head around why it would prove *far* more efficacious
against certain cancers and parasitic infections if left
untampered with and as part of the bio complex, but they
don't provide big enough exam jotters for that. Your '*couple
of people*' ought to able to take it from there. But those so-
called 'Gods of the Market Place' are *so* fastidious and
demanding when it comes to patents, aren't they? You used
the first-person plural, but I reckon that '*they*' would have
been much more appropriate for your conveyed insistence
that the medical treatments available to Joe Public be, at best,
attenuated." Then, for emphasis, I added "And to be
absolutely clear, that was '*patents*', not *patients* … sadly."

197

"Come *on* now," he struck back cynically, "you can never discount the power of the *placebo!*"

"What really *worthwhile* material rewards or enlightening insights do *you* get out of your ongoing contribution to such crimes against humanity?" I persevered. "How do you *imagine* yourself: *cognoscenti*?

His returned look was one of manifest contempt.

"*Illuminati*?" I laughed. "So, your delusion, like your training, is *clinical*, is it?"

Lost in some, catch-up process, as he was, there showed upon his countenance no sign of any conscious grasp of the final part of my remark. And as he began to regain his earlier air of complacent rapacity, there returned to me that queasy feeling that presaged my having vomited in the gents' washroom of the Boyd-Orr building, almost three years previously. Angry at myself for even *contemplating* his specious offers, I immediately changed tack.

"I *see* now that your proposals constituted little more than persiflage. Taking you up on them would, ultimately, only have set me back *further*. Given your already-stated attitude to '*extravagant*' gifts, I must conclude that *mine* was ill- judged. Permit me if you will, though, to tell you something of *another* location that may be of *greater* worth to you. But first, a question. When were you first recruited into Freemasonry?"

"At university," he snapped back, with alacrity and a hint of pride. "My *father* was a freemason."

"Thank you. Whom do you serve, and to what ultimate end?"

His face darkened.

"I can see that you have at least some *inkling*," I pressed. "With Christ's redemptive act, your master lost. *Sure*, this still dense material earth remains, for now, subject to his blight: *largely* because of the machinations of *your* kind on his behalf. But not for *so* much longer."

I gave him a moment to digest that, before completing.

"In the innermost part of every soul is the heart of purity: the incorruptible core of being. It guarantees each person the return to the eternal homeland, sooner or … *later*. There exist *incontrovertible* Divine Laws; and *later* could therefore turn out to be a *great deal* later for someone on *your* current misguided path: stuck for aeons – and, all the while, *suffering* – in the midst of some appalling insubstantial state of being, as you pay your dues for all the chaos and misery that you have contributed towards. Unable to reincarnate on a more highly vibrating earth, where you once had repeated opportunities to make up for your crimes all the more quickly, there would be nothing for it but to *endure*. I'm no *judge*, but I'd wager that as *your* book currently stands, this will almost certainly be your last time round on earth. *And*, on the topic of endangering families, you may even have dragged your *own* family into your sad little catastrophe."

The chimpanzee dashed the snow globe to the ground.

"*Humph*! And what would *you* have me do, Goody Two-shoes?" he asked, looking piqued.

"*I* would have you do *nothing*. I've strayed as far enough into the role of proselytizer as I care to. But if I *was* in your position, I would at least *consider* abandoning those regrettably *human* leanings towards the timid, the generically iniquitous and the abacus; and undertaking to look *within* myself: maybe even *repenting* and starting on the process of unfolding myself, by fulfilling the Laws."

By that point, he appeared to be shifting beyond 'piqued'.

"*Look*," I added, perceiving a strategic opportunity, "I've been walking all night and I'm weary, so I'm only now coming to realise that my being quite so bluntly doctrinaire with you has been disingenuous of me. How about something to our mutual benefit: to give all involved some *breathing* space … to see whether there can yet emerge *common ground* between us? Consider it as you might the prospect of a colonoscopy: a little distasteful while it's happening, but in your best interests in the long run. And, who knows," I ginned louchely "maybe not as altogether an *unpleasant* ongoing experience as you might have first imagined?"

"What form might this '*something* to our mutual benefit' take?" he demanded, unadmiring of my impishness.

"*Well*, you could get Bela Lugosi and his familiars off my case for a *start*: as a sign of your *sincerity*. From *your* perspective it would be simple *pragmatism*, as it might yet result in my intuiting *some* … mutual accommodation."

Of a sudden, I checked myself. A sequence of his facial tics had specified another stinging backfire that caused me immediately to wish that I had, *long* before, reconsidered my long-standing view – first adopted at age twelve – that dedication to the playing of board games such as *chess*, although purposed to develop tactical skills, was of little more worth in relation to *real life* than as an indicator of egotism and possible psychopathy.

However, I was not without at least one other string to my bow.

"*Ah, of course*, I see it now: he's quite a bit *higher* than you on the shit stack. You're a specialist in *this* sort of thing. Oh well, it is what it *is*. I really *have* to curb that inclination towards *wishful thinking*: it *will* impair one's focus."

"You've *lost* me," he lied.

"*Have* I? Each thing has its ... what's that word you people seem to like? Oh yes, '*proper*'... its proper signs and signals. Yet, *knowing* that – and *smart* as you think you *are* – you *do* give your signals and signs away *so* readily, *don't* you. Why might *that* be? What *is* it that you're after? Is it, as I surmised, *salvation* ... *doctor*? Or, as we've been chatting so *informally*, should I just call you *John*?"

His smirk was *long*-gone by then.

"What *is* this, Brian: some sort of *head game*? I'm getting tired of your maunderings!"

You started this '*head game*', as you have it!" I pointed out. "In the Great Turn of Time, *redemption* is something that every *one* of us shall be afforded. But for the *switherer*, the vacillator ... the *dilettante*, the *now* can prove that bit more difficult than for those currently on either side of the metaphorical fence. That *said*, I reckon that the combined goodwill of *enough* people on the *right* side of that fence could achieve *such* great things. It could even deflect *comets*."

As I began to walk off, I hit him with my final volley.

"*Me*, I don't much *like* games, but I'm not averse to the odd *gamble*. And I'm willing to wager that you and your cronies *don't* have Medicine all sewn up: not even *yet*. MacSween or *no* MacSween, I'm going to try and get back on my own merit."

I feared, however, that that was going to prove impossible; but I just wanted to give him pause for reflection.

"For now, though, you chaos-promoting, cataclysm-precipitating *ninny*, let's you and I play a *new* game," I called back, as I began a slow anti-clockwise rotation through 360°. "I'm going to call it '*hide-but-not-seek*'. I'll go hide first. You stay *here*, cover your eyes and count up to a hundred, while you wait for your two uniformed muttonheads to return and take you back to wherever you came from."

"*You lanky fucking ingrate!*" came back his ill-tempered reply. Then cackling, near-crazily and nervously … haltingly: "*Thaumaturge!* You'll *need* to be!"

But he was already out of sight, and I affirmed to myself with some relief, that if I could just make it back to my bed, he – *and* his contumely – would also be out of *mind* for a good few hours to come.

As I walked up through the cemetery and onto Manse Road, I sang softly in an attempt to buoy my spirits, which had begun to sink slowly into a sea of despair:

As the sound – not unlike roaring lions – right at the song's[5] end, suffused me, it made me think again of the Augmenter and of how she had just that hint of the *lioness* about her.

On reaching the flat, I went straight to bed and slept for nearly thirteen hours.

Because I was deemed to have completed two academic years in Medicine, some years previously, I had not been awarded a grant throughout the first two years of the BSc. course The entire *third* year grant payment eventually arrived – overly late, and redundant in terms of presumed purpose – at the end of the first week of September 1989.

---

[5] *Kotton Crown*, by Sonic Youth

Like the capitalist consumer scum that I was, I invested a substantial part of it in a four-day trip across an ocean and a continent, to a destination almost as far west as I could go without getting to be *east*: in order at least to *try* to gain some sense of perspective; and also, if I *could*, to claw back some reserve of strength.

I was going to need *both*.

Chapter Twenty

"Believe me, my young friend, there is *nothing* – absolutely nothing – half so much worth doing as simply messing about in boats."

Ratty (to Mole) in *The Wind in the Willows*, by Kenneth Grahame

One afternoon, just a few days later, in the mid-September of '89, I was sitting in a small boat off Vancouver Island in Canada, while indulging in a pastime that was not quite as distasteful to me then as it is now: I was fishing for salmon with a friend who had moved out there to live and work less than a year before. I had been best man at his wedding in Vancouver, and this was my second visit to British Columbia.

"I'm curious about something," I said to him. "Vancouver seems a fairly cosmopolitan city. I've seen plenty of white faces, various oriental types, autochthonous Indian folk – insofar as there *are* truly indigenous people in the Americas – and numerous faces that you, here, would describe as 'east Indian'. But I've hardly seen any African-Canadians. I can't imagine today's Canada as being a selectively *racist* country, so why should that *be*?" I asked him.

"I dunno," replied my fishing companion, distractedly. He was concentrating on unravelling some tangled nylon line. Then he paused and looked up and to one side: vaguely emotive, as he appeared to give the question a little more thought.

"Maybe the winters are just too cold for them up here," he speculated aloud. His answer struck me as less than wholly satisfactory, but I let it go at that.

For a little while thereafter, we sat trolling calmly along in the warm afternoon sun. Then, he piped up again.

"There's a friend of my dad's: a professor of neurology. He was over at my folks' place in Bearsden one night a while back there, and he was rabbiting on about this theory he had: that differences in the skulls of blacks shows that they're less evolved than *white* people."

"So what was *his* story, then: some sort of misplaced interest in comparative phrenology, or something more *sinister*?" I asked.

"Beats *me*, but you're going on about African-Canadians just put me in *mind* of him."

"What's his *name*?"

"Peter Behan. He's an Irish guy, keen on fishing. He was the one who helped to get Mrs Howatt's son into Glasgow."

I sat back quietly for a moment or so, in order to take all this in. Then I spoke again. "I had a *lecture* from him, just a few months ago, in the pathology department at Glasgow. His wife runs the 'Unusual and Rare Diseases of the Central Nervous System' module in the course. You have to love that *nepotism* thing: they indulge it *so* brazenly at Glasgow."

I saw no point in bringing up the matter of my earlier encounter with Behan, years before.

"I say *lecture*," I continued, "but all he did was draw a circle on the marker board, to represent the viral genome. Then he just talked witless twaddle for a further fifty minutes. I suspected that he might have been unwell or severely hung-over. It was *so* profoundly bad that uncomfortable looks were being exchanged between the other students in the room. Early on, I came close to walking out, but at least in deciding to suspend my disbelief and submit for the duration to his particular brand of dumb-assery, my right brain was freed up to make socio-poetic leaps. *That* was the only way that I could see to keep myself either from laughing aloud or, worse, getting into an ill temper throughout that awful hour. I *tell* you: had *Brian Blessed* been in Glasgow that morning, to deliver a lecture on '*The Art of Whispering*', I would have learned more by …"

"*Who?*"

"*What?*"

My friend said nothing more. He just *smiled* and we trolled on into the afternoon.

A mere three hours before, I had been sitting in a meadow overlooking the sea: far beyond and several hundred feet below. Through the sepia-like haze of the early afternoon, a peaceful sense of rural idyll had come about in me. Soon afterwards, we had been drawn down by the magic of the water, and that tranquil mood had continued a while longer. *Now*, however, all that had suddenly vanished, to be replaced by a stifling apprehensive air.

With the reappearance of Behan in that tutorial room, one day during the third year – another 'non-lecture' that had not been worth getting out of bed for – I had let the matter go as an insignificant coincidence, but now there was again that rare sense of foreboding.

I quickly resolved, however, to let mood and emotion go, and simply to relax out there on the water. Holidays *are*, after all, for *unwinding*.

'Burning ice, biting flame; that is how life began ...'

From: Snorri Sturluson's *Edda* (circa 1220)

By the nineteen eighties, Fred Hoyle and Chandra Wickramasinghe had put a modern twist on the same idea, with their propounding of a radical model of the vaguely pornographic-sounding '*panspermia*' theory of the origins of the biological life present in the earth's biosphere.

'What goes around comes around'; 'there is nothing new under the sun'; 'In space, no-one can hear you ...'; ...

From June to September, after my third year, I had worked (unpaid) on a project in the pathology department. The whole show had been run by a visiting Cambridge-educated medic and someone up at Biochemistry. The project concerned the development of a glycerol-based medium: to replace liquid nitrogen for the transport of prostatic tissue biopsies from theatre to pathology. Immersion in liquid nitrogen can result in a degree of crystallisation, which can hinder the pathologist's job of discerning whether malignancy is present.

I had undertaken to work as a research assistant that summer because I felt that it would be a good addition to my record for medical school applications. I daresay that my contribution to the design of the new medium was at least greater than *negligible*.

This Cambridge chap, whose name now escapes me, appeared hurriedly round the door of the lab one morning in early September. He was unusually pallid and his hands were shaking.

"What's the matter?" I asked, sitting him down.

There were specially sealed vacuum flasks for transporting liquid nitrogen from the reservoir tank, located at the entrance to the department. Throughout the summer, he had not until then had cause to work directly with tissue samples. He had therefore been unaware of the existence of these flasks, and had decided to fill his own domestic thermos with some of the very low temperature, liquefied element.

The liquid nitrogen-filled thermos had immediately exploded in his hands, and although he had fortunately escaped any 'burning' injury, he had received quite a fright.

I chatted calmly and cheerfully to him for a few minutes and gradually he settled down.

"I just wanted to thank you for what you've contributed here over the summer, Brian; and I can tell you that your name will be there along with the others, when we publish."

The ensuing paper was to be forwarded to various urology journals, but I heard nothing more about it.

A week later, I went to Canada for the aforementioned holiday, before the commencement of the fourth academic year.

At the beginning of the second term of the fourth year, I finally received an interview for medical school. It was at Glasgow. I was disappointed that none had been forthcoming from anywhere else. It seemed to go well and I awaited their reply patiently.

With April having arrived and the honours exams well in sight, I had still heard nothing from the medical faculty: so, one morning I took a walk over to the faculty office. There, I talked with the clerk.

He spoke in a cold disapproving tone.

"It was my understanding that a letter had already been sent out to you, Mr MacKinnon."

"Well I haven't *received* any letter."

He went into his office and returned with an envelope addressed to me, but he offered no apology. I was about to leave and open it in private, when he announced, once again *reproachfully*, "I'm afraid that your application was not successful."

"Oh."

Chapter Twenty-One

"I've been looking for you for half the morning, Brian. Where have you *been*?"

It was Professor Whaley. He had just shown up in the doorway of the small room where I did much of my work. I had been sitting there, staring blankly at nothing in particular, since returning from my brief discussion with the medical faculty clerk.

"I've got that kidney paper from the journal you couldn't obtain on inter-library loan. What's the *matter*, Brian? Come on over to my office."

I had been careful to conceal any signs of distress, but there was no discernible reason why he could not have been every bit as good – or *better* – a reader of micro-expressions as I was.

In his office, I told him the bad news.

"You know, Brian, you're probably just as well *shot* of Medicine. It's a *thankless* profession anyway."

As he had spoken, I had been looking up, out of his office window. I looked up, and it was the *sky* that I saw; and me in it.

With a great part of the power of the element that runs so strongly within me, I turned on this stern, yet kindly man, who had never done me any harm.

"That's all right for *you* to say! You've *got* your degree: and *more*. I want the knowledge and experience too, so that I can make my *own* decisions on that. It's not as if I don't have the *ability*. It's hardly *my* fault that I once became incapacitated because some roguish *aberration* tried to have me killed. As for 'thanks' … that's something I've never needed or wanted from *anybody*!"

I checked myself. That sort of outburst just would not *do*.

My head sank forwards and I stared down at nothing in particular, as I awaited his order to get out.

The order never came.

"Look, maybe you just offended the wrong people, Brian!" he continued, stabbing his uninjured thumb upwards at an angle.

For a moment, I took it that he was indicating Jennett's former residence in the old quadrangle at the top of the hill; but it quickly registered that he could equally have been pointing up to MacSween's office, one floor above us.

As it turned out, Whaley's economical thumb jerk had been employed to identify *both* men.

"What do you mean?" I asked.

"*You're* a smart lad, Brian. Don't you know that MacSween and Jennett had a certain … *co-dependency*?"

"I heard *something* about it."

"Do you imagine that things are much different *now*, just because *Jennett's* gone? MacSween has more levers at his disposal than the control room of a major rail network junction; and right now, he's *off his head*! He's on *steroids*!"

It was the ridiculous, metaphor-spoiling and unavailing thought that such rooms must have been switch- or push-button-controlled by then that first occupied my conscious mind, while on some deeper level I came to terms with what Whaley had just confirmed and expanded upon.

"Oh, for *goodness* sake, could you not have clued me in on some of this a little earlier, sir?" I replied, irritatedly, after a brief hesitation.

'Sir' hardly seemed in keeping with how the general tone of our conversation must have sounded by then, but I had added it for precisely the reason that I had felt strangely uncomfortable with how *informal* things had suddenly become.

"*Goodness* plays no part in your predicament, Brian," he snapped back with an expression that suggested some puzzlement at seeming naïveté on my part. "If I were you, I would just get out."

With that, he paused for a moment. He had spoken softly and without a hint of menace, or even ill temper. Plainly, his words were not an order to get out of his office. Rather, they were words of advice to get out of the *course*.

As I stepped towards the door, he spoke again in the same soft tones: "Things could only get worse for you here. I'm sorry."

After a sombre lunch, I composed a short letter, which I left on Whaley's desk.

Dear Sir,

I am writing to inform you that I am withdrawing from the Experimental Pathology course.

Yours sincerely,

B. L. MacKinnon

Taking an indirect route towards my bus stop, I paused on the grassy patch bound by Lilybank Gardens and Great George Street. There – and thereabouts – throughout the previous year, she and I had found one another on many a lunchtime. Catching sight of her, not quite *slinking* – I can do no better than *graceful* to characterize her gait – into view with that sinuous tread that she had, would never fail to gladden my heart: 'just that hint of the lioness', evolved and upright.

By her bearing *alone*, I could have picked her out of any crowd. Indeed, I *still* occasionally find myself looking for her in a crowd: the inducement of one of those (hypothesized) engrams that *stay* with you ... *change* you somehow?

Sometimes startled – although always delighted – at how heightened all of my senses would become around her, I would, after a while of her being near, close my eyes for a little: just to bask in the fascination of it.

I had trembled the first time I saw her, and again when first she had spoken to me. No one had ever had that effect on me before, or ever has since.

And always, when the inceptive thrill had settled to a glow, and our eyes would meet again, I would – with recognition of that correspondence in her – settle to my ease: some deep sense of being *home*.

Contentment is – as I have heard Irish folk panegyrize on other subjects – '*grand, so it is*': particularly for one previously divested of same (and, thus, engendered *malcontent*), and who was not, at twenty-five, even looking for it ... not even *envisaging* that it was something that he would experience again: at least not like *that* — that *quantum* of it: *restorative*; an oasis in a vast desert, the greater part of which I had yet to traverse.

On the track, *Success*, Iggy Pop sings of the one that he thinks of 'in the last ditch'. In *my* life, there have been more seeming 'last ditches' over the years since those salad days than I care to count; with almost as many self-evidently seasonable wonders having prolonged my life. But to what – if any – consequential culmination, I know not yet. 'You make your bed, you *die* in it', pronounced some smarty-pants wag once upon a time. That's as may be, but I *do* know that no matter how long I may live, *she* – and that all too brief interlude that I had with her – will always be the great light of my life.

"Okay, *here's* a thing!" I had mooted. "It's not that I don't appreciate that I'm the most *fortunate* creature alive; and as far as *I'm* concerned it's just *without compare* how you …"

"Y-e-s …?" she had enquired, her interest piqued by my prevarication.

"*Well*, a challenge … *no*, too strong: an *invitation*!"

"*Uh huh,*" she had delved, her eyes narrowing with amused suspicion.

"*Okay*, okay. Uh, once you're those final few inches away, why not have a go at … *seeing* if you can resist that …"

"That *what*?"

Well, that sort of *pounce* that you do. I mean, *just* if you're *comfortable* with trying it.

Alone together in a room, we had been kissing; and I had failed to consider the import of the lazy 'why not?', before I had given voice to it.

She had looked momentarily puzzled by the request, but as she coolly arched an eyebrow, I could see that she was preparing to meet the provocation with obliging good will.

It was just about the only time that I witnessed her fail at *anything*.

Unaccountably struck by a burst of giggles and, loopily, extricating myself from the investing lux of her munificent maul, I persevered:

"Try it just *once* more!"

In the further witnessing of her returned look of mild puzzlement, and its development into one of nonplussed perplexity, I was swiftly edified by realisation of the iniquity of what I had ventured.

"Oh I'm *so* sorry, _____!" I blurted. "I had no *right* to suggest that. Your kisses are heaven sent: just like everything *else* about you," I reassured. "I'll never again try and change a *thing!*"

Gathering her to me, I felt the high, prominent zygomatic arch of her cheek pressed against mine, and the wondrous Pitta-Kapha rhythm and beat of her heart once again harmonising my own.

Whispering into her ear, I asked her to forgive me.

Alone on the grassy knoll, on that day the following year – and in spite of the grim revisionary task that I had gone about on my return to the course – my feelings for her had merely deepened. Whenever we would meet, there would still be that unimpaired connection between us: seemingly invulnerable to curtailment by worldly vicissitudes and afflictions.

Standing there, it struck me keenly how I *still* cared about and liked all the differences between us. What did it *matter* if I had never been able to sit through *The Rocky Horror Picture Show*, or that I had formed some (no doubt unjustified) association between Leonard Nimoy and the descent of later seasons of Mission: Impossible into 'style over substance'?

I did, though, have a soft spot for the *original* Star Trek (of which she was a fan).

Distraught, and once again – as in childhood – oblivious to the dodgy politics, I began to wonder how Dan Briggs or any of his 'I. M. force' might have gone about finding a solution. Immediately thereupon, however, I chastised myself for thinking that way. She was neither a commodity nor a 'prize' to be schemed over or planned for: she was the being that I had come to love above all others. Because of that, I wanted what might be best for *her*, whether I was destined to be a part of her future or not. Therefore, had it not been for two unexpected occurrences some months before my lonely return to that patch of urban green, I might have paid heed to that 'well-kent' imperative of my otherwise impersonal nature: "Walk away!"

The American artist, Martin Mull, once commented that 'writing about music is like dancing about architecture'. I think that, with some merit, the same could be claimed for writing about *love*. Certainly, I am at an *utter* loss to convey the *precise* nature of what it was that had convinced me that I must not – *could* not – 'walk away'. It had, however, emerged from two events on two consecutive days: her having chased me with a golf putting iron, and a short spoken exchange between us on a train back from the location where she had swung the offending club.

The golf club incident might have seemed, on the face of it, to have been little more than a slight overreaction to some high jinks on my part: but *on edge* as I was too, I found extra speed that day, for both the avoidance of my deserved braining and a quick clear read of her micro-expressions … and of those cool green-flame *eyes* that would for most of the time conceal much; then, just once in a blue moon, reveal *all*.

On the return journey to Glasgow the next day, I noticed her looking a little irritated and I approached her to ask what was wrong. A supercilious girl in our party had said something insulting to her.

I cannot now remember whether it was a hundred, a thousand or a million that I cited to her as being the multiple that she was worth more than the offender could ever have been, but neither can I forget what I encountered in her returned look.

In as much as I have ever been able to *know* anything completely, I just knew from those two events that she loved me. Maybe qualitatively and/or quantitatively it was other than what *I* felt. *Who*, after all, *can* be *quite* sure of the precise nature of *anyone* else's sensations, thoughts or feelings? *Somehow*, though, I realised that her affection for me *corresponded to* mine for her, whatever her general reticence/inability to express in words her innermost feelings: an establishing trait that I *did* hold that Vulcan character as probably having had a hand in. However, *if* – ears aside – my passing resemblance to him had any bearing *at all* on her having been drawn to me in the first place, then 'Hail Mr Spock!' I say.

So, although I believed in *providence* in its spiritual sense, I resolved anew that I was, thereafter – and in terms of timely preparations for future eventualities – also going to do all that I could to facilitate our being together: if that was what she was *also* inclined to by the time that I could bring propitious circumstances to bear. I guess that's what you do when you find the being that you are inclined to – that you *ache* to – share life's adventures with.

Before I walked off the grass and towards the bus stop for what I imagined would be the last time for the foreseeable future, I remembered something that I had once read about each Spirit/Light Being (what we are each finally revealed to be, when our 'soul garments' are, at last, fully thrown off) having a 'Dual': a specific, unique, eternal, 'yin-yang', 'other half'.

Other than *actual* emetics, few things in life have been more effective at making me feel queasy than love-struck individuals' talk of 'the one', or their 'soul mate': *that*, and some of the insufferable, self-penned marriage vows, which have offended the ears of the poor blighters unfortunate enough to have found themselves in attendance at the 'joining together' of those over-sentimental, mutually-beguiled nincompoops.

But I *did* wonder whether in some big, unassailable, ultimately-authoritative document far from this world – the content of which HLA and MHC class II are merely faint, far-off, lawful reflections – she and I had once been designated 'Duals'.

I wondered and, rightly or wrongly, I rather *hoped*.

Chapter Twenty-Two

The day after I submitted the letter to Whaley, I received a call from MacSween.

"You know, you really *must* stay on to sit the final exams, Brian," he insisted.

I was determined not to add to his enjoyment of whatever perverse excitement his tone was revealing of.

"I'm sorry, but I don't see any point in doing so. My objective was to study and later practise medicine. *That*, it would appear, has been denied me."

"A first or an upper second would still provide you with the means of applying successfully elsewhere, you know," he persevered, but we *both* knew that he was not going to permit that.

Nevertheless, with my mother still 'in the dark' regarding MacSween – my father had, quite rightly, not wanted her subjected to any more trauma after the nightmare of 1981-'83 – and with my continuing to be at a loss over how to enlighten her without causing her harm, I agreed to sit the finals.

Over the next few weeks, I divided my time between preparation for the final examinations and the completion of my project thesis.

The finals came and went and I knew that I had gained a first.

I had supplied compendious, accurate, up-to-date facts: identifying and quoting from relevant papers; and – here and there – even generating further possible explanations (on certain points directly related to the questions asked) by cross-referencing from many available sources.

By way of winding down, I went climbing with three friends, with whom I had been on various expeditions since the mid-eighties.

On this occasion, I had only a week before the fifteen-minute oral exam for the project component: with the posting of the results taking place later on the same day. I had therefore suggested to my friends that we confine ourselves to Scotland, and they were agreeable to that.

I knew that I had presented an excellent thesis: even on a subject that had yielded nothing but negative results. And by *that* time anyway, I was well prepared for any question that they might throw at me in the oral. Nevertheless, I decided that after each day's climb, I would go over everything again during the evenings, while the others were in the bar or wherever.

We went first to the island of Skye, where we climbed Sgurr Alasdair and Sgurr nan Gillean. Then, on the third day, we crossed back to the mainland and headed up to Sutherland and the gentle ascent of Ben Hope, Scotland's most northerly Munro.

At the end of day four, I phoned home. My mother told me that MacSween had called: something about a problem regarding the comprehension of my handwriting, in part of one of the final examination papers. He wanted to see me.

It was not any 'problem' with my handwriting that left me unsurprised by his communication of this further impediment to my progress. There had *been* no problem. It had all been good.

That night I drove back to Glasgow.

"Will we be seeing you for the project orals, Brian?" he asked me the following morning, as I got up to leave his office at the end of our brief interview.

"Yes, Professor MacSween," I answered as evenly as I could. Then, with probably more than a hint of unintended resignation in my voice, "I wouldn't miss it for the world!"

Bold and brazen as he comfortably felt that he could get away with being, he had presented me with my answer booklet for a question set by Peter Behan's wife, as part of the 'Unusual and Rare Diseases of the Central Nervous System' module.

"As you can see, Brian, these later pages are illegible," he declared, as he fleetingly flicked two or three of them in the general direction of my field of vision.

"Would you mind letting me have a *proper* look?" I asked flatly.

To this, he gave no reply, but instead just sat there staring at me with a vehement intensity in his expression.

"O-o-kay. Why don't we take the answer booklet down to Professor Whaley, then: see if *he* has any problems reading it?" I suggested.

"Professor Whaley isn't *in* the department today."

"Any *other* member of staff then?"

Again, there came no answer: just that same unblinking vicious glower.

After another few seconds of that, I began to feel that my *Gelassenheit* was beginning to desert me. It had been at that point that I had gotten up to leave.

Later that day, while I was at the supermarket, my father – having heard from my mother about the matter of an alleged issue with my handwriting, and having become concerned about it – spoke on the telephone with Professor Whaley.

Whaley intimated to him that in the other papers – all of which *he* had assessed – the work that I had produced had been of the standard of a 'good first', and that I should not concern myself unduly.

He gave my father his home phone number and insisted that either of us could call him at any time.

I never saw or spoke to Whaley again. I gathered that he took up a post at The University of Leicester not long after that.

Chapter Twenty-Three

"Normal is an illusion. What is normal for the spider is
chaos for the fly."

— Charles Addams

Orals for final honours exams are purportedly designed as
fifteen-minute, quick-fire, Q&A sessions whereby a few
more percentage points may be gained by a candidate.
Sometimes they make up the difference between one class of
degree and another.

Inside the small tutorial room on the ground-floor
extension of the pathology department, were seated Dr
Lindop, who was nominally my project supervisor, and
MacSween; but no sign of Whaley. There was also an
external examiner from Edinburgh University, plus another
professor of pathology – an even more diminutive 'mini-me'
version of MacSween, who likewise sported suspiciously
black hair for a man of such advanced years – from
Glasgow's Royal Infirmary. I recall him as being the
individual who was featured briefly in the Scottish news, a
couple of years later, for having invented a brassiere fitted
with electronic sensors and bleepers, whereby women could
have early warning of suspect breast lumps. I do not think

that his 'innovation' ever caught womankind's imagination, or met with its collective favour.

After the first few minutes, during which they did nothing but chat and joke amongst themselves, I began to think that they had forgotten that I was *there*. Since I had been told to come in and sit down, no one had even glanced in my direction.

Then MacSween suddenly looked up and smiled: a big, forced, crocodile-like grin.

"Well, Brian, do you think these cells really *exist?*"

The cells to which he referred were podocyte-like kidney cells for which distinct morphological and physiological qualities had been theorised by teams of researchers at Glasgow and in Melbourne.

"Well, sir, I can only express an opinion as regards the damaged and degraded *murine* kidneys that I had to work with," I replied. Professor MacSween had – from the outset of the project, in my third year – vetoed all access on my part, as a non-medical student, to any *human* tissue. During the summer between the third and fourth years, however, when I had worked unpaid in his department, he had raised no such objection to my collecting, preparing and examining human prostatic tissue.

"My answer would have to be *no*. I have found no evidence of a new and distinct podocyte cell in the rat kidney tissue samples, which I had access to," I continued.

MacSween and Lindop looked first at one another, and then united in scowling at me, in lazy preference to any attempt at a dismissive reply to my having dared to answer in the negative.

"I notice from this page of results, that you have in one instance quoted a figure to one more decimal place than your data allows for." It was the especially small guy in the corner, and he had the sort of look on his face that most people reserve for those rare occasions when someone insults their mother.

The page in question contained nothing but rows of blood pressure results taken from hypotensive rats. At the end of each row was a calculated mean result. I was justified in quoting to four decimal places, but in one instance the computer had thrown up a '2' after the four zeros following the decimal point. I had included it, with an asterisk betokening an explanatory note, on the following page.

"That shows your *ignorance*, doesn't it?" shouted the small guy, with considerable venom in his voice.

"Well, if you'd just look over the ..."

"*Doesn't it?*" he roared, launching himself up from his seat and leaning across the table. It was like being mauled by a toothless munchkin.

"Uh ..." I looked across in astonishment at the external examiner, to see if he might bring some sense of order back to the proceedings, but he, like MacSween and Lindop, had bowed his head and appeared to be perusing some paper or other on the desk in front of him.

I suppose that I ought just to have stood up and walked out at that point, but I was determined to see this through to the bitter end, if only to maintain my own sense of dignity: whatever good *that* was going to do me. Still, I wished that at least *one* of them would soon say *something*, as I was beginning to feel a little bit like a lamp post in a room full of pooches.

It was MacSween who broke the icy silence, with the same big, forced cheesy grin. He seemed to be in his 'normal' element; and if that *was* his element, then he was *welcome* to it.

"*Right*, that's *fine*, Brian. You can go now!"

I got up and left without a word.

Half an hour later, I was making my way back to Pathology from the Western Infirmary canteen.

We had been told that we could expect an 'indication' of our grades from our project supervisors, before the official list went up.

When I reached the lab, Lindop had not yet arrived; but he came in after a few minutes.

"You missed a 2:1 by a ba' hair, Brian," he grinned.

I just smiled and walked home. I did not feel particularly bad. I was certain that I should have been awarded a first. The real *degrading* had been done by MacSween and his carefully selected little *ad hoc* cadre: the further degrading of themselves, G.U. and the medical profession in Scotland. At least I had caused them a little bother in return for the nasty fashion in which they had, in *one* sense only, 'degraded' *me*.

As I paced the four miles or so from the West End to Bearsden, I considered the reality of the scenario that I had suspected increasingly throughout the course of those past two years as being inevitable. Were I to have graduated, I would have effectively cast the final stitch in MacSween and his cronies' little embroidery. And there was *no way* I was going to do that.

An hour or so later, my father telephoned the department again and asked to speak with MacSween. Instead (and once more), he got *Whaley*, who reiterated that almost all of the work that I had submitted in the finals – i.e. that relating to the subjects that he had taught, and the papers which he had assessed – had been of the standard of a '*good* first'. On that basis, I decided to submit a first stage appeal to the senate.

MacSween showed up in the foyer on the day that it took place, and he entered the chamber ahead of me. The grinning loon sitting at the centre of the table in front of me was a familiar face from around three-and-a-half years before.

In the first examination (in Biology) in the first year of the course, I had scored 79.5%, which might have been regarded as respectable enough. However, I had been given a *very* low mark for one of my two essay answers. It included the comment: 'Doesn't really answer the question!' I had twice re-read the question and my answer; then I had shown it to the lecturer in the Biology lab, and then to my Adviser of Studies. Both men had agreed with me that I had answered the question very well and that the mark awarded seemed inappropriately low. 'Remarkable' had been the term used by my Adviser of Studies, on consideration of the mark awarded, after he had read the question and my answer to it. So, off I had trotted to the professor who had set the question. Upon meeting with him, it had soon become apparent that no matter in how many ways – each presented with courtesy and diplomacy – I would point out that I had answered his question appositely, germanely and cogently, he was not going to budge an inch. Moreover, there had been 'written all over his face' – his big, long, sallow, viciously grinning, dumb face – an undisguised wicked intent: and I pride myself on reading facial micro-expressions accurately. I remembered leaving his office and wondering how such a fellow could ever have been made a professor, *even* at Glasgow. It just didn't make *any* sense at all.

And there he was again, chairing that senate appeal.

I became aware of MacSween looking towards me from my left side. I turned to scrutinize him first: the same broad, thin-lipped, baleful, co-opted, franchised grin. Turning my attention to the two individuals flanking the other professor, I found that neither would meet my gaze. Both remained determinedly focussed on whatever papers sat in front of them: committedly grey cyphers disappearing into the pages.

227

That was *that* then. They could collectively shove their BSc. It was not, in any case, a qualification that I had sought as anything other than a means of regaining a medical school place. Of course, with that resolution, there came the realisation that I was again back to square one. *That much*, however, I could cope with: if only to be rid of the whole rats' nest of them.

In one sense though, finding myself in that position was my own fault. *That* was what made it so gut-wrenching. No one had twisted my arm to go back to Glasgow. It was just me and – in some appreciable measure – my superannuated ideas about integrity and justice.

But there *had* been those precious few days of heaven; and for *those* – and those *alone* – I would have borne all the rest of it a *million* times over.

Chapter Twenty-Four

In August of 1990, I took my mother up to visit my maternal grandmother on Mull. My father had undergone a hip replacement operation shortly before, and between that and his overall health declining inexorably, he was not up to driving the distances involved.

I had, around then, been weighing up how to broach the matter of this impinging imposed status of 'cabbie' that had been landed in my lap. I did not mind helping out *occasionally*, and in general I got along famously with my mother, but this was not what I wanted out of life. I had lived away from the family home between late 1983 and the autumn of '86, but I had returned when I had gone back to University in that latter year. By 1990, I was minded that it was high time for me to stike out on my own: and there was still that *someone* with whom I still desperately wanted to make a *life … somehow*.

The challenge was just how to broach the topic with my father. He and I did not always 'see eye to eye', and I knew that I would be obliged to bring to bear the greatest susceptivity in propounding my position with this 'maimed bull' of a man.

Aside from one east-coast stretch between the villages of Salen and Craignure, all the roads on Mull were – back then at least – single track, with passing places.

One afternoon, on the north side of the island, not far from the building near Dervaig where my mother was born, I was slowly rounding a tight bend on one such road. Just as I was coming out of the turn, an old Austin Princess car hove suddenly into view. It was approaching us head on, on the wrong side of the widening in the road, and it was travelling very fast. I had the merest instant to reduce my already low speed towards zero, and turn slightly away from a head-on collision.

When he hit us, the windscreen of his car fell out in one piece. Ours shattered and sprayed inwards.

It felt like the warning
Of what I feel now.

From: *When We Two Parted*, by George Gordon Byron

For most of that morning, and in moments throughout the earlier part of the abruptly halted car journey, I had been troubled by sinistrous feelings of trepidation, accompanied by a series of unfamiliar 'hot flushes'. Then, no more than half a mile from the collision location – and with contrasting urgency – there supervened a manner of '*frozen* warning' that all but caused me to pull over.

Had I not been so taken up by thoughts of how *exactly* to go about my envisaged approach to my father on the aforementioned matter, those self-same feelings may well have found more credence with me. Alas, focussing on the road was as much mindfulness as gained traction with me that day.

When the police arrived on the scene, the other driver admitted to having had five pints of beer in the public bar of the Bellachroy Hotel in Dervaig, before having set out on his journey; and he was subsequently arrested.

My grandmother, previously a remarkably fit ninety-six year old, had been sitting in the front passenger seat. She had her eye surgically removed two days later in Glasgow's Western Infirmary, and she died ten days after that.

My mother sustained broken ribs and back injuries.

After a cursory examination at the surgery in Tobermory, I was hastily diagnosed as having suffered nothing more serious than minor face and head wounds, and 'whiplash' injuries.

Earlier that summer, a friend of mine from the Experimental Pathology course had died.

It was a bad time.

One of the aphorisms from *Daybreak*, by the German philosopher, Friedrich Nietzsche reads: 'Field-dispensary of the soul... What is the strongest remedy? ... Victory.'

At times during the late summer of 1990, I felt as though a little victory – for a change – might have come in handy, but I had already begun to accept that all that we have is *given* to us. It was not what Nietzsche called 'sublimated will to power' that I was in need of, but total surrender of my human will to all that was good: to *providence*, in both senses of that term; plus the reaffirmation that worldly power is an illusion.

For much of the next few months, I rested and looked within myself. During that time, I was for the most part quite resigned to having to be what the Americans call a 'shut-in', and my Visitor/Guardian, although by then firmly ensconced, seemed to loosen a little his not-always-welcome numbing grip on me. Whatever else I knew, or felt – or was *denied* feeling – I stilll *missed* the Augmenter; and in certain moments, I missed her such that I just could not *bear* it.

One day, quite early on in that period, I found myself thinking of the tale of Dersu Uzala, and how, if he and Arseniev could have found one another again in the vast Sikhote-Alin of Russia's Far East, then – even though it was a Saturday morning – just *maybe* I might have been able to find *her* on the Gilmorehill campus.

Whether I *ought* to have or not, I just *had* to get myself out that day. 'Whiplash', 'decompartmentalisation', 'discombobulation': *give it a name*: any jargon you like – it was unpleasant. I was *jiggered*, but determined to rally.

I sat myself on the low wall near to where we had first met over two years before, and began to entertain initially vexing thoughts about the fascination of the unreformable, elemental, birling, hydrargyrum quicksilver; and of how that allure masks cytotoxicity not so far behind certain radionuclides in its lethality. Defiantly habile, however, an inchoate and lightening sense of anticipation led me to grasp that 'un*re*' need not necessarily imply 'untrans'.

Then I saw her approaching, smiling; and I rediscovered at once how effortlessly she could transfigure me. Any attempt to trace her means of doing that had always seemed like a *sin*: a sin that I was glad not to have been appreciably inclined to. But those means – *whatever* they may have been – nonetheless struck me as something *far* finer than indecorous containment. And even if she effected it – as she unfailingly *would* effect it – *consciously*, then that *shift* was surely as to *deft*, as arch is to camp.

Naturally, as ever we did, we fell to mutually captivating conversation: up on that tightrope of nervous anticipation, with those confidence-inspiring trampolines marked 'comfortable' and 'comfort*ing*' never too far below. From the last time I saw her until I was sat, one cold winter's night around fifteen years later, watching what may have been the best-ever episode of *Wallander* (the Krister Henriksson version), I never once caught a sense of quite such manner of wonderment again.

She was on her way to an extracurricular computing class. I was hardly going to detain her. I had been selfish even in having 'run into' her like that, but our brief encounter seemed to please *her* as well.

This world of (largely) fallen souls may well still be greatly ravaged by the widespread application of 'divide, bind and rule', but between *us* there was ever the spontaneous arising of that divine principle, '*link and be*'. No other person can fully comprehend the content of the feeling, sensing, thinking, speaking and even *acting* of another, but I reckon that we came pretty close: *simpatico*, as the Italians have it. I fully realised, though, that I had confused and frustrated her in the late Summer of the previous year: a few months after our encounter with MacSween at the rugby club function; and, no doubt, I had caused her further anguish with the steps I had taken to ensure that MacSween was apprised that the apparent close association between us, throughout the '88/'89 academic year, was *no more* thereafter.

She had, I think, waited fairly patiently for me, while I had done what I chose to do. I hope that it was the *right* thing that I eventually did. Try as *hard* as I did, I just could not find a workable alternative.

All human relationships are, inevitably, unique in their qualities. The remarkable effect(s) that someone might have on one person in particular might not register as anything *at all* on most others. I am impersonal; and I have at certain times thought of that as an absolute and immutable quality

233

of my nature. But there have been three exceptions to the rule: my Redeemer, my mother and *her*. And in relation to her, that quality seemed, for a fleeting moment that morning (and for the *only* time in my life) to feel like *selfishness*.

Like an ailing animal, which instinctively seeks out that *one* healing herb in the forest that will cure its ill, I instinctively sought her out, in the certainty that mere contact with her would aid me greatly: *that*, and I just wanted to see her anyway – like I did *every* day.

The requisite coronal mass ejection was furnished poste-haste and unstintingly to one mantled as wounded Mercury, fain to find his way back into close orbit around his beloved, The Sun. And just as that incandescent star, she was magnanimous; and *more*: magical ... music-filled. There was certainly always something of music in that laughter of hers: and *love*. And out of that love there came stillness, and *healing*: *always* healing of me she was.

Just as I had so many times before, I gave myself over to all of it: to *her*.

A few minutes after we parted company, I had to stop momentarily, due to a peculiar sensation of loss of proprioception: with respect to the position of my head. For a disconcerting few seconds, I felt as if it was going to slide forwards and off my shoulders: just one of a number of peculiar feelings that would arise over the course of the following months, as a result of the injuries sustained in the car crash. There was something else, though: something wholly *positive,* welcome and invigorating: like a cloud of music created out of a collision of Ravel's *Le jardin féerique* and the Cocteau Twins' *The Spangle Maker*, with her laughter overseeing the birth. I inhaled deeply of that cloud that she had surrounded me with, as I would the best kind oxygen. *You* know, reader: the *not* 'bundled as O_3', *non*-'free radical-/oxidative stress-producing', *good* 'quantum' stuff that you get with the likes of an 'Airnergy+' or around the cresting curl of an ocean wave. It exhilarated and filled me with a manner of energy that could do but one thing: *improve* me, as *ever* she improved me.

"Oh Brian, you're *incorrigible!*" she would sometimes declare, laughing heartily. Heaven knows I *had* to be back then, or my spirit would simply have crumbled. But because time spent with her did *so* much to ameliorate the sheer oppressiveness of just about everything else, I would usually try to dial it back a little. That *laughter* though … so just a *little!*

Not in the Abbey of Perlevresse; nor in the combination of base pairs that go to make up the so-called 'fountain of youth gene', Lin28a; nor in an as yet to be discovered derivative of metformin – nor even, I suspect, *anywhere* on this earth – could there be waiting to be discovered an elixir to rival her; just *her*: none other for me.

*

Chapter Twenty-Five

With the passing of the summer of 1991, I was back on form and I felt more strongly than ever about what I ought to do with my life.

My plan was to try to gain a medical school place abroad.

I applied far and wide and managed to obtain what appeared to be tentative interest from the University of Alberta, in Edmonton, Canada. They specified, however, that at least one year of study in their faculty of science was required before a student could gain admission to medicine. The outlook was not altogether grim though, as they further indicated that it was their adopted policy to accept a small number (three per cent of the total intake) of foreign students to their medical school each year.

They also stipulated that in order to be considered for their 'pre-med' course, I would first have to undertake one year on a Biological Sciences course at a British college of higher education.

Prompted by an advertisement in a local newspaper, I approached the Biosciences department at Glasgow Polytechnic, which later that year – and in common with other polytechnics nationwide – was to be accorded university status. It became Caledonian University in the course of my time there.

I showed them my Higher results from 1980, and in order to dampen any tendency on their part to look into my more *recent* past, I said that I had been living and working in Canada since shortly after leaving school. I informed them of my desire to study medicine and of how I felt that a degree in the area of biological science would provide a good initial foundation, with respect to that ambition.

They were happy to accept me. I paid my fees, matriculated, passed through the year with the highest marks in all subjects, and was given a great report from Dr Kinsman, the course coordinator.

In late August of 1992, I received an acceptance from Edmonton and I flew out a couple of days later.

It was not such an attractive undertaking as it might have been. In May of that year, my father had been diagnosed as having terminal cancer and I was therefore uncertain as to whether he and I would ever meet again. There was also the prospect of living four thousand miles away from the young woman for whom my love had not diminished. The perplexing nature of what had once seemed to me surely *specious* in its nature – *romantic* love – was perplexing no more: just heartbreaking.

Having eventually arrived at the University of Alberta, I paid my annual fees and enrolled in classes, which I thought would be commensurate with a future progression to medical studies. This was not as straightforward as it *might* have been, since their acceptance of me had been at the 'last minute', before the beginning of term. Therefore, when I arrived, enrolment had long since begun and many of the classes were full.

I managed, after some trying, to obtain an appointment with a medical school adviser, as I was anxious to make sure that I had chosen the right subjects. The earliest that she could see me was in the afternoon of the seventh day after my arrival.

In addition to existing on a diet of nothing but haggis and deep-fried Mars bars, drinking excessive volumes of whisky, fighting, and wearing a kilt at every possible opportunity, Scotsmen are most often stereotyped as being dour skinflints. In the main, such lampooning is most unfair, and I daresay that, in common with most of my countrymen and women, I have a fairly sunny disposition. *Money* simply is not in itself something that I ever think much about. Although raised, for the most part, in a household that was in certain senses idiosyncratically *removed* from the British class system, I had until then – and perhaps inappropriately – always assumed that monetary wealth was something that I was not going to *have to* concern myself about throughout my life.

I had gone to Edmonton with my savings of around six thousand pounds. Between university- and accommodation fees and buying books and equipment, I began to notice that my funds seemed to be haemorrhaging out in every direction.

I decided that as soon as I had seen the Adviser of Studies, I would look into the possibility of obtaining part-time work as a foreign visitor; and with time to spare at the beginning of the first term, I had been working on a business plan based on the application of two synergistic technologies that I had been developing throughout the preceding year. Their (joint) purpose was the location and pinpointing of sub-surface deposits of platinum group metals.

From the outside, to the disinterested observer in a world full of everyman chancers, it could have appeared to have been a whimsical unrealistic hope, but I'm not even sure that it *was* merely a *hope* that, by then, I harboured that the

Augmenter and I would be reunited. It was more like *faith* … and *knowing*. There was still that invisible *something* that, sometimes, I felt so *strongly*; and when it would come – as it did at least once each day – and I could sense her close in the aether, I would always embrace it: even though there would follow such *sadness* at her continuing absence from my daily life, over four thousand miles- and eight hours of 'time zones' separated as we then were.

In those rare moments of relaxation when I would sit down for a tea or a coffee, it would always be the *travel* section of a newspaper or magazine that I would turn to in search of far-flung unfamiliar places that we might one day visit together.

As well as feeding into a specific aspiration, the developing practice was also undoubtedly emblematic of my having so much enjoyed – and my continuing to want to re-establish – the sharing of time and space and ideas, and so much else with her: her *alone*. But I felt strongly that I just *had* to get to where I knew that I could be – *had* to be – in (adult) life, in order to be able to offer all of it to her: dauntlessly, equitably and in ongoing fashion.

I knew that she was due to graduate in '93, and I had resolved that if I could make good academic progress, and maybe get this business up and running, I would, upon my return visit home in the winter, ask her if she might consider me, and Canada, as options: *life* options. After all, without even having been able to stop myself from doing so, I had told her that I loved her, not so many months after we had first met: and *that* had not put her off; so, "why *not*?" I had thought.

Then, with tea break over, I would turn again to working towards doing some measure of good for humanity, in the one way that I knew I could.

The night before my visit to the adviser's office, I went for a meal with some of the other students whom I had met.

They seemed a cheerier and somehow more easy-going lot than many of my acquaintances back home, and I felt very much at ease in the general company. I already knew a few Canadians from my earlier visits to Vancouver, and the atmosphere felt much the same as there: laid-back and good-humoured.

The conversation was not in any way 'highbrow', though.

As pudding ('dessert') arrived, the main thrust of the developing (or, more accurately, *degenerating*) discussion, somehow turned towards identifying as many slang words as had ever been coined for 'vomiting' and 'vomit'.

I forget most of them now, but 'chunder' and 'blow chunks' still cling grimly to the walls of my mind. For my own part, I offered up 'Hughie', which seemed to go down (or rather, *come out*) quite well. I considered adding 'Green', but it struck me that the cultural reference would, in any case, have been lost on them. They were an okay bunch, I suppose: not the sort who asked you what you did, immediately upon meeting. But the subject did eventually arise over coffee.

"What're you majorin' in, dude?" asked the jolly, grossly overweight fellow from directly across the table.

"Well, I'm enrolled in science subjects, but I'm aiming to go on to study medicine," I replied.

"Well, good luck to ya man! But *shit*, I wouldn't go gettin' your hopes up … *unless* … you ain't Hong Kong Chinese, are ya?"

"No."

"Are you *rich*?"

"Not *particularly*, no."

I was suddenly finding his line of questioning a little discomfiting.

"Well, like I say, dude, gettin' landed immigrant status and a place in med. school ain't gonna be the easiest thing in the world for *you*. Good luck to ya anyway, though!" His attention then turned immediately from me to one of his friends down at the end of the table, before I could get the chance to question him on what he had said.

"Hey, *Pete*! Did you catch that Seahawks game last night: third quarter? I can't remember an *entire game* where I've seen so many fuckin' defensive errors!"

The next afternoon, the speculations of my foul-mouthed, 'armchair quarterback', dinner companion proved entirely accurate.

As I would soon thereafter discover, the stark reality was that in the preceding four years, only *one* European student had been admitted to the medical school there, and she (an Irish woman, then in her third year) was facing the prospect of having to give up, because she was finding it impossible to gain the aforementioned – and prerequisite – certification for continuing to study and work in Canada: 'landed immigrant status'.

To allude once more to the work of Joseph Heller, it was a classic *Catch 22* situation for many people coming from abroad to study in Canada: without prior qualification in some area which was of use to the Canadian economy, you could not gain landed immigrant status; and without landed immigrant status, you could not stay, study or work in Canada for any longer than a year at a time. And in addition to *that* paradox, tightening restrictions were by then greatly diminishing the odds of even *visitor* status being renewed after the first or second year.

The expedient, of course, was to have a lot of money: a quarter of a million dollars, plus a small investment in a new or established business, could buy immigrant status (and eventual citizenship) for a sufficiently wealthy individual and his or her dependants.

I wrote earlier that money is not something that I often think about. I did *then*, and with regret that I had not devoted more of my time to amassing it. *Poverty*, then – and in the face of this constantly shifting 'Brave New World' – had been the (universal and) personal Achilles' heel that I had failed to cognize.

I was disconsolate.

The next day, I booked a flight back to Scotland.

Past, present, future: all can be in *present* form: *present, past present, future present.*

Time is merely an *extension*. But an extension of *what*?

The grief that comes with the loss of a loved one – through death, in *one* form or another – can spur an individual to processes of *actualisation*, which may bring at least *some* degree of comprehension.

For me, the 'stepping stones' were: my sensing that, with nothing to offer her, I would thereby lose her; and, with that cognizance, there immediately ensued the further *absolute* loss of a tendency that had been marked in me right up until that point: my proclivity for forming emotional attachments to *places*.

I loved her; and her *alone*; and I suddenly realised that since the advent of that love, nothing else had mattered to me anymore, except in relation to that specific state of being.

Now that I could perceive no remaining path towards our being together in the world, I discerned that all that was *worldly* – time and space included – would, almost *automatically*, begin to leave me; and vice versa.

I knew too that in endeavouring to desist from continuing to take the matter of my human survival into my *own* hands, the process of my becoming 'not of the world' would, consequently ... *stepwise*, commence.

Stepwise *indeed*!

Chapter Twenty-Six

It is, of course, an impossible thing to convey the totality of one's experience using language.

After my return to Scotland, in September 1992, I spent the next seven months helping my mother to nurse my father. It was at the end of that period that my plan to re-enter medicine, via a belated and incognito return to school, eventually welled up in me. As to the precise course of its evolution, or the minutiae of its refinement, I would not know quite where to begin.

I would, however, state that, terrible as it might seem, it was not *merely* the dissolution of a loved one's human personality, or the stench involved in the cleaning up of melaena faeces; the chaos or the waste, or even the callous aggression of Strathclyde Regional Council that offended me most back then. It was also the *lie*: the propagated and entrenched lie that I could not 'cut the mustard', as was later reported by the *Daily Mail*, a rag which outdoes even *The Telegraph* or *The Guardian* in the running for the title of Britain's vilest newspaper.

MacSween and his servile cronies had effectively labelled me a 'failed medical student'. Yet, it was *they* who had failed: they had failed *me*.

The more that I considered what they had done to me, the more I hated lies; and the more I was in awe of the persistence of ego: one's *own* ego.

It had neither escaped my attention that, driven by a likewise persistent zeitgeist of resurgent, so-called 'neoliberalism', there had also become clearly apparent a prevailing political praxis, which audaciously *encouraged* the seeking and grasping of opportunity from fluid catastrophic states: another devolving pitch, soon to be reified as the terrible triumvirate of abysmal Blairism, egregious Britpop and Harry 'brain deadening' Potter.

Then it *hit* me. If they could make me the victim of their *lie*, in *their* system – the *only* system – then perhaps the only way that I could yet win through would be to create my own role in their hardball, lying game, and *play* for *all* that I was worth.

It would require counterattitudinal behaviour, over a considerable period of time; and *that*, in turn, would necessitate great patience, plus the placement of a little *iron* in my soul.

I quickly realised that, in spite of my sadness at the prospect of the concomitant necessity of temporarily becoming as sly a mizzler as the *best* (worst) of them, I might well have had within me *all* that it would take.

One may sometimes have to risk much for just a little piece of life. And I *wanted* my life. I still do.

In view of all that it threw open to public scrutiny; and, especially, the gross distortions for the purpose of public consumption – via aforementioned Hypodermic needle model, D.I.P.s and a number of other ever-'evolving' consciousness-manipulating techniques, that even back then were firmly in play – I am now minded to write the remainder of this account of key events, as they took place, up until 1999.

Chapter Twenty-Seven

One late December night, in 1995 – and for the first time in memory – I paid heed to the cold. Through the living room window, there was no sign of spring buds on the willow tree, no shooting crocuses or daffodils: nothing like that would arrive for a couple of months.

That year's winter had been particularly severe. In its depths, around Christmas, an old friend came to visit. Over the preceding years, we had lost touch with one another and it was good to see him again. From time to time, we had gone hillwalking together.

On the previous night's news, I had heard tell of the third death on a Scottish mountain that year. Throughout the previous year, there had been thirty. I had hoped that sensibilities were refining amongst climbers, to the extent that there would be markedly fewer such fatalities by the end of '96.

In a light-hearted, dark-humoured moment, it once occurred to me that broadcast reports of severe weather in the Scottish Highlands somehow activated an as yet unidentified 'lemming gene' in certain susceptible individuals around the country. Such people, I visualized as falling promptly into a hypnotic trance; then, automaton-like, packing T-shirt, shorts and plimsolls into a backpack, before driving inexorably northwards to an inescapable, high-altitude doom. That sort of flippancy of course serves little purpose, in view of the devastating effects that these avoidable deaths must have on loved ones.

> The north cannot undo them
> With a sleety whistle through them;
> Nor frozen thawings glue them

From: *In drear-nighted December*, by John Keats

I do not suppose that either my friend or I fell into the 'lemming' category: both of us invariably had a good idea of what we were undertaking. But as I walked with him to the junction of Drymen and Stockiemuir road in what must have been about minus twenty degrees, I remembered how harsh it had sometimes been on the hills and mountains: the snow and the ice, the relentless, biting wind, and that rare, peculiar sensation of generalised numbness, when it suddenly and unnervingly occurs to you that one side of your scrotum may just have frozen to your thigh.

As I stood chatting with my friend at the side of the road, the cold still did not particularly bother me, but somehow I had a fuller appreciation of what it could mean for many. It was late. An old lady passed by, walking her dog. I could well-nigh *feel* her discomfort.

Some nights later, on Hogmanay, I was standing in my mother's front room and looking up out of the window at a dark orange sky that hinted at more snow. I thought again of my former climbing companion, who by then was reaching the end of a mountain craft training week near Aviemore. He had always appeared to me as a creature of fine substance. Not all the folk who had turned up on the doorstep in the preceding months had seemed so.

I reached down for a letter, which lay on the table beside the window. It had been hand-delivered earlier that day, while my mother and I had visited friends for a pre-New Year's dinner.

It was from Stuart Kelly: one of the boys who had been in the fifth year at Bearsden Academy during 1993/'94.

Kelly and his contemporary, Timmy Perman, from the sixth year, were a couple of lads who, for reasons best known to themselves, had sought out my company on a disconcertingly regular basis throughout the '93/'94 school year.

While it was not the most difficult challenge to foil Timmy's frequent enthusiastic entreaties that we 'go for a beer sometime', it was not always so easy to keep smiling under an all-out aural onslaught from Kelly's intensely monotonous drone.

There are of course all sorts of reasons why people speak in the manner that they do.

Nonetheless, I had seen David Lynch movies that made more immediate sense than I could derive from wondering why either of those two had been inflicted upon me.

However, when I later heard of – and subsequently read – their paid contributions to the Press canon, I could at least trace a manner of grim *causality*.

In his missive, Kelly intimated that he was: '... writing to you [me] as I spend my Christmas vacation from my studies in Edinburgh.'

He continued:

'... Since I have come back here (*sic*) my thoughts have turned in a big way to my actions following the breaking of the story concerning you.

I am unsure of your exact feelings over your aquaintances (*sic*) talking to the newspapers but I have heard that you are annoyed and I imagine that would be the case. I would like to sincerely apologize to you for any offence or annoyance I have caused you in talking to The Daily Record. The Daily Record got my name from my brother Robert, who is now thirty, who had decided to talk to them as he had met you at a school speaking contest when he was fifteen.(*sic*) He did not consult me before doing this and I had already made up my mind not to approach the media. I had decided that it would not be the right thing to do. After they approached me, I was persuaded to say something minor without giving my name, but after that (*sic*) things spiralled out of control and the resulting article was not my intention nor expectation. (*sic*) What happened was not what I wanted and in view of the press' (*sic*) treatment of you in print and the harassment of you and your mother, I think of the incident with deep regret. To me personally, it was a very unpleasant and traumatic experience and I was deeply hurt and shocked by the treatment I was given by the reporters and by what was printed in the end. I would like to explain to you in greater detail why it was that things got to the stage they did sometime (*sic*) but I want to keep this letter brief.

I hope this letter finds you and your mother in good health.'

He signed off: 'yours sincerely, Stuart Kelly' (*sic*), but I could not help but wonder as to his sincerity.

On the afternoon of the day after the story broke, in September 1995, my mother – watching from her living room window – saw Kelly approach a group of reporters on the public green outside. After chatting to them for a while, he walked over to the payphone on the corner and dialled what turned out to be my mother's telephone number.

He asked her if she knew where I was. When she said 'No', he replaced the receiver without a further word, and walked back towards the gathered hacks.

Later, my mother described that particular experience to me as having been 'creepy'.

While I bore Kelly no ill-feeling, neither did I feel inclined to meet with him to listen to his explanation: although I had done my *utmost* to remain entirely impersonal in every human interaction that I had engaged in throughout 1993-'94, my *own* substance could no doubt still have borne some refining.

"Move on! *Move on*!" commanded the Black Witch, having ceased her giggling. But, ridiculously, she had grossly overestimated the extent of her power over him.

— From a fairy tale read to me in early childhood (title and author's name undetermined).

Back in October of '95, and thereafter, I had been careful to minimise my contact with reporters. Aside from those of Glasgow's *Herald* newspaper, I spoke briefly – at 11 Whitehurst – with only *one* other journalist.

I had two particular reasons for doing so. Primarily, it was an attempt at further discovery about MacSween's connections (as they extended into the *English* establishment). Unsurprisingly, it soon became apparent that they *were* extensive. The secondary spur, which motivated the specific choice of *hack* – or 'hackette', as it turned out to be – was curiosity about any significance concerning the recurrence of a particular surname: 'Gillan'.

In her article in *esquire* magazine, Audrey Gillan, the *one* dour, unsavoury ghoulish creature – of the many such persistently stalking wights – whom I had selected to admit to the flat in order to make those determinations, began by describing the house as wearing 'an expression of simplicity'. Looking around the living room on Hogmanay, I recalled a time when the inside of the dwelling was almost as 'minimalist' as the outside walls.

Chapter Twenty-Eight

A week after my father's funeral in late April of '93, I helped my mother move house.

While I transported most of her household goods and other possessions from the old flat to the new one, she set about cleaning the old place in preparation for the incoming warden.

There were three clear days between receipt of the new house keys and her being ready to move in. I decided that that was long enough for me to conduct the immediate business that, by then, I had firmly in mind.

I bought a telephone/fax machine and opened a BT line at 11 Whitehurst: my mother's new flat. Then, through the pages of *Private Eye* magazine, I set up a mailing address at 281 City Road, London. I gave my real name and I requested that any mail, telephone or fax messages for either myself or a Professor William Lee – whose private secretary I claimed to be – should be forwarded to me at Whitehurst. This was agreed to, and suddenly almost everything that I required to actualise my purpose was in place.

The next step was a little trickier.

Imitation is not an art upon which I place much value, yet I would appear to be adept at it. Some sustained 'received pronunciation' tinged with more than a hint of pomposity seemed to be in order.

Even then, as I sat on the uncarpeted floor and dialled up the number of Douglas Academy in nearby Milngavie, I felt sledgehammered by the dual prospect of pretending to be someone that I was not, and thereby attempting to overcome odds of success that I suddenly sensed as being on a par with those of a tadpole in an arse kicking contest. Still, I held fast to my intention and persevered. Perhaps, in the course of one's spiritual development, there are appropriate moments for great willfulness.

At the other end of the line, a woman's voice answered, "Hello, Douglas Academy!"

"Hello, this is Professor Bill Lee. I'm calling from London. I wonder if I might speak with the head teacher."

As it turned out, Douglas Academy had a policy of sixth year exit. I had by then reasoned that an approach from a prospective sixth year student, with no prior qualifications, would have been subject to in-depth investigation. Furthermore, I was unwilling to get caught up in an undertaking extending over two years.

That left Boclair Academy, situated within Bearsden and about two miles from my mother's place.

Again in the character of the fictitious Professor Lee, eager that his son, Brandon, should gain a school placement, I spoke firstly with a Mrs Marker.

I wondered if she was the same Mrs Marker who had taught at Bearsden Academy during my time there between 1975 and '80.

She seemed hopeful about the prospect of admission, but indicated that she first had to consult with the head teacher, Mr Aitcheson. He was away from the school that day, but she indicated that if I were to call back the next morning, he would then be able to speak with me.

The following morning, I got through to the head. The voice was unmistakable: it was the same Mr Aitcheson who had taught me German throughout my third year at Bearsden Academy, between 1977 and '78.

Boclair, however, was not to be my destination throughout '93/'94.

Aitcheson expressed his regret that it was not his school's policy to accept pupils from outside its catchment area. Whitehurst lay within that of Bearsden Academy.

Well, I was hardly going to let a little bit of extra *weirdness* get the better of me. It may not have been 'do or die', but it surely was 'do or *fade away*'. And I was *not* for fading.

My Alma Mater, perforce, could not have been more accommodating.

Again, by replying to an advertisement in the classifieds – this time of a national newspaper – I had the following letter of introduction typed, and faxed to 11 Whitehurst. The typing service also posted a couple of laser-quality copies to me, but they did not arrive in time for my aforementioned interview with Mrs Holmes. Nevertheless, the faxed copy worked well enough.

W. Lee PhD, DSc, FRS, FRSE
Professor emeritus of Zoology

281 City Road
London
ECIV ILA

10 May 1993

Dear Mrs Holmes,

This is to introduce my son, Brandon, who is currently staying with his grandmother, Mrs M. MacLean, at 11 Whitehurst, Bearsden.

He is a very bright young man, with excellent analytical powers, great perseverance and disciplined study habits. His ambition is to win a place at a university medical school and to become a doctor. To these ends, he is eager to undertake the Scottish Higher study courses and examinations in English, Mathematics, Chemistry, Physics and Biology. It is my hope that you can thus accommodate him.

Please find included with this letter, reports on Brandon's recent progress, from Ms Martha Hunt, BSc.; and from his former Science tutor.

Yours sincerely,

William Lee

With these simple measures followed through to completion, I was in.

Chapter Twenty-Nine

Being 'in' was by no means a bed of roses though.

Around the second week of June 1993, not long after my thirtieth birthday, I found myself standing close to a corner in the school canteen. In front of me, two fifth year boys were arguing over the correct method for tackling a particular type of physics problem involving vector resolution.

"That's not the way to do it," said the first lad. "It should be the other way round." He gave the impression that this was a generally accepted principle, in an attempt to distance himself ironically from his own statement; but people, young and not so young alike, are not always sensitive to these things.

They had both drifted a little towards me, and just as the first finished speaking, they each glanced in my direction with almost identical expressions of mild entreaty.

By way of clarification, I supplied the smile that the first boy had forgotten to add. But it was not reciprocated.

"Well anyway, let's say different people do it differently." I qualified the first boy's statement, because I felt that this was the kind of thing that prevents rows.

"Ah'm *tellin'* ye: *that's* how you do it!" said the second boy, gesturing to the working on the page of his own jotter, which he had retrieved from his backpack. This he did, while exhibiting in his voice a note which was pitched somewhere between supplication and annoyance.

"Not necessarily," I observed, slightly hurt that my offer of conciliation had been so peremptorily rejected.

"He's right," said a third youngster, drawn, iron filing-like, by the magnetism of our incisive debate.

"*That* is how it's done!" reaffirmed number two, his hand flapping against his own page of largely illegible scrawl that he upheld as gospel. By now, the tone was simply of vexation.

"On the *contrary*, *that's* how it's done," persevered number one. "In the solutions to these kinda problems, at the back of the textbook, they always follow the sequence of steps that *I've* got and ..."

"Aye, well maybe in *your* textbook, but not in *mine*," interjected number three, smirking impishly.

"Anyway, I'm sure that *either* of these methods will get you to the right solution eventually," I said, because things were really starting to get out of hand. However, it was obvious that there was no such easy way out of it. Moreover, I was also concerned about my being increasingly hemmed into the corner. I feared that the inquisitiveness of one or other protagonist, heightened by the heat of argument, would suddenly switch focus to the close-range perusal of the fine lines on my allegedly seventeen-year-old face.

"Vector problems get solved the way *I* solve 'em," number one countered, addressing his remark to number two. "If Gunn wants it done some *other* way, I'll *do* it, but I doubt that he *will*. I spent nearly three hours doin' the fuckin' things last night, so I should know the right way by *now*!"

"In that case then, you spent nearly three hours doing them *wrong*," replied number two, coldly.

"Wrong*ly*," I found myself thinking, ridiculously and against my own inclination. Of course, I did not give voice to such rogue pedantry, especially in view of the fact that number two's latest retort had been spoken as though he had been waiting for years for the chance to voice it. Then, in order to make his perceived victory the sweeter – despite the risk of giving number one (and, indeed, number three) an ally – he called to a passing *fourth* boy, who, as I gathered even *then*, had a pre-established reputation as a bookworm.

Whether fortuitously or otherwise, the fourth boy came up with what I discerned to be the best method.

Bookworm or not, he still lacked both the good grace and sense to resist adding, '*Everyone* knows that. I'm surprised that you're even *asking*!'

Number two was visibly happy with this reply and with the last part in particular, because it gave him the chance to turn a defence of himself into a further attack on number one, "It's not me, it's *him*! He says you resolve them right at the *beginning*."

"I never said 'right at the beginning'," protested number one. Then, not content with having set the record straight, he plumped for outright perjury. "I said at the *halfway* point."

With number one's position appearing to have collapsed, that might have been an end to the whole ridiculous fiasco, but number two was unwilling to let his sparring partner off so lightly.

"What d'ye mean, 'at the *halfway* point'? Are you on *drugs*?"

"*No*," replied number one, stubbornly. "If you don't resolve them at the halfway point in the trajectory, you simply cannot arrive at the correct solution," he decreed.

"*Drugs*!" affirmed number two, almost crowing.

"*Shite*!" This was number one again. Having been left with no way out, he was retreating into some bizarre form of dogma and would brook no variation.

By now, number three was rising irresistibly to virtuoso heights.

"What ye *actually* do is just take it to Gunn and get him to do it on the blackboard."

It was a mediocre joke, but everyone laughed anyway. Unfortunately, however, nobody laughed in quite the right way: number two and number three passed up the opportunity of laughing with a sense of self-irony – which would have invited number one to a moment of cathartic solidarity – preferring instead to laugh in celebration of their complicity in having made an *idiot* of number one. Number one was laughing sarcastically at the absurdity of what number three had said, and I was attempting to *ease* the atmosphere by laughing in such a way as to convert the others' laughter to a higher plane of meaning. But it was obvious that I was not succeeding, because everyone was continuing to laugh in ways that were contradictory and therefore inflammatory.

"They probably did something along the lines of what you're claiming before *trig.* calculators were invented," resumed number one. Far from giving ground, this was actually a statement of manifest contempt.

"That's right. Perhaps that's *true*," I said, as I endeavoured to extricate myself, physically, from the corner into which I seemed to have become wedged; while, figuratively, I was trying to carve an opening through number one's contempt, in the hope of finding space for mediation.

"The way *you* two say it should be done," said number one, revealing a certain disregard for the pliable definitional qualities of language – and a possible interest in the original Star Trek – "is *illogical*."

"Well, actually, *Mr Spock*, it's the *only* way!" shouted number two.

"The only way amongst those with any brains," added number three indignantly.

"Physics problems are done the way *I* do them." This was number one again, and his stubborn insistence upon shunning linguistic relativism suggested a degree of essentialism that an impartial observer might have identified as the start of the whole wretched dispute.

"Hi Brandon!"

It was Stephen Addo: a pleasant fellow who sat beside me in Biology class. He had introduced himself to me on the first or second day. Sometimes one just feels instantly at ease with certain people, regardless of circumstances. Stephen was such a person, and he had come over to bail me out.

At the beginning of the fourth week of September 1995, while my mother was hemmed into another corner (the flat where she then lived) by the so-called 'media circus', and I was still in the throes of a necessarily tortuous route back to Scotland, he popped an uplifting note through the door. In it, he conveyed his sympathy for the troubles that we were going through at the time, and he wrote that:

'... it [is] at times like this that you know who your friends are (the ones that don't go to the newspapers and slander you with lies).'

His letter concluded with the offer to meet up for a chat or a drink.

Just as he approached and spoke to me in the school canteen that day, over two years before the commencement of those troubling times, the bell rang, marking the end of the morning break.

259

I smiled in his direction, slipped my cordon of embryonic rocket scientists, and walked with him to the exit.

"What's next period?" I asked, as we passed through the swing doors and out of the dinner hall.

"*Physics*," he grinned.

"Terrific!" I sighed. And then, again – and in keeping with the 'proper' *British* way of thus proclaiming – in a tone that sounded simultaneously peeved, but also kind of stoically resigned; and at the same time smugly omniscient (as though thoroughly pleased that one's prediction had been fulfilled); and, of course, *effortlessly* 'numb': "Just *terrific!*"

Chapter Thirty

The year back at school certainly constituted an unexpectedly intense refresher course in the art of detachment, and thereby, the artless – and, at first, seemingly paradoxical – process of being impersonal.

The apparent necessity of being intensely self-conscious, day in, day out, quickly and briefly took on the quality of a joke. That experience afforded me a fresh perspective on the axiom that I could never see this through to completion by trying to '*be* someone'. I had to try to relax and trust entirely to my belief in the essential (moral) rightness of what I was doing. I had become aware that only by loosening up would I manage as far as the first year of medical school, before having the profile of my endeavour raised into public awareness, and being able one day to continue my intended course of study, free from the indignity of a false identity.

After all, common sense alone tells us that we can become overly elaborate in our methods to achieve a goal: with the all too inevitable result that we make little or no headway. Take the music industry, for example: if you can manage something as novel as playing two instruments simultaneously, such as the guitar and the mouth harmonica, then you have a shot at being hailed as a musical genius, like Bob Dylan or Neil Young. But as *soon* as you go that extra few yards, by strapping on a snare drum and tying a couple of cymbals to the inner aspect of each knee ...

Even now, much of the remaining experience of that year strikes me as little more than an ordeal: the settlement of some *soul debt* ... *karma*. Perhaps the most astonishing thing about the whole interlude was that it did not turn my hair *completely* grey.

In the turn of time, the year eventually passed by. May it rest in peace!

With the arrival of the summer and the last performance of the school show, it only remained for me to await the arrival by post of the Higher examination results.

Earlier in the year, I had attended interviews at both Dundee and Aberdeen universities. Both had gone well and I was offered provisional acceptances. Dundee required that I gain at least 3 'A's and 2 'B's. Aberdeen wanted 4 'A's and a 'B', as I was applying from the fifth year and it was not their 'usual policy to accept students before they had completed a sixth year'. As it turned out, I was awarded 5 'A's.

Back at the end of my original fifth year at school (1979/'80), I had gained 4 'A's and 2 'B's, before going on to study medicine at Glasgow University. However, Paddy Christie, a reporter for Scottish Television's *Scotland Today* news programme, presented her own contrived version of my original schooldays.

A few days before my arrival back in Scotland on September 23rd, 1995, she appeared on camera outside Bearsden Academy, to tell viewers that 'Brandon Lee was originally enrolled here as Brian MacKinnon in 1975, but he left after his third year, with no qualifications.'

On the following Monday, September 25th, two days before the deadline for me to present an explanation of my actions to Dundee University, Ms Christie appeared again for *Scotland Today*. This time she was standing in the road, outside my mother's flat. From there, she announced, "According to May MacKinnon, Brian has said that the time he spent at Bearsden Academy was the happiest year of his life. It was his father's dying wish that Brian become a doctor; and Mrs MacKinnon said that she promised that she would do all she could to help him."

Up until the time of Ms Christie's report, on September 25th – and for several days thereafter – my mother had spoken to neither reporters nor anyone else, on *any* matter. In addition, the alleged utterances were spoken by neither my mother nor me.

I am sure that my father *had* wished for my success in medicine, but beyond that, Ms Christie's other above-documented declarations are lies.

The following is a quote from *The Herald* of September 27th 1995, the deadline day for my letter of explanation to Dundee.

'Dr Brian Potter, Scottish secretary of the British Medical Association, yesterday expressed sympathy with Mr MacKinnon's plight and said he hoped Dundee University would 'take a broad view' in considering whether to take him back.

"Practising as a doctor, you have to have a high level of integrity and trustworthiness, but I would hate to see someone with such a compelling urge to be a doctor barred because it had led him to enter this subterfuge," he said.

No doubt any latent sympathy that may have existed amongst those judging me at Dundee University Medical Faculty would have been erased by the very public announcement of such false claims by the likes of Ms Christie, for *Scotland Today* and Leslie Anderson, for *Reporting Scotland*.

And who says that journalists do not always perform righteous and worthwhile roles in society?

In any case – and by way of appropriate and necessary expansion – there follows below an account written as an 'epilogue' (begun in August 1997 and completed in January '98) to my original text.

Epilogue (of yesteryear)

Towards the end of January this year (1997), there was a break-in at my mother's flat. The room which I occupy whenever I return home was ransacked, and disks and hard copy of my typescript were stolen. An old video camera, a 'telerecorder' and some tapes were also taken. The policeman who visited on the following day – a DS Boyd, as I recall – expressed the view that I might receive some form of communication threatening blackmail. Having had previously outlined to him the typescript's contents, I found myself unable to follow whatever path of deductive reasoning that the detective sergeant had forged towards his conclusion: because there *wasn't* one.

Shortly afterwards, I wrote to Dr. Brian Potter, the Scottish Secretary of the BMA, primarily to (belatedly) thank him for his considered and supportive remarks to the press, in September '95, but also in order to formally register my deep disquiet at all that had been wrought upon me by Professors MacSween, Jennett and the shabby little Scottish establishment of which they are a part. I ended my letter to Doctor Potter with the request that the whole matter might one day be thoroughly and impartially investigated by a suitably empowered body, such as the BMA.

"*Some* hope!" I remember thinking as I popped the letter into the post box.

About a week later, I was pointedly reminded of my cynicism, when Doctor Potter called with the good news that he had spoken on my behalf with Professor Graeme Catto, the Dean of Medicine at Aberdeen University; and that Catto, sympathetic to my position, wanted to see me for interview. Dr. Potter further intimated that he had first pleaded my case (to no avail) with the Dean at Glasgow University. Despite my absolute faith in Potter's best intentions, I did find *that* additional news quite disconcerting.

Six days after Potter's call, however, my meeting with Catto could not have gone better. He told me that I would have to apply formally through UCAS, but that I could expect to receive confirmation of my acceptance to Aberdeen for September.

On the 10th of June, there appeared in *The Scotsman* newspaper an article which began, 'Brian MacKinnon has still not learned his lesson'; and which included the quote (attributed to me), 'fuck identity!' Its remaining contents were based upon another, then forthcoming article, which was to appear in the June edition of *Granta* – a publication that until then had concerned itself *exclusively* with the reviewing of *published* works – and in *The Sunday Telegraph* magazine, on the last Sunday in June. The author's name was Ian Parker.

On the 11th of June, I wrote to Professor Catto, to assure him that I had not spoken with any journalist, either since or for many months *before* my interview with him. In March of this year, I had declined Parker's request for interview, just as I had declined all such requests from journalists since as far back as September '96.

On the 16th of June, Catto wrote back, indicating that he had seen the article in *The Scotsman*, but that he did not know how they had come by the information. Shortly afterwards, I received a rejection slip via UCAS, and Catto followed up with a letter expressing the view that I would 'never be admitted to a British medical school.'

Needless to say, my complaints (in all instances, via both telephone and letter) to *The Scotsman*, *Granta* and *The Sunday Telegraph*, elicited neither retraction nor apology from any of them.

The one interesting aspect of Parker's concoction was that it was only the second occasion on which Professor Bryan Jennett had deigned – or was otherwise *compelled* – to make public comment.

Fifty thousand is a number that has come repeatedly to my attention this past while. It is a factor of the total amount of (taxpayers') money thus far spent by Glasgow University on preventing the continuation of my education. It was also the sum offered to me by the *Mail on Sunday*, in May '96, for the privilege of 'serialising' my typescript, in its then state of development.

With the prospect of having to finance myself through any medical school to which I might yet gain admission, I accepted their offer. They also asked to interview me. I was somewhat wary about that, but they were at pains to stress that it was merely to provide a brief introduction to the extracts from my text.

Over two weekends (9th and 16th July '96), and with no prior reference to me, the *Mail on Sunday* ran a narrative, which bore resemblance to neither my text nor the interview which I had granted them. A literary agent of my acquaintance described it as being 'sub-edited out of recognition'. I could not think of an appropriate descriptor for it, but I noted with interest that its conclusion, on the 16th of July, provided the first platform for Professor Jennett to make pronouncement on matters pertaining. Strangely (by my reckoning of the man), he admitted then – and for the first time – that I had had a virus. I could only *guess* at which of the two viral infections he was referring to.

26th August 1997

As I conclude this epilogue, the calendar has moved on to 1998.

In the months following the appearance of Robert McNeil's article in *The Scotsman* of June 10th, 1997, 1 maintained a vested interest in the daily perusal of said rag. Thereby, I gained further insights into three areas of personal concern that might otherwise have remained inscrutable.

Professor Catto's sudden and unexplained turnaround on the matter of my admission to Aberdeen University had left me wondering as to the particular design of political hothouse that he must have suddenly found himself inhabiting. I was already familiar with the barrage of spurious argument set forth by McDevitt (the Dundee dean), Whiting and (indirectly) Jennett, via the so-called 'Council of Deans'. However, *The Scotsman* of October 2nd revealed yet another aspect of Catto's new, uncomfortable and unexpectedly confounding habitation. Even in its impalpable form, that aspect constituted a *mirror* in which he was forced to confront his own ambition.

The article, by Frank Urquhart, bore the headline: 'Aberdeen professor takes over as Chief Scientist'.

It began: 'A LEADING Aberdeen academic, Professor Graeme Catto, has been appointed the Government's Chief Scientist in Scotland.

Prof Catto, The Vice-Principal and Dean of the Faculty of Medicine at the University of Aberdeen, will be responsible for advising the Scottish Office on funding for medical research projects throughout the country.

He succeeds Professor Jan Bouchier, who retired on Monday.'

It continued: 'Prof Catto, who is 52, will continue his new duties with his current post at Aberdeen University. He said: "I'm delighted to be taking up the challenge and I look forward to working closely with colleagues all over the country. There is an enormous opportunity at present in

Scotland to assess how best to take forward research and development within Scotland to improve patient care.'"

I guess that I can hardly blame a seemingly honnête homme for exhibiting the sort of moment of frailty so commonplace amongst humanity in general.

Tim Luckhurst was the BBC Scotland editor of *The Lives of Brian* programme, to which I contributed some eighty minutes of taped interview in the late September of 1995.

Almost immediately after our being introduced, back then, he intimated that his brother, a Cambridge medical student, had some years before – and in the face of overwhelming work pressure – committed suicide. That is not a disclosure which I repeat lightly here.

Luckhurst's cynical editing and the grossly distorted, biased and trivialized version of events which his programme conveyed, shocked me at the time; but I quickly came to understand the broad motivation behind his crime, as deriving from more than mere BBC face-saving. Indeed, I strongly suspected that his personal history had not been overlooked, before his selection as the Corporation's character assassin for that week. It is not that I have any particular leaning towards the popular art of psychological profiling, but when someone whom you have not provoked acts viciously towards you, you feel compelled to deduce the reason(s) for their actions.

In the first half of last year (1997), Luckhurst began writing for *The Scotsman*. Shortly afterwards, he was summarily dismissed by BBC Scotland: only to be immediately installed in a senior editorial capacity with … *The Scotsman*. On October 28th, 1997, he produced therein an impassioned article bemoaning the government plan for English students to pay full fees in Scotland, for four-year courses where Scottish students would be exempt from fees in the fourth year. This, he insisted would be a disaster, as it would deter large numbers of students from England from going to Scottish universities: notably, St. Andrews and Edinburgh. At one point, he described any diminution in numbers of students from England as being a 'body-blow'.

In common with many people, I am enlightened as to the somewhat opposed arguments about the so-called 'Englishing' of Scottish universities, on the one hand, and those extolling the benefits of cultural diversity in universities generally, on the other. In relation to these concerns, and again (I suspect) in common with many others, I was no further edified by Mr Luckhurst's article.

Over the past couple of years, I have clung to a diminishing hope – some days, almost an expectation – of a call or a letter indicating that MacSween and his compadres have at last been found out, and that I will be given back my life.

Towards the end of last year – and as an indirect result of yet another report in *The Scotsman* – I had first sight of a twelve-point 'media statement' (reproduced below), released by Glasgow University in September 1995. In reading it, I was pointedly reminded that expectation is a state of mind generally best avoided.

UNIVERSITY
of
GLASGOW

MEDIA INFORMATION

Statement: Brian Mackinnon (*sic*)

1. By his own admission Brian McKinnon's (*sic*) record of events is vague. He says in the Herald article: "I do not remember much about the following year to 18 months (March 1981 onwards) although the memories of a few events stay with me."

2. In his first year in medicine (1980-81) he reported no medical problems. He failed all his exams but passed them on resit.

3. During the second year (1981-82) he reported health problems. Far from being summoned to one meeting there (*sic*) were in fact several meetings to discuss his position and he was referred for help to the chief adviser of studies, a student counsellor, the student health service, a consultant physician, and the student psychiatrist. In the light of their advice he was persuaded to withdraw from the course. He was told that he could seek re-entry but that this could not be guaranteed.

4. In his account to the Herald he omitted to say that in a letter dated 15 July 1982 he asked to be considered for re-entry to the course. In the letter he said: "I am now feeling very well and I am writing to apply for re-admission to study in the faculty of medicine." He was given the opportunity of a repeat year and readmitted to retake the second year course in October 1982.

5. In his third year at the University (1982-83) he took the second year course. He reported no health problems during that year. He sat four exams and failed them. On resitting them he passed only one.

6. Based on the rules and regulations applying to all students he was advised that he faced exclusion from the course. He made a written and personal appeal to the Appeals Committee. When he appeared before the Committee he (*sic*) claimed that he had in fact been ill but had concealed his ill-health. His appeal was rejected in October 1983.

7. His appeal to the Senate was rejected.

8. He then appealed to the University Court and this was rejected in November 1983.

9. There then followed a succession of letters from the student and his mother to the University and a number of meetings were arranged at which it was explained that no further action could be taken.

10. In 1985 he (*sic*) submitted a further medical report seeking a re-opening of the Court appeal but (*sic*) it was ruled that this did not constitute new evidence.

11. In 1986 he (*sic*) returned to study in the Science Faculty. He successfully completed the course but did not graduate. He qualified for a lower second class honours degree. A limited number of science graduates with first and upper second degrees are allowed to transfer to medicine but he (*sic*) did not qualify for this.

12. The correspondence with the University continued until 1991.

To be attributed to a "University spokesperson"

Point 4 in particular perplexed me.

I knew that I had not written any letter in which I had applied for re-admission to study in the faculty of medicine in the 1982-83 academic year; and it sickened me to realise that for over two years past, those concerned had been thus able to use their 'official' status to reinforce their lies.

As I have already stated, I was coerced into signing a form presented to me at a meeting with Jennett, but I wrote no letter of application.

The assertions (point 5 and 6) that I reported no health problems during 1982-'83, and that I sat the second year exams twice, are simply downright brazen lies.

Point 1 attributes to me words that I have never spoken or written.

The day after I first saw the above media statement, I obtained a photocopy (also reproduced below) of the letter referred to in point 4. An individual calling himself 'Iain X. Maciver' provided it. He first telephoned, claiming to be a 'public relations agent' who was keen to represent me; and he thereupon faxed me copy of the forged letter, reproduced on the following page.

BRIAN L. MAC KINNON
16 OLD NORTH COURT
MANSE ROAD,
BEARSDEN,
GLASGOW
G61 3RQ
15/7/82.

Dear Dr. Miller,

Following upon a period of ill-health, which prevented me from attending University from late ...ber 1981, it transpired during the early part of this year that I should withdraw from the second year of the MBChB course, with the aim in view of returning at the beginning of the new academic year this October.

I am now feeling very well and I am writing to apply for re-admission to study in the faculty of medicine.

Yours sincerely,

Brian L. MacKinnon.

It was a dual shock to behold such a sham, even while being acutely aware of the wicked audacity behind its contrivance and advent. Although insufficiently absorbent for the use to which I was initially inclined to put it, it *was* nonetheless – as I soon came to realise – something worth holding onto.

Given Mr Maciver's pronounced Lewis accent, my immediate suspicion was (and remains) that this latest ex-directory number-snaffling opportunist was another member of MacSween's outer island mafia: a suspicion much reinforced by my having never heard from him again.

I did not write the letter reproduced on the previous page. The handwriting is not even a *near* approximation of my own, either as it was in 1982 or at any other stage of my life.

I immediately sought legal advice from a solicitor, as to how I could challenge this. He advised me that it would be a matter for investigation under criminal law, but that in the first instance it would be important to identify the letter's author. To that end, he further advised me to write to the University.

This I did: addressing my letter to Professor Whiting, the Dean of the medical faculty.

With two weeks having elapsed without any reply from Whiting, I reported the matter to Strathclyde Police.

Insisting that these were 'civil matters', the police officers with whom I spoke were as indifferent to this portion of my account as they were to that concerning the facts that Ian Parker – a journalist whose request for interview I had declined – had gained access to my typescript before its publication on the Internet; and, apparently, to my medical records: he wrote of an operation, which I had undergone in my mid-twenties, to remove benign growths from my arms.

With MacSween et al's continuing access to G.U. and BBC slush funds, in an age when the so-called 'culture of denigration' is propagated increasingly via corrupt – and therefore easily *bribable* – journalists, I can perhaps look forward to further salvos fired off by those curious, little, remotely controlled subhumans that constitute the press and television.

In any case, this written account ends here, as I find myself stilled by a gem of wisdom imparted by one of

America's most prolific philosophers, Bugs Bunny: 'If you can't say nuthin' nice, don't say nuthin' at all!'

17th January 1998

If you are interested in knowing the sad tale of what next befell Dr Brian Potter as a direct result of his having dared to assume the role of advocate for me, then you might care to check online. Ditto with respect to Giles Gordon, the Edinburgh-based literary agent who went to great lengths to try and get my original typescript published in the conventional manner.

I cannot be certain as to whether it was simply because he had been a high-profile *medic*, but at least they let Potter keep his *life*.

Having been made aware again, in 2004 (by my G.U. contact, 'Tom'), that the letter reproduced two pages back, plus two other similar (and similarly, *forged*) letters, were soon thereafter to be used in a planned article about me in a Scottish newspaper – and especially in view of the particularly determined and vicious attempt that followed on the lives of both myself and my mother, two days after my having recived that information – I contacted Strathclyde Police (as they were then 'branded') about the physical attack and the planned fraud.

Detective Sergeant Weir was, from the outset, mindlessly aggressive, less than helpful, and only fully *comprehensible* 'thanks' to my Glasgow upbringing.

"Whit it boils doon tae, Brian, is *their* sayin' 'Aye he did!' and your sayin' 'Naw ah *didnae*!'"

In the light of such dazzlingly rarefied insight, I could envisage a bright future for the detective sergeant in the modern force.

By way of a last-ditch attempt to appeal to any hitherto undetectable modicum of decency residing in the man, I offered to submit to handwriting analysis and a polygraph test.

In the face of that offer, he looked momentarily bemused: as though the gates were up and the lights were flashing, but no train was as yet in sight of the station. Then, to his apparent relief, it *arrived*.

He took considerable delight in informing me that results of neither of those types of investigation were considered as admissible evidence by Scottish courts.

Should they ever be deemed *otherwise*, my offer stands.

Chapter Thirty-One

Near the beginning of August 1994, Dundee University offered me a place on their MBChB course, beginning in October of that year.

I accepted their offer, without hesitation: only because no offer from any other university had been forthcoming. Then, on August 25th, a letter arrived from the admissions office. It indicated that:

'... the number of places available in any Medical School is limited, not least by the number of students who can be accommodated in First Year laboratories and the Anatomy Dissecting Room.'

It continued :

'The results of school examinations this year have been outstanding, so we have had to confirm our conditional offers to a larger number of students than we had anticipated, and have exceeded the number of students whom we should admit this year.

We are therefore writing to students holding places to ask if you would like to defer your entry to the Medical School until October 1995, instead of coming this year.

If you agreed to postpone your admission, your place here would be held for you, and you would not have to apply again through UCAS. We would write to you again about your admission in March or April next year. We would be responsible for cancelling any arrangement you have already made with the University Residences office, and you would have an early opportunity to apply for your first choice of accommodation next year.

However, if you have already applied for a student's grant, you would have to notify the awarding authority that your admission to university had been deferred for a year.

We would not specify what you would have to do during your year 'out' – further studies would not be necessary. Paid or voluntary work in a medical-related field might be possible for some of the time, but would not be required. Any work which involved meeting and dealing with people would be useful preparation for a medical career. Most students who have had a year out in the past have found that it was beneficial to have a breather between school and university – there is little opportunity for taking a year out any later in a medical course and career.

Another aspect of deferring entry for a year would be the possibility of saving some money towards the costs of being a student. With the reduction in students' grants which is taking place, all students are facing increasing problems, and there is no doubt that you would find it advantageous to begin studies at university with some funds in hand.'

The letter concluded with an offer for me to defer entry until 1995.

For one reason in particular, it was a *tempting* offer.

That reason was the very one alluded to at the letter's end: my finances were beginning to run worryingly low.

My plan, at that time, was to finance my studies by trading on the American Futures/Commodities markets, which I had also been studying since late 1990. I had reasoned that, allowing for payment of my academic fees, accommodation and other essentials, such as meals and textbooks, I would have had enough left in the bank for such a venture

I applied to a brokerage in order to open a trading account, but discovered to my dismay that for prospective *UK* clients at least, the minimum threshold capital required had recently been reset to a considerably higher level than previously.

I told my mother that I would have to defer entry for another year. She offered the following solution: if I paid my own academic fees and used the remainder of my money to cover any other expenses that I might incur throughout the year, she would take care of accommodation costs. In return, she wanted to come up to Dundee with me.

She did not exactly *relish* the prospect of remaining alone in Glasgow, with no car (she did not drive) and the nearest supermarket almost two miles distant.

I could see her point; and *besides*, we got on well together. It was agreed. We would head up to Dundee towards the end of September.

At that time, she was in the process of selling her holiday home beside Loch Fyne to a young couple from Yorkshire. Since initially they could neither afford the asking price nor manage to obtain a mortgage for that amount, she had agreed that they could pay one thousand pounds per month, until a level was reached where the bank would give them a loan.

It was this monthly income of one thousand pounds which would cover our rent and food bills in Dundee.

She further suggested that the following summer, when the rest of the money from the house sale would be paid, she would be in a position to provide the necessary top-up collateral for a broker's account, and we could split the profits from successful trades.

I insisted that she first read a substantial part of the literature that I had amassed on Futures/Commodities trading, in order for her to become familiar with both the

279

techniques and the risks involved; and that when she had done this, we would discuss the matter again, the following June.

From the 'Accommodation to Let' section of a local (Dundee) newspaper, we were both drawn to one particular advertisement for a place to rent in nearby Tayport.

The landlord was a Mr Roy. He was asking for £330 per month, in advance, and with no deposit required. The flat itself was on the ground floor of a block of four flats, in the part of the village known as Cowgate.

On the day that we arrived to have a look, it was very cold – and not only *outside* – but upon brief inspection, the place seemed habitable enough, and we took it.

We were ready to move in almost immediately. My mother paid Mr Roy the first month's rent, and he parted from us amicably and with the promise that he would have a short-term lease agreement drawn up and forwarded to her by the end of the month.

If ever there was an accommodation that could be described as a 'summer dwelling', then *that* flat was *it*. No matter how high – or for how *long* – one turned up the heating, the inside temperature seemed to deviate by not as much as a single degree from that outside. As if that was not challenging *enough*, the place was infested with little grey insects called woodlice. As a child, I used to call them slaters. There were quite a few spiders as well, but their numbers paled alongside those of the slaters, which crawled with disconcerting regularity from almost every nook and cranny. The best that I could say about the lodging was that it was very well ventilated.

Nevertheless, we were neither of us to be put off by those developments. Sweaters and coats were adopted for indoor – in addition to outdoor – wear. I proceeded with my studies and my mother went ahead with her daily routine.

I rather enjoyed my short time at Dundee University. The work was engrossing and I did not drop a single mark in my assessments throughout the course of the first term.

That focus and precision was sharpened considerably by my awareness that the Dean of Medicine there was a Dennis McDevitt: one of MacSween's *fidus Achates*, whose name had featured in the dossier that I had handed to Strathclyde Police in early '93. *That* discovery had been more than a little reinforcing of my (by then) long-adopted maxim: 'Be *constantly* alert and *stay under the radar*!'

On Friday evenings, we would return to Glasgow for the weekend: driving back up to Tayport on the following Sunday night. What I recall most vividly from our Glasgow-bound trips each Friday was the enormous vistas that would open up as we drove over the top of the rise beyond Perth, and down into the wide glen below. The sky was always full of flocks of a variety of different species of birds; and the scenes occasioned by the commingling of fading, slanted sunlight and prevailing air conditions at day's end, seemed continually diverse and spectacular.

We would have left Dundee earlier each Friday, had it not been for an oddity in my timetable.

Whereas my other classes usually finished by the early afternoon on the last day of the working week, there occurred, out on its own, the week's only Anatomy tutorial: from four o'clock until five. Around the end of the third week of the first term, there was a 'spot test' set on the subject of the thorax. This involved moving, at two minute intervals, between fifty locations or 'spots' along the benches in the histology lab. At each spot sat either a prosection (a pre-dissected body part) from the region of the chest, or an X-ray. Each had an attached pointer, indicating the structure to be identified by the student.

I completed without error and was able to contribute quite a bit during the ensuing tutorial that afternoon.

As I arrived down at the car a short while afterwards, I was – as I clearly recall now – suddenly suffused with a very real and almost forgotten sense that embodied both self-worth and purpose. But it was other than just ego. I really felt that I was back on track towards what I was somehow 'meant' to do in life: the work that I was *made* for.

As we took off in the car for Glasgow, I said to my mother: "You know, I'm *glad* that I didn't have to leave it for another year. Medicine still seems to me like such an exciting and challenging field of endeavour."

"Well, I'm glad you're happy in what you're doing," she replied.

A few days later, a letter arrived from our landlord, Mr Roy. Therein, he thanked my mother for her cheque (made payable, at his request, to his mother, who owned the flat), covering the first month's rent.

His letter continued with a request for a deposit, to the value of one month's rental (£330). Beforehand, in speaking with her on the telephone, and also in the course of his conversation with us both when we had come to inspect the flat, he had been quite explicit about a deposit *not* being a requirement. This had immediately struck us as an *unusual* but nevertheless welcome aspect of the deal on offer.

The final part of Mr Roy's letter was also 'the final straw' As tenant, my mother would, according to Mr Roy, have to be responsible for the payment of 'rates' for the flat: a previously unmentioned addendum, which Mr Roy was now having incorporated into the contract that his lawyer would draw up.

My mother wrote back to Mr Roy, informing him of our shared intention to quit his premises forthwith.

We left the flat at Cowgate in Tayport, a few days before the end of our first month there. Thereafter, we moved straight into bed and breakfast accommodation in Dundee.

There, we stayed during weekdays for much of the rest of the term. We spent what mutual spare time we could afford in looking for another flat, but there was not much on offer at that time of year.

Much later, on September 20th 1995, Glasgow's *Daily Record* newspaper quoted the then current tenant of the Tayport flat where we had stayed, as having said that 'they [we] went away without paying rent for two months'.

Chapter Thirty-Two

"Enjoy the little things in life because one day you'll look
back and realize they were the big things."

— Kurt Vonnegut

One morning, towards the end of November '94, just as the
Anatomy lecture had concluded, a group of students from
maybe the third or fourth year came into the lecture theatre.
Between them, they carried several piles of The Oxford
Reference Concise Medical Dictionary: freebies from the
MDDUS (The Medical and Dental Defence Union of
Scotland), for its annual batch of new, first-year members.

With the instantaneous and unbridled enthusiasm of a
famine-stricken community which had found itself suddenly
transported to a restaurant on buffet night, almost the entire
first year surged forward and down towards their union
representative peers and the promised tomes.

"Fuck that for a game 'a soldiers," sighed one young
man wearily, from his seat in the row behind me.

"So wisdom isn't a *complete* stranger to the young, after
all," I thought with an accompanying smile.

There were dictionaries for only about half of the class,
but the speaker was at pains to reassure all present that
further copies would be sent out to all of the unticked names.

About a week later, while we were in Dundee, the postman arrived at 11 Whitehurst with a package addressed to Brandon Lee. It was my copy of the free dictionary: not the world's *bulkiest* book, but just too big to fit through the letter box.

Shortly after our return to Bearsden the following weekend, there was a knock on the door. My mother answered it. It was Mrs Hanlon from no. 12, the upstairs flat. She had the undelivered package in her hand. From the kitchen, where I was preparing dinner, I overheard the short conversation at the doorway.

Before my mother could even say hello, Mrs Hanlon began: "This arrived with yesterday's post and I took it in. It has your address on it, but the name at the top is 'Brandon Lee'."

By my mother's report, she reached forward at that point, in order to take hold of the package, which her neighbour appeared to be offering to her; but Mrs Hanlon held firmly to it.

"I'm going down to the post office in the morning and I'll hand it in then!" asserted Mrs Hanlon stridently.

"If it's addressed to number eleven, Mrs Hanlon, it's for *me* to do that," I heard my mother reply, with a hint of determination creeping into her *own* voice. Then, "Good evening." Mrs Hanlon made no reply and the next sound that I heard was that of the door closing gently.

One night, a couple of years later, I would involve myself in saving Mrs Hanlon's daughter's life. I made up my mind to call the police quickly after her abusive boyfriend decided that his fists were insufficient for the task of the beating he had just begun to give her. He moved on to what sounded like a kitchen chair, which he either threw at- or smashed down upon her. One cannot hear someone screaming like that and not do *something* about it. I was later given to understand that the mother had been out at the time.

"Mum, I think that we ought to part company," I said as she came into my room to pass me the package. "For a *while*, anyway. Perhaps as much as a year. The thing *is* ... my remaining here any longer could well create problems for you."

"What sort of problems?"

"I can't yet foresee their precise nature. That's what makes the situation worrying."

But I could clearly foresee the *fundamental* problem. If, as I then had begun to envisage, this was set to reach public consciousness on *any* level, then to have doled out to *me* similar treatment as MacSween had had meted out to my father, was *one* thing: but now it was time to protect my mother at all costs.

"I have no desire to spend the winter on my own here!"

Finding myself letting out a sigh, I perceived a break from lowly human calculation as being propitious.

"I have a bottle of a favourably appraised Armagnac which I somehow haven't gotten round to opening in the six months since I bought it. Will you have a small measure with me ... *with* a little water?"

"No thanks, I'm just going to have a cup of tea."

"Well, if you've no objection, I think *I'll* have a little."

My mother was an Aries, and possessed of a natural air of authority that demanded one's attention. She was a wise, often clever, tough-minded pragmatist: and one of only two people remaining on earth whom I loved unconditionally. Maybe it was *because* she was *so* averse to (and disapproving of) violence as a solution to *anything*, that I would sometimes picture her as a warrior in some past incarnation. The soundness and force of her conviction impressed me *so* much, that by my early teens it had also become mine. I sensed strongly that, like the Gnostics, *that* soul had *lived* it … *actualised* it, to have become what she was: poised and graceful as a swan, and kind and gentle; even in the light of that fierce, bright blue Arian flame that would sometimes make itself apparent amidst the sea-green of her aura.

I most vividly remember that latter quality in relation to a discomfiting event that occurred in the late summer of 1975: not long after I had turned twelve and begun my first year at Bearsden Academy.

At the beginning of the lunch hour, I had reluctantly gone along to the school chess club with a fellow from my class. I was not particularly keen, but my cousin had shown me how to play during a visit one rainy afternoon years before; and on what was *another* rainy day – not *uncommonly*: it being *Scotland* – it was something *different* to do. We were placed in a group with seven other kids and arranged along one side of a long table, which had chessboards laid out on it. On the other side of the table were two sixth-formers – a girl and a boy – who each took on four opponents, with a short (sixty seconds) maximum interval between moves having been imposed.

I was in the half that played the older *boy*. I recall that the girl won all of her games, with the lad who was the school champion winning three out of four.

With a couple of minutes of the lunch hour left, he resigned in his game against me.

I will never forget the look on that young chap's face as he extended his hand to congratulate me: it was as though I had taken *everything* from him.

On the spot, I resolved that although there was no escaping *football* (an activity that I barely noticed *anyway* as being anything more than keeping possession of a ball en route to kicking it between two posts), *competition* was not for me. I had long since realised that the notion of competition, as being a beneficial and desirable phenomenon – with dedication to the ethos giving rise to improvement and innovation – was nothing but part of a rising tide of agitprop, promulgated with the specific intent of stifling creativity, advancement and breakthrough, via the gradual imposition of stressful, hectic and, ultimately, *malefic* states.

The little pointy-faced, pointy-bearded, irascible teacher who ran the club, though, was not one to take 'no' as an answer to his insistent 'offer' to me of a place on the school chess team.

Here was a *dilemma*. High school felt like this wonderful opportunity to do well and go on to study Medicine. I was therefore at pains not to do anything that might blot my copybook just as I was starting out. But I could envisage *no* good arising from my undertaking to waste my time indulging in an activity designed, on the *one* hand, to *sublimate-*, and on the *other*, to *foster* and *hone* some ghastly instinctual impulse that I was fortunate enough not to be possessed of?

I was *twelve*; and as it then seemed like too big a dilemma to tackle on my own, I took the easy way out and made my predicament known to that fount of all wisdom: my mother.

To my further displeasure, she informed me that she had already received a call for her to see the head teacher about my refusal to join the club.

As there usually *is* between mother and child, there was a deep connection between my mother and me. We used spoken language only for the conveyance of detail, when something unusual and/or new would arise. Even before the appointment, perception of that reassuring bright blue flame began to ease my mind with regard to outcome.

On the evening after the meeting had taken place, I was sitting cross-legged on my bedroom floor, with my head in a book of numbers, when I sensed her in the doorway behind me. "How'd *that* go?" I asked.

"Oh, they *huffed* and *puffed* a little, but they eventually came round to the point of view that, with it being something distasteful to you – and with it not being part of the curriculum – your choosing to have nothing to do with it ought not to be something that you should be penalised over."

Then, after regarding the back of my head for another moment or two, she added that there was nothing that I needed to worry about.

I was content to take her word for it, and I let her know as much with a warm smile as I at last turned to look at her.

There was, however, one further game that I *did* indulge in throughout the remainder of my first five years at Bearsden Academy: the strenuous avoidance of the bearded teacher who ran the chess club; and who, thankfully, never taught any class that I was part of. My success in that endeavour was such that I suspect that the only time that he ever caught sight of me again was once each year, when I would step up to collect my certificates at the annual prize-giving ceremony.

As a child, my mother had had a Chinese nanny who taught her Mandarin. The Chinese have a saying: 'To bend like a tree in the wind: that is *true* strength.' *That* was my mother: right up until the beginning of her eighty-third year, when, perhaps as much as another decade before the completion of what would have been her natural span, she was cut down by cowards, killing on behalf of an even more despicable coward.

From the aforementioned day (in late 1994) forth, there was to be no further discussion of our parting company.

Chapter Thirty-Three

"As a rule," said Holmes, "the more bizarre a thing is,
the less mysterious it proves to be."

From: *The Adventure of the Red-Headed League* by
Arthur Conan Doyle

I believe that it was Moses who was accredited with the declaration that, 'there is nothing new under the sun'. On the other hand, the American President, Harry S. Truman, is sometimes *misquoted* as having once commented that 'the only new things are the history that we don't already know'. Of course, there was no way that Moses could have known that Truman *wasn't* going to say that!

As for my own duff attempt at treading the fine line between banality and profundity, I would first state that history always has a way of getting wherever it is going next. Furthermore, *here's* a thing about the future (for those granted the gift of occasionally glimpsing one or other aspect of it): generally, when you look *closely* at it, it begins to permute ... *because* you looked at it. And *that*, I glean, is as it *should* be: it is *spiritually lawful* for us, as human beings, to live in the present ... in the *moment*.

In the second week of December 1994, a hand-addressed envelope arrived at Whitehurst for my mother.

As she read the contents, her complexion transformed alarmingly from a fairly healthy bloom to a sickly shade, approaching ashen grey.

"What's the matter?" I asked, moving quickly across to where she stood on the living room floor: having begun to fear that she might collapse.

She made no spoken reply, but just handed the letter to me as she sat down on the sofa.

"Can I *get* you something?" I persisted.

"No, I'll be all right. I just need to sit for a moment."

The letter was from the Fullers, the young couple who had been in the process of buying my mother's house beside Loch Fyne. Mr Fuller wrote that because of recent financial shortcomings, they would have to discontinue their monthly £1000 payments until the spring.

"This is just a piece of *nonsense*!" I remonstrated. "Surely they signed a legal contract with you before they moved in?"

"No, our agreement was based on goodwill."

"You should pass this on to a solicitor."

"Yes."

"Are you all right for ready money, short-term?"

"Well, I have my pension, and I've other money invested. I'll get *by* all right, but I don't see how I can keep us both going, up at Dundee. I was working to a close budget with that monthly thousand. What about you?"

"I've got just over four hundred left in the bank."

"What will we do?"

In as placid a voice as I could muster, I intimated that I would sleep on it, and hopefully come up with something in the morning. The calm veneer was for the sake of preserving my mother's newly regained composure. Behind the façade, however, I was slipping from desultoriness towards desolation.

"There's nothing like a good night's sleep!" I have heard people say. Absolutely right! I slept a dreamless sleep: no images, no words.

Back in the conscious world, I considered my sleep as a cue: no *words*, therefore lose the semantics and choose what looks right … or at least *workable*.

I had already informed the school and the university that I lived with my grandmother. That morning, I called Dundee, to inform the faculty office that my grandmother had died in the night. A few days later, I wrote to them, indicating that as she had died intestate, I would be without available funds for up to six months.

Sometime afterwards, they wrote back to let me know that I could recommence the course the following autumn.

I had at least bought myself some 'wriggle' time.

The solicitor to whom my mother passed on Mr Fuller's letter, was a Mr George Hunter of Morris Hunter & Co., a Glaswegian firm with offices in Crow Road, on the city's north side.

Much later, on the 18th September 1995, Mr Hunter telephoned my mother on another matter. When she professed absolutely no interest in the subject broached by her former solicitor, the firm followed up with a letter, the next day. It began with a reference to '… our Mr Hunter's telephone conversation with you [my mother] on the 18th September 1995.' and continued by affirming that they appreciated 'that they had no instructions from my mother or myself … in connection with any matter currently ongoing.'

They went on to indicate that both their offices had '... been contacted by two radio stations and one national newspaper' with regard to an interest in a story, which they understood related to me; and that it was:

'... quite clear from the level of interest in the 'story' that the media companies concerned would be willing to pay a substantial figure for an exclusive story.'

The second paragraph of their letter concluded with the intelligence that 'This contact with us has been completely unsolicited on our part, although it would appear that someone has mentioned to the media that we acted on behalf of a family member.'

<u>Shyster</u>

Origin:

GERMAN

Mid-19th century: said to be from Scheuster, the name of a lawyer whose behaviour provoked accusations of 'scheuster' practices, perhaps reinforced by German *Scheisser*, meaning 'worthless person'.

Example usage: "But aren't *all* lawyers shysters?" she queried incredulously.

Chapter Thirty-Four

As I made my way towards Bearsden Cross, immediately after the final paper of the last Higher examination (Biology) that I sat in May of 1994, I was waylaid by a small group of girls from the fifth year. Amongst their number were Nicola Walker, whom I was by then familiar with from the school play, and her friend Gillian MacCallum. They were about to head into Gillian's house, and they wanted me to come with them. I immediately made the excuse that I had to pick up something for dinner at the Cross. They insisted that I come in 'for just a few minutes'. I remonstrated.

What followed actually culminated in my having the sleeve of my jacket forcibly *tugged*. As *that* was happening, I remember there flashing into my 'cartoon head' a scene from one of those natural history shows, where one of a group of ambush predators clamp onto the nose of a large herbivore – such as a bison – with their jaws: as part of a group effort to drag it off its feet.

Throughout my year at the school, I had been assiduous in my efforts to maintain an impersonal attitude of remoteness, with respect to the bona fide pupils there, but in order to avoid any more of a scene, I capitulated and stepped inside for the juice and cake that had been offered. That may have been a mistake, but simply dodging and running off just did not feel like an acceptably elegant option.

Although I made sure that I remained only briefly, my reluctant participation *did* seem thereafter to give rise to a presumption of familiarity on the part of those in that particular coterie, whenever I would run into one or other of them on the street, in the supermarket, or wherever.

Nicola was a bright spark and, for her *age*, a talented actress. I hope that latter description does not read as being redolent of some manner of dark, Victorian perversity: it is of course not *meant* to, but when you have been at the receiving end of as much male, midlife crisis-driven 'journalism' as I have, it becomes difficult not to acknowledge the pervasiveness of that peculiarly deranged mindset.

Nicola played the character of Bloody Mary in the school production of *South Pacific*, and by my acquaintance with Nicola, I came to know Gillian. Nonetheless, with my being obliged to attend at the school for a couple of weeks beyond the Biology examination, I was careful to avoid any further involvement with either of them outside of school hours.

One day, in late September of '94, I bumped into Gillian on the street and she asked me to drop her a line from wherever I ended up staying. This, I later did: in the form of a postcard.

When she first called me, the following January – having gotten the number from Nicola, to whom I had given same because she once had said that she was concerned about fleshing out some aspects of the scenes we shared in the play – Gillian mentioned that she had sent three letters to the Tayport address. Presumably, they had arrived there after my mother and I had moved out. Certainly, one of them was eventually forwarded to Whitehurst.

Not long after her calls began, Gillian confided in me that her mother was seriously ill with cancer.

Regardless of whatever feelings well up in oneself, it impresses me as an appalling flaw of character – sanctimonious hypocrisy – to express the sentiment of 'feeling sorry for' another; but having watched my own father die from the effects of widespread malignancy, I could at least *empathize* with this girl.

Right from when we first met, there was a real but unspoken understanding between Gillian and me that she knew that I was other than what I purported to be; but I never sensed any threat from her.

Shortly after her first call, near the beginning of 1995, she began to be very forthcoming – with accompanying ominous forewarnings – about the ill-intent towards me of the mother of a girl called Sheila Louden. According to Gillian, the Louden woman had somehow found out about my real identity, and she would 'stop at nothing' to obtain a medical school place for her daughter, who had applied, unsuccessfully, to Glasgow. Apparently, Sheila Louden had been in the same mathematics class as me throughout the previous year, but her's was not a face to which I had ever bothered to put a name.

Just as I had in relation to my continuing concerns relating to MacSween (in late 1992), I once again 'suited up' and went on a fact-finding mission: well, *several*, actually. The logistical challenges involved in doing so were, in their multiplicity – with several subjects yielding at least one more requiring to be looked into – much more daunting than they had been in 1992. However, this time around I was granted some considerable, subtle, but nonetheless *perceptible* support: '… To *light* and *guard*, to rule and *guide*.'

The short version of the salient events and interconnectedness that I divined, might be most elegantly conveyed by a (drawn) 'Mind Map'. But as this is prose …

Our 'good' neighbour, Mrs Hanlon had – not *unremarkably* – observed evidence of my identity switch: one day when she had espied me bedecked with (if hardly *resplendent in*) the academy tie.

She had thereafter informed her sister, who worked as a teller at the local bank where I had an account. The teller knew the Louden woman, and the Louden woman's husband – himself a school headmaster – had both media connections and an acquaintance with MacLeod, the (then) headmaster at Bearsden Academy.

Depressingly, I also discovered that a deal had already had been done to expose my deception, in return for a place in Medicine for the Louden girl at Dundee.

Additionally, I further uncovered that Richard Louden was also a former sports reporter at *The Herald*, with connection to the BBC (including Leslie Anderson and their sacrificial 'lamb', Alan Douglas) via an intermediary named Douglas Gillan ('Gillan' being a surname that would come up again later).

So far, so '*Dirk Gently*'; but furthermore (and unsurprisingly), what they (the men) all had in common was their dedication to *freemasonry*.

I make no apology at all for harping on about this aspect of the tribulations that I – *and* those close to me – have endured: *someone* has to! And you can be sure that it will not hereafter be any member of the supine power-worshipping media of *this* country at least.

I do not resile from that. Neither am I afraid of being chided (or worse) by low individuals (or groups of same), as a consequence of my doing so: even as that most abominable of organisations has now all but succeeded in realising its master's heinous complot for humankind.

In their letter to me of June 23rd, 1995, and headed up: 'admission to the university in October 1995 – medicine', the University Admissions Office at Dundee introduced a new requisite for annual student matriculation, which had not been present the previous year. Under the subheading, 'Matriculation and Enrolment for Classes', was the new requirement for each student to present the original – photocopies would not be accepted – of his/her birth certificate (or passport, if he/she was born outside the UK).

Even *then*, such an introduction, *that* year in particular, might have seemed to me to have been quite a coincidence. However, I do not believe in coincidences.

In the (donated to me) tabloid newspaper, the *Daily Star*, of September 21st, 1995, I read that the mother of Sheila Louden

'... was terrified the teenager would have to study in the same class as the sad conman.'

And that she:

'... immediately called uni. bosses and alerted them about the 32-year-old conning them into giving him a place.'

The following passages from my original text ought to allow you, reader, to make the links for a fuller understanding of the correlations: the *interconnectedness*.

The embellished tale had been 'brokered' to BBC Scotland's Alan Douglas by Douglas Gillan, and on behalf of Richard Louden. One or other of the latter two had been in the process of taking up a position with the BBC. *The Herald*'s Ron Mackenna claimed not to know which one, adding that the appointment was currently (then) 'on ice', as it had quickly become apparent that the claims about my having had two passports, brawling in a bar and being arrested could not be substantiated.

"That's because they're not true," I remember cutting in angrily. "And how come you are so out in the open about this?"

"Well it's no skin off *our* noses," offered Mackenna. "The Loudens could hardly deny their involvement: one of the American TV stations has its satellite dish set up practically on their *doorstep*."

Furthermore, Louden's future position as a contributor to *The Herald*'s education section (he was freelance) was also, by then, 'in grave doubt'.

Even on subject matter outside of his *immediate* agenda, my conversations with Ron Mackenna were invariably limited by his childish enthusiasm for exigently addressing only his own concerns. On that first night, he was eager to move directly on to his interview with me. He had already assented to my demand that my letter would not be published in *The Herald* until after it had been considered by the Dean at Dundee (and, for that matter, MacLeod), and he thereafter deemed it his established right to exact his pound of flesh with all due haste.

Ridiculously – if not unexpectedly – most of his questions concerned the subject of my holiday with the girls, in Tenerife.

As his main line of pursuit became quickly apparent, I began to wonder at the madness of what was going on all around us.

In *The Herald* missive, which had arrived through my mother's letter box, along with all the others, they had claimed that their coverage had 'been less sensational and more factual than any other newspaper'.

'Of course,' I thought, 'I'm forgetting all about that little supra-heading on many of its pages: 'Scotland's Independent Newspaper'. *Poppycock*!'

A deal is a deal though, and I responded to Mackenna's questions honestly and directly. I do not think that either he or his paymasters particularly expected or liked that.

Our interview concluded after some three hours: at about midnight on the Sunday.

Such was the volume of what was asked and answered, that it required *two* of those old-fashioned (even back *then*) Tandy word processors, which he used to store it all.

At around half past three in the morning, Mackenna returned to 11 Whitehurst with the outrageous claim that both Tandys had 'crashed': with all the information having been lost irretrievably.

"They *both* crashed did they, Ron?" I asked, mouth agape, feigning incredulity.

"Yes, I'm *afraid* so," he replied, feigning veracity.

By mid-morning, I had finished answering his questions for the second time, and in language true to the dummy run, which had been intended to wear me down.

After a couple of days of further imposition and monotony, *The Herald* representatives began to hint that they would like to take my mother and I to a hotel at an as then undisclosed location.

For their part, they had delivered my letter to Dundee and they wanted exclusivity regarding both the Dean's response and any other comments that I might care to make. Besides that, I had already let them sense, on a couple of occasions, that I was on the verge of showing them the door.

My leaning in that direction was prompted by one event in particular.

Late on the night of Monday 25th September, I had discovered my mother crying bitterly in a corner of her room. I had never seen my mother cry before. It simply was not something that she *did*: not in *company* at least.

301

I was too stunned at seeing her in this state even to ask her what the matter was. For a fleeting moment, it occurred to me that it was just the accumulation of events getting the better of her; but that was not the case.

She spoke first.

"I want that Mackenna fellow out of the house."

"Okay," I acceded, instantly and in earnest, but I could not help asking, "Any specific reason?"

"This afternoon, he asked me if I wouldn't mind making coffee."

"Uh huh."

"He came down and cornered me in the kitchen and said, 'You'll never get the Loudens, May!'"

"Is that *all* that he said?"

"Once he saw that I wasn't having any of his bullying, his manner suddenly softened and he said something else about all this being difficult for 'Dick'."

In the course of a purportedly 'supportive' telephone call to my mother, the headmaster of Bearsden Academy, Norman MacLeod, had also been distinctly cagey regarding Richard Louden: 'Ah, yes … *Well*, Mrs MacKinnon … poor Dick Louden,' were, by my mother's report, his precise words. He possibly recognised his 'former headmaster' peer as a mere 'trigger man', playing the stooge for his unhinged and domineeringly aggressive wife; but I already knew that there were also even more determinedly motivated pressures being applied to *both* men: pressures under which they had each *readily* yielded.

"We can say 'cheerio' to them in the morning, if that's what you really want. But you perhaps ought to weigh that against the likelihood that they'll want to whisk us off somewhere: probably *tomorrow*. That would at least give you the chance to get away for a few days: away from all those other meatheads outside. *And* it would, hopefully, result in their permanent dispersal."

"Maybe *that* would be for the best then," my mother acquiesced thoughtfully.

"It might well *be*," I agreed, although by then I was becoming increasingly doubtful about any 'best' outcome being achievable.

"Do you think that they might take us to the *sea*, Brian?" she asked in a faraway voice. "I miss the sea, you know."

There were tears running down her cheeks again, but she was silent now: all played out. Then and there, I had the vaguest fleeting sense of what it might be like to be approaching seventy in a state of anguish.

I helped her to get into bed and offered to make her a cup of tea (something of a 'cure-all' for upsets in what was once the MacKinnon household). This, she readily accepted, and I sat at the foot of her bed while she drank it.

"Did you notice that Australian girl: the one who Mackenna brought in with him: the *photographer*?" she asked me.

"Yes, of course," I replied. "Patrina Malone. I spoke with her briefly. She asked me to pose for a photograph, but I declined. I said that she could take them, at her discretion, while I was either writing or talking with Mackenna."

"Well, I was watching her; and after you brought out that medical dictionary to check the spelling of something in your letter, she waited until you were sat cross-legged on the settee, and then she started snapping away *wholesale*."

"So what's the big deal about *that*? They already *have* my image. There's nothing I can do about that for now."

"It's that 'Peter Pan' headline that some of the other papers had. She was capitalising on that. Just you wait and see!"

"It's the replacement for the 'Walter Mitty' one: after they realised that my having once been a bona fide medical student could not be concealed. They're just elements of what they themselves term *disinformation protocols*: usually manifested by those manner of less blatantly introduced lies that you'll already have read or heard broadcast. *You* know, the ones that begin with the likes of, 'However, it has been suggested that …' or 'A source close to MacKinnon said today that …'. They even have an *acronym* for it: same as in that song you liked, " I prompted, feeling suddenly a little nervous. "I'm sick 'a all the *dips*, I'm bored," I began to sing, almost tunelessly; and, throughout that short burst, barely managing to check a wave of bitter sadness that had started to rise in my craw. "Now, that *is* funny," I laughed as my attempt at song petered out. But neither amused nor even 'bored', I had managed to laugh only feebly, bleakly, and without any conviction.

My mother, though, was even *further* past seeing the funny side of *any* it than *I* was; and it was clear to me that she dearly needed to sleep.

The Herald promised an 'all expenses paid' week at a 'good hotel'.

Our arranged 'break for freedom' was fairly consistent with the ongoing fiasco of the preceding days.

For the purposes of 'disguise and surprise', a large white van, marked '*The Herald* and the *Evening Times*' in large bold lettering, arrived and parked outside the entrance to 11 Whitehurst.

For a few minutes, one of its occupants fiddled unsuccessfully with his mobile phone, in a vain attempt to inform one of the reporters (via *his* mobile phone), who waited inside the flat with my mother and me, that the 'getaway vehicle' had arrived.

I was to be driven in the van, to Glasgow Airport, where a helicopter awaited for the next leg of the journey: which, for me, was to be to Prestwick. My mother, meanwhile, would be driven away later, in a 'decoy' car; and we would all eventually converge on a hotel on the Ayrshire coast.

By some miracle, I made it past the awaiting multitude of reporters outside the door, and into the van. Inevitably, a Keystone Cops-style chase immediately ensued. The chosen mode of transport was, after all, hardly difficult to spot or keep up with.

Behind the driver's seat, the interior was all bare metal: no seats, no ledge, *nothing* except a steel-lined cage with two intruding wheel arch bulges, which at speed became zones to be avoided at any cost.

I spent much of this first ten-mile trip either bouncing violently up and down or spinning around like a top: with my coccyx more often than not the central pivot. 'Smooth as a baby's bottom' is not a phrase that springs first to mind for the purpose of describing either the quality of the ride or, indeed, *my* bottom by the time that we reached Glasgow Airport.

To continue in a typically British 'Carry On' vein, I heard later in the day from one of *The Herald* reporters, that in the sudden mêlée at Whitehurst, there had been a couple of 'rear endings'. With sexual innuendo the furthest thing from my mind at that time, I instantly accepted that he was talking about reporters' cars. In that one respect at least, some modicum of natural justice had already emerged from the developments of the preceding days. On hearing of this further chaos at the scene that I had been involved in only hours before, I felt my chest tighten; and at that unnerving moment – as I moved to re-establish equilibrium – I thought of the Augmenter and of her amusement at those famous lines from *Doctor at Large*:

"Big breaths!"

"Yeth, and I'm only thixthteen!"

She had been twenty at the time, and the joke had been at least a decade older, but *still* she had been able to make it infectiously funny.

Yup, I guess that there is a lot to be said for the old comedy tropes! As to how much of it might be commendatory, I could not possibly speculate. But that flash of remembrance certainly helped *my* breathing that evening.

I used to like to dance, but I was no Nijinsky. I believe that Ron Mackenna fancied himself as something of a Sergei Diaghilev, though. For all I know, his preposterously inflated opinion of himself may well have afforded him the self-perception of some manner of latter-day Svengali.

"I'd like to do the book of this, Brian."

'Well,' I thought, 'what good fortune that I have the likes of *you* around, Ron, to *do* the book for me.'

By that point – our second day in the Ayrshire hotel – I had read some of what Mackenna had written, concerning *me*, in *The Herald*. Even allowing for the heavily pro-establishment bias and the inaccuracies, he did not strike me as a particularly able writer.

"I'll want the going rate of course," Mackenna quickly pitched in, interrupting my train of thought.

"*Sure* Ron! What might that be, anyway?" I enquired; adopting an 'innocent in a bordello' expression, while wondering if perhaps he *did*, after all, intend to churn out some watered-down and distorted version of my chronicle, after a conveniently lengthy period.

"*Fifty-fifty*," he ventured, his customary veneer of self-confidence faltering somewhat for a moment. "We'll have to move fast though," he emphasised gravely.

"I don't think that's going to *happen*, Ron," I smiled.

Inevitably, *The Herald* condensed their promised week into three days, before handing us over to television.

I was keen to take up the offer to appear on Sir David Frost's Sunday morning programme: *regardless* of his knighted status. The show was live, I was familiar with his interviewing style, and I reasoned that it would provide me with dual opportunities: I could publicly repudiate the BBC Scotland lies, and *that* sort of exposure might finally kill off press interest to the extent that they would no longer bother my mother at all hours of the day and night, when she returned to her flat.

"*I'll* arrange it," insisted Mackenna, in his usual, self-important manner.

"Fine, Ron," I agreed a little wearily. By then, I had not slept for longer than I cared to remember, and I was hardly fit to arrange finger bowls at a banquet.

Mackenna returned to the room a little while later, with the news that Frost's researchers 'seemed to have no idea about the security measures necessary' for getting me down there and back.

"I'll take up one of the ITV offers then," I proffered.

"*No!*"

Mackenna had gone almost as white as one of those (post-wash) sheets on the television soap powder ads. "They'll just have you on one of those *freak shows*, like Richard and Judy."

"Huh? I've heard that they're rather *good*. That might be just the *thing* ..." It had been my turn to lie: at *that* time, I had no idea who Richard and Judy were.

"Look, you really *must* use the BBC, Brian," blurted out Mackenna in an exasperated fashion. "They're much more professional. And it really *has* to be Jackie Bird."

"Oh, really," I thought, "it *has* to be Jackie Bird, does it?"

I suppose that, by then, I must have seen the BBC's *Reporting Scotland* news programme at least once, because I *did* know who Jackie Bird was. I was also aware that she was married to the editor of *The Sun* (Scottish edition), one of the tabloid 'newspapers'.

"Would it be *live*?" I asked.

"*Oh yeah*," he lied.

'If it's pre-recorded, then it will subsequently be edited,' I reasoned. 'Therefore, even the slightest gaffe on my part will be edited *in* to *their* best advantage. BBC Scotland will probably not currently be looking to use any programme as a means of publicly refuting and apologising for Alan Douglas' and Leslie Anderson's misconduct on the 18th. Therefore … I'll do it anyway, because I love a challenge.'

"Okay, Ron, you set it up," I said.

Mackenna let out the sigh of a man whose tissue biopsy has just come back from the lab with an 'all clear' tag attached. I doubt that he would have pondered that in Glasgow's Western Infirmary, that sort of 'good news' can constitute the *sickest* of jokes.

The distinction between individuals and the organisations that they work for can sometimes seem blurred. This perception is not a fault which lies with the observer, but rather with those observed. Work for an organisation and, whether you like it or not, you become 'bound' to it.

The programme's editor, Tim Luckhurst assured me at our first meeting that BBC Scotland's reported claims of misconduct on my part while I was in Tenerife, having proven to be wholly without foundation, meant that the BBC would be conducting an investigation into how these claims were allowed to be broadcast. He further emphasised that this intended programme (which, *surprise, surprise*, was to be pre-recorded) would provide me with a deserved opportunity to personally and publicly 'lay to rest' those false claims. That I *did – twice*, as I recall – in the course of the eighty minutes of taped interview that they conducted with me. I was equally clear in addressing all of the other false claims made – at the behest of MacSween – by Glasgow University. Needless to say, following upon their inevitably inimical editing process, those sections were not included in their programme: just another bunch of 'Old Boys' closing ranks in an attempt to bury another, major, odious – and obvious – misdirection.

With the benefit of hindsight, I could clearly recognise that it wasn't anything that I hadn't seen before. But, for anyone who should ever feel obliged to appear on television: make sure it's *live*!

Chapter Thirty-Five

One day in February 1995, Gillian MacCallum asked me out for a drink. Near desperate as I had become to divine *any* overlooked detail that might prove useful to me in any effort that I could conceivably make to keep my head above water, I said 'okay'. The outcome of my investigations had left me in *no* doubt that disaster was looming for me, and had I by then secured the funds to do so, I would simply have arranged for my mother and I to 'disappear' to some new life somewhere else: leaving the rats to their sewer. As things then stood, however, I could only hope that a close-up demonstration of nonchalant bravado might make them think twice: *that*, and at a pinch, an attempt at a series of quickly executed manoeuvres which would leave even today's 'state' and 'non-state' theorists alike, *wondering*.

Towards the end of the hour – and a little later than I had anticipated – Gillian brought up the idea of our going on holiday together that summer.

"Well, I shall be going to Germany at some point, so I'll have to see how much money I have," I replied with a smile. Our outing had been congenial enough, and I did not want to present anything that might dampen her raised spirits.

On a sunny evening in late March 1995, Gillian invited me to her family's house, in order to look at some holiday brochures that she had collected. By way of gently subduing her obvious enthusiasm over this shared trip abroad, I intimated that I could not foresee my having enough money for an extra summer holiday.

She persisted that 'it wouldn't hurt to look', and that *besides*, there was someone else coming over who wanted to go on holiday *with* us. That someone else was one Sheila Louden, whose idea, according to Gillian, the whole thing had been in the first place.

"Why," I asked, "would someone whom I had never met want to go on *holiday* with me?"

"Come and judge for yourself! I mean, there can't be any harm in taking a closer look, *can* there?"

"Well, that's just *it*: I can see potential for *plenty* of harm … But maybe I *have* to get closer now."

Women, and even girls, may have a few more pantomimes for disguising what they know or feel than do men, but I have never known anyone who could conceal fear, hatred or shame *completely*. As we were introduced, all three shone out clearly enough from Sheila's eyes during the short time that she allowed her gaze to fix on mine.

"She *knows*," declared Gillian, afterwards.

"I know," I retorted at once.

"She's a bitch and she's *nuts*!" she blurted. "Sheila may have been left on the tilt-and-whirl a bit too long as a baby, but her mum pushes her to study constantly. When Sheila didn't get into Glasgow to study medicine this year, her mum phoned them up to *demand* that they give her a place."

"Interesting tactic," I offered. "Do they get on well together?"

"They're more often than not at one another's throats. But *rest assured*, if Sheila knows about you – and she *does*

– then '*Mummy*' does too. And right *now*, you're her ticket for getting her darling little daughter into Dundee."

"What about the father?"

"They're separated: no surprise there. He used to be a school headmaster."

"Retired?"

"I don't know. I think he's a journalist now. Will you come?"

"First of all," I said, "I have two more questions."

"Shoot!"

"Where is it that you're going?"

"Tenerife."

"I've *been* there once: in 1986. We stayed in a little village called El Médano, on the south-east coast. It had a good beach, Playa del Médano: big with German and Scandinavian windsurfers ..."

"Yeah, yeah. What's question number two?"

"How long have you known Sheila Louden?"

"Long enough, and *too* long," grinned Gillian, ear to ear. "You *are* coming, *aren't* you?"

"Well, let me *see* now: either I get dumped on in such a manner that there is nothing I can do about it, or I get dumped on under circumstances where I might possibly have some recourse towards self-preservation; *or*, best of *all*, I manage to engineer matters such that I don't get dumped on *at all*."

"You mean, you think they might *panic* ... and back down?"

"Who knows," I sighed, "but I'll *be* there. Are you *hell-bent* on Tenerife, though?"

"Yeah. Why?"

"No reason. One place is as good as another, I suppose," I said gravely; then, touched by the absurdity of it all, "You know, Gillian, I do believe that you may have something of the *witch* about you … a *white* witch, of course."

Outside, as we walked back towards the car, Gillian proclaimed, in a loud singing voice, "They should just *give* you a medical degree!"

"But I need the *knowledge*," I replied. "And, moreover, I want to *know* that I know: hence my requirement to study at an accredited medical school."

"*That* sounds like a plan," she laughed.

Chapter Thirty-Six

The Tenerife trip was booked one stiflingly hot afternoon in mid-July.

The three of us were standing together on the hot asphalt halfway down Buchanan Street's pedestrian precinct, when I put it to Sheila that I gathered she knew that my name was Brian MacKinnon, not Brandon Lee; and that in June of that year I had turned thirty-two, rather than eighteen.

"That's cool," she said quickly and nervously, while avoiding any eye contact.

"Are you *okay* with that?" I inquired.

"*Yeahitscool*," she reiterated, condensing the three words into one non-word.

I had brought my (only) passport along, lest it was required for booking. Almost immediately after coming out of the travel agent's, Sheila asked if she could have a look at it. I passed it to her and she examined its contents for a few minutes.

"You've been around a bit," she said, as she eventually handed it back.

"S-a-y no *more*!" I flashed back, unsmiling and in what I was sure was an at least *recognisable* impression of Eric Idle.

She stared blankly back at me.

"Right enough," I thought to myself, "before your time."

Gillian cut through the moment's uncomfortable silence with the suggestion that we all three should adjourn to the upper level of Prince's Square mall, for frozen yoghurts.

On the evening of August 17th, the night before our departure for the Canaries, Gillian telephoned with the news that Nicola Walker wanted to join us for a week in the middle of the two weeks that we had booked.

"Would that be okay?" she asked.

"Sure, Gillian," I said. "Nicola and I get on fine."

"It's just that Sheila gets so *moody*. I think that it would be much better with Nicola there."

"Yes," I agreed. "Are you sure that all this is okay for *you*? I mean, besides everything else, it is after all your *holiday*."

"Don't worry about *me*," countered Gillian. "*I'll* enjoy myself all right: but I'll be glad if Nicola *does* come along too."

"You realise that I probably won't need to stay for the duration?"

"Alright."

"And you're okay with that *too*?"

"Yeah, but I hope you *do* stay."

Whether or not Nicola could come was to depend upon last minute flight availability.

"There's something *else*," added Gillian, with suddenly diminished enthusiasm. "Sheila's mother wants us both to come over for dinner, a few hours before our late-night flight out of Glasgow.

315

"Wants a close *look* …" I mused.

"You *up* for it?"

"Yes."

Aside from differing hair colour, Sheila and her mum looked *so* alike that it was impossible for me not to dwell on the words that another mythical professor – F. J. Lewis of *History Today* – had been inclined to utter, to great comic effect.

The harsh, flinty tension around the mother's mouth and in her eyes matched the mendacious smile with which she greeted me at the door. I had seen vicars take brass rubbings of gentler features. Her expression prompted the recollection of another that I had once beheld on the face of a Soviet negotiator, in some archive footage from the time of the Cuban Missile Crisis.

The meal, to which I brought a bottle of organic Australian fizz, almost didn't come off, when, apparently over nothing at all, Sheila threw a tantrum and insisted that her mother should leave the three of us to dine alone.

Mrs Louden seemed none too happy about this demand, and she asked Sheila to come to the kitchen with her for a minute or two: presumably, in order to settle their dispute.

Gillian and I were thus left to chat with Sheila's little brother. After a couple of minutes, he went out as well: leaving us alone, save for the household's tiny yappy dog.

"Looking forward to St Andrews, next month?" I asked of Gillian, who was due to commence reading Sociology there at the end of the coming September.

"Yeah, I guess so," she replied, pococurante.

"Well, if – God forbid – you ever have the misfortune to be seriously ill, I sincerely hope that it doesn't happen to you until *after* you graduate."

"Thanks ... I *think*!" she replied.

Outside the car, in front of the airport terminal, Mrs Louden hugged first Sheila and then Gillian. For an instant, I could not understand why Gillian was suddenly returning my own devilish grin: borne of my mirth at her barely disguised disgust upon being manhandled by this appalling woman. Then I realised, to my *own* horror, that the mother was heading in my direction.

She seized me after the fashion of a snobbish arachnophobe obliged to hold on to a net bag full of spiders. Condescension, abhorrence, martyrdom — they were all there on that odd, self-concerned countenance, as she released me from her alarming embrace.

"Oh dear," I found myself thinking, "this whole thing is becoming decidedly *Russian*!"

Chapter Thirty-Seven

Having touched down sometime after three o'clock on the morning of August 19th, we finally stepped off the bus at Playa de las Américas, in Tenerife, at around four thirty. Tired by the journey, we all went straight to our beds; and at about ten in the morning, I got up and went for a walk.

I always feel that it is best to look for positive aspects in any experience or place.

Playa de las Américas was built inwards and upwards from the Atlantic Ocean and, inevitably, it was the magic of the sea that determined the initial direction of my stroll.

There was precious little in the way of *olde worlde* Spanish charm en route to the beach, but even long before the trip had been booked, I had realised that such would be the reality.

Past the traffic, down onto the long promenade, and I had the smell of clean sea air in my nostrils. As *ever* it was, *that* much was good. All the way along the front, I do not recall having once looked landwards to the high-rise hotels and everything else that lay beyond.

On a balmy night almost a decade before, I had been close to that same spot above the beach. My companion and I had tried to find a last-minute deal for The Azores, that September. With nothing available, we had settled for Tenerife, and this resort had been one of our briefer stopovers as we explored the island in a hired car.

Wandering further along, my head filled with thoughts of big fish under the waves, and some imagined conception of the multitude of different folk that must have passed that way, both before and since I had last been there: all the *people*, their lives, their changing; moving forwards ... *unrestrained*.

At further stages in my own, lesser journey, I caught the odours of calamari and garlic; then, later, fresh crêpes. Eventually, from the point at the promenade's end, I espied an oil tanker: only just visible as such, and moving with barely perceptible motion along the far horizon. The sight of it triggered Brian Eno's *The Big Ship* in my mind, and that provided the engine to propel me inland and uphill.

Addressing a chance acquaintance in an Amsterdam bar, Albert Camus' character, Jean-Baptiste Clamence – in the novel, *The Fall* – asks, "'Have you noticed that Amsterdam's concentric canals resemble the circles of hell? A middle-class hell, of course.'"

'Not so different for Playa de las Américas' concentric apartment block 'developments',' I reflected: although hardly a *middle-class* hell.

"*Nah*, I'm too *old* for all that nonsense," I protested, in response to Sheila Louden's repeated insistence that I accompany her and Gillian when they went out clubbing on that first night. "And besides, I always get sleepy on my first day by the sea. You guys will fare much better without me."

"Well, you've *got* to come tomorrow!" she persisted.

"Okay, sure. Just tap on the patio door when you get back, and I'll let you in."

"Don't you mind being woken up?"

"No."

The next afternoon, I went down to the beach for a swim. Somewhere out in the middle of the bay, I eventually stopped, to tread water.

"Hiya!" sounded a girl's voice from behind me. It was Sheila, who, having arrived on the beach with Gillian, had decided to hit the waves. In the distance, I could just make out Gillian sitting on the sand. I swam further out.

I have heard surfers refer to the ocean as 'The House'. Although I much prefer being beside – or atop – *ocean* waves, over like proximity to those of any inland body of fresh water, the ocean is certainly not *my* house! Water is not my 'natural' element, so I think that it must have been because I do not feel particularly at home in it (beyond immersion in a nice hot bath), that early on in life I took up the challenge to become a strong swimmer .

Out beyond the crowds, I dropped under about ten feet or so: just to feel the cold ocean around me. After about a minute, I powered upwards, projecting about two thirds of my body above the swell, and then began to swim flat out for the shore. Once there, I sank down onto one knee and plunged my fist into the sand, to steady myself in position while I got my breath back.

Eventually raising my head, I noticed Gillian directly up ahead of me, sitting on a beach towel. With her striped one-piece, her hair tied up under a headscarf, and white-rimmed Gucci sunglasses, she looked rather like some time-travelling visitor from the fifties.

"You surely can't be *cold?*" I asked her, as I walked past the spot where she sat.

"No," she replied impassively. "Why do you ask?"

"You're so *white*!" And she was: *parchment* white.

I was thinking, as I so often did, of *another*. But I was hardly going to say anything about *that* to the girl. Instead, I opted for a reference to Linda Fiorentino in *The Last Seduction*, a neo-noir film that I had gone to see a few months before. That seemed to meet with her approval. I guessed that she had seen the film too.

It had turned out to be my last visit to the cinema for some sixteen years. As I had emerged back into the foyer, I had, in a moment of forgetfulness, looked to one side, expecting to see my treasured erstwhile companion. She had of course not been there. 'Neo-noir' had, then, been appropriate for my 'last picture show': for me, the world had indeed been drained of its entire palette of once-vibrant colour.

Continuing up to the top of the beach and the promenade, I stopped again for a moment. Amongst the thronging crowds of that foreign holiday resort, it came to me that I was *quite alone*. That sensation hit me hard; so, rather than go off somewhere on my own, I opted to head back to where Gillian was lounging.

Sheila had arrived quickly after me onto the shore, and as I returned, she was proceeding to pull on a pair of cut-off denims over her swimsuit. We stood up and waited while she tried to do up the buttons. In this, she was experiencing considerable difficulty, as the shorts were about two sizes too small for her. Eventually, fearing that Gillian was about to say something that would be construed as offensive, I felt that I had to pre-empt her with some manner of benign remark.

"Are you sure they're not too *big*?" I joked.

"*Fuck off*, ya little *shit*!" retorted Sheila vehemently. Then, discerning no reaction in me, she became quickly agitated, such that I thought that she was going to cry.

"I'm sorry," I said, sensible that my levity had been less than respectful; then I turned in the direction of the café alongside the promenade.

Inside, a green tablecloth covered the table around which we sat. I was glad to lose myself in the swathe of colour for all of the twenty minutes that we remained there.

Back at the villa, Sheila's apparent mood had changed again.

"You've *got* to go clubbing with us tonight!" she enthused.

"*Really*? Well … okay," I conceded, "but just for a *little* while."

> "1,000 years from now there will be no guys and no girls, just wankers."

> — Mark Renton, *Trainspotting*

As best as I could recall, the last time before that evening that I had visited a nightclub, was in 1989, with the Augmenter.

Oops: I sense a generation gap thing coming on here! However, as Magnus Magnusson often used to say, 'I've started, so I'll finish!'

As we stepped inside the first nightclub on the boulevard, the sound was not unlike that of a Nintendo suspended about a hundred feet down a well and cranked up to at least the same number of decibels; and what met the *eyes* seemed more like a vision of something once envisaged by Mark Mothersbaugh of Devo, than anything suggesting a likely venue for a worthwhile night out. It was so jam-packed with bodies in there, that there was precious little room to dance: even if one had been so *inclined*.

After a few more moments' exposure to this monotonous drone, I began to remember myself back in Glasgow's Pavilion Theatre, around the Spring of 1992. I had been watching Bill Hicks running through (amongst other things) his 'Suck Satan's Cock' routine. It seemed that there was quite a queue of the talentless – in the music business as well as in medicine – lined up, down through the years to come: each hoping in vain for their modicum of inspiration from the demoniacal seed. *Still*, there is indeed *no accounting* for taste.

I fancied that the late, great Texan would somehow have managed to see the funny side of it all; and I endeavoured to do the same.

Around two hours, two more clubs and three or four rehydrating bottled waters later, I looked across at Gillian. She knew that I was for heading back, and I could see that *she* was too. She grabbed Sheila's arm. Sheila, however, did not seem much pleased at the prospect of leaving: she appeared to be looking around frantically for something or someone. Gillian appeared to be in charge though, and the three of us moved out across the road to the local McDonald's, for some fries and another soft drink.

"I guess that one early night won't kill us," affirmed Gillian, as she squeezed the last from a sachet of tomato sauce.

"But it's nearly *three* o'clock in the morning, Gillian," I protested, laughing.

"You *old* guys," she retorted, "you just can't handle the pace!"

"*Listen*!" I protested, with a self-disparaging smile as I thought of one of George Burns' funnier lines, "There isn't a thing I can't do today, that I couldn't do at eighteen." Then, after a short pause, "That'll give you an idea of just what a raver I was at eighteen!"

Thus concluded my only night 'on the town', while in Tenerife. Neither then, nor at any other point, was I involved in any brawls, 'bar-room' or otherwise. Nor was I arrested, discovered to have had two passports (which I did not have anyway), or deported.

During the week that I was there, Gillian and Sheila (and, upon her later arrival, Nicola) occupied the villa's only bedroom, while I slept each night on the sofa in the living area.

On the third morning, Sheila awakened me very early, as she pulled a chair up to the table across from where I lay. As I came round, she was in the act of sitting down, with her back to me. Seemingly oblivious to the fact that I was awake, she started examining something on the table in front of her. I could hear the sound of pages being flicked through. I looked towards my watch on the coffee table beside me, but it was gone: as was my notebook, on the top of which it had been sitting.

Sheila remained at the table for maybe ten minutes, during the latter part of which she started writing. As she stood up and turned, I watched her through the narrowest manageable opening of my eyelids.

First of all, she folded up a piece of notepaper – about A4 size – which she had lifted from the table, and proceeded to tuck it into the back of her waistband. Then, reaching again towards the table top, she lifted my notebook and watch. Seeing her head begin to turn in my direction, I closed my eyes completely. I listened, as she returned the notebook to its overnight position. Next, there came the scraping sound of the coffee table being eased a little way along the floor.

I opened my eyes wide and saw her checking my watch, which she held about a foot out from her face. Her right foot still rested on the coffee table leg; and somehow, her overall stance looked preposterously contrived.

"Good morning," I said evenly.

She made no reply, but just stood there for a moment, staring blankly at me. I returned her gaze for a few seconds, and then I asked, "Find whatever you were looking for?"

Whatever little colour had been in it drained rapidly from Sheila's face and she turned quickly back towards the bedroom. I think that she mumbled *something* on the way, but I could not make out what. Possibly, it was just a gasp.

I picked up my notebook and had a look through its pages. Gillian had offered me a note of Sheila's address and telephone number, on the night before our departure: in case there were any problems about the dinner invitation. At the end of '3 Cromarty Crescent, Bearsden', Sheila had now added 'G61 3LU (by the way)!' Beyond that, my notebook was as it had been before.

At Gillian's request, I had brought along my CD/cassette player, and, mostly, it was the girls who played their CDs on it. On those occasions when I was in the villa on my own, I would pop on one of three cassettes that I had thrown into my bag just before leaving home.

"Your taste in music's *shit*!" It was Sheila again, and she had just staggered in through the open patio door. She had been gone since mid-morning and it was now late in the afternoon. Aside from an early morning swim, I had spent the greater part of the day lounging around the villa, reading.

It was still day three. Gillian had gone off for a walk almost an hour earlier.

"I'll switch it off," I offered, moving towards the source of the music. As I did so, I caught the whiff of unmetabolized alcohol on her breath.

'Each to their own,' I thought, and thereupon found myself wishing that Gillian would show up; but she didn't.

"And *how* do you suppose that you're going to manage to get back into *Dundee*?" continued Sheila, with an accompanying look of brattish defiance-cum-ascendancy that could surely have soured milk.

I did not answer. I just stood there, smiling serenely in the face of a misfiring cannonade: her waning petulant gaze.

Then, she seemed to wither entirely, but her despondent look lasted only for a moment. The next thing I knew, she was hyperventilating, in a manner not unlike that of an asthma attack sufferer. However, it just seemed too forced, too *voluntary* to be the genuine article.

Seeing that I was not buying her act, she abandoned her gasping routine just as suddenly as she had launched into it, and then stormed into the bedroom, slamming the door behind her.

"You're a *fucking schizo*!" she roared, from behind the door.

That seemed like an appropriate juncture for me to leave her to stew in her self-induced derangement. Whatever manner and level of near-term grief that was still to come my way, was, however, something that I could only *guess* at.

Much later, in a number of the tabloid newspapers of September 23rd '95, I would read that I had admitted, while on holiday, that I was a schizophrenic. This was certainly not true. Neither was it a pleasant experience to read such a thing written about oneself. *So* much for Dean McDevitt's later comments about the public expecting 'the medical profession to demonstrate both knowledge and integrity!'

Without resorting to scaling walls or crossing other holidaymakers' patios, there was only one path into and out of the villa: around the side and out onto the road. The route took me past the girls' bedroom window.

"You *filthy* little *wanker!*" shrieked the charming Sheila from the bedroom, as I passed by. I walked on and out of the apartment complex, making no reply.

Nicola was due to arrive at around noon on day four: Tuesday August 22nd.

Sometime before three that morning, I had unsnibbed and opened the patio door, to let Gillian. After that, I read for a little while; and then I fell into a deep sleep. Presumably, Gillian admitted Sheila, when *she* arrived later.

"Sheila won't get out of her bed. She says she's not feeling well."

"That's okay," I said, handing Gillian a glass of orange juice. "If you want to stay with her, I'll take a cab and meet Nicola."

"No, that wouldn't be *right*. I'll see if I can coax her into getting up."

At the airport, Gillian took Sheila for a reviving cup of coffee, while I waited for Nicola at the arrivals gate.

"That guy's got a *cup*."

"Huh?"

"*Him!*."

"So he *has*," I observed. "Aren't you going to let him *in*?"

"I suppose so," said Gillian.

327

Sheila had gone back to the bedroom, in order to sleep off whatever ailed her, and Nicola was unpacking.

The guy on the other side of the glass patio doors was one of the group of four or five Lancastrian lads, who occupied the adjoining villa. They had been partying noisily, and more or less constantly, since we had arrived. I supposed that Gillian's hesitation had stemmed from the fact that the four until eleven a.m. 'window' was her preferred period of repose, and she had not appreciated having it interrupted during the previous three nights.

Our visitor seemed heavily influenced by *The Last of the Mohicans* school of fashion: extreme short back and sides hairdo, multiple earrings through cartilage, compulsory tattoo, no clothes above the waist.

"Have ye got any washing-up liquid we could borrow?" he asked gruffly.

"I'm sure that we could manage that," I heard myself reply, with an accompanying feeling of embarrassment at my *own* adoption of an avuncular tone, which, until I actually heard myself effectuate it, I wouldn't have thought myself capable of.

"Where were ye all *earlier*?" he inquired.

"We were picking up Nicola up at the airport," I continued, nodding in her direction.

"Ah, *right*," he said and sidled out again.

That evening, Gillian passed up on dinner, professing no appetite. Sheila had emerged from her repose shortly after the departure of our visitor, and had then gone off somewhere. Nicola and I dined together at one of the open-air restaurants on the seafront promenade. As we were finishing off a couple of complementary *Frangelico* hazelnut liqueurs, Sheila arrived and flopped down in one of the two empty places at the table.

"That older waitress says Gillian looks like Claudia Schiffer," she giggled, stabbing her thumb backwards over her shoulder. By then, though, the waitress had moved on, and it was only Gillian who stood there: a little way off and scowling sulkily. Evidently, she was not much impressed by the looks of that so-called 'supermodel'.

Somehow, we all reached the villa at roughly the same time. The patio doors looked like they had been abandoned by an amnesia-struck window cleaner. They were covered in thick foam, which shared a distinctive 'lemon-fresh' scent with a certain brand of washing up liquid: a volume of which we had bestowed upon our 'needful' neighbours earlier in the day.

All heads turned towards the adjoining villa, whence emanated loudly the pre-recorded sound of another number from the vast – yet vastly *limited* – repertoire of the 'Suck Satan's Cock' cult.

"I'll fucking *kill* them!" promised Sheila, as she staggered in the direction of the machine-gun beat. But it was an *empty* promise.

"Wait!" I shouted, suddenly fearful of what might develop. I ran past her and stood, blocking her way. "Let's just get into a *landing pattern* here, Shiela, and wait until the morning!" I entreated. "Who knows what these guys are *on*, or how they might react at this time of night?"

"Don't you *fucking* threaten *me*!" she yelled back.

"*Threaten*? I'm not threatening you," I replied, taking a step back. But she seemed oblivious to my advice as she jostled forwards relentlessly, towards our neighbours' patio.

I realised then that if pleading was to cut no ice with this inebriated hothead, then perhaps a little 'ice' would work.

Speedily repositioning myself in front of her again, and bringing my face swiftly up close to hers, I spoke with as much feigned menace as I could muster.

"If *you* want to commit suicide, do it on your *own* time. Don't drag *other* people into it."

In human terms, tragedy and comedy are often identified as opposite sides of the same coin: diametrically *opposed* – as might seem to be the case on first consideration – but somehow *so* close in their essential natures as to be inextricably linked. Suddenly embroiled in what was, by *that* paradigm, both a very *human and* 'tragic' situation, there came to me the inevitable powerful impulse just to laugh at the thought of some poor devil, six years down the line, having the misfortune to regain consciousness on a trolley in an A&E department, only to be faced with the looming fizzog of this unstable, hysteria-prone termagant.

It was that impulse that finally let me realise that there was nothing that I could – or *ought* – to do there. I might as well have attempted to condition the behaviour patterns of a baboon. And even an *attempt* to contain and manipulate female teenage hysteria would have made me no better than those *already* manipulating the girl: *whatever* way one looked at it.

The only remaining hope that I could envisage was that whatever lies would be fed to the media about this sojourn would be quickly revealed as such, thus affording me an opportunity to demonstrate exactly what had been perpetrated by MacSween et al since 1980. Even at that, it still seemed like a tall order; and I finally had to accept that, boxed in on all sides as I then was, there was no remaining effective option for preventing MacSween, or any of his marauding trigger men – from McDevitt and Whiting, downwards – from acting according to their planned schedule.

Evidently, however, I must have stifled that powerful impulse to laugh at the Louden girl's antics to the extent that I overdid the *menace* bit. She promptly ran crying into the villa, and her bedroom, slamming the door behind her. Even her constant and unimaginative use of the word 'fucking' – with consistent emphasis on the '*ing*' – was something that I found preferable to her tedious penchant for slamming doors.

Her modesty knew no beginning. But given that that great swathe (from Newcastle to Glasgow and beyond) of what yet remains the UK, is *world-renowned* for its denizen's particularly imaginative use of foul language, then *who knows*: maybe the door slamming was merely expression of her frustration at her own creative shortcomings? Whatever the case, I could at least be relieved that, early in the emanation of the inflicted horrors of the preceding fourteen years, I had managed to summon the wherewithal to abjure my allegiance to – and identification with – the UK as a whole. By 1995, I had realised that my true homeland was The Light: yet, without the one I loved, even the *concept* of 'home' had become as *nothing* to me?

Staying on had become more trouble than it was worth. And *moreover*, I reasoned that Sheila had already worked herself into a sufficiently uninhibited state of frenzy for her to petition and reassure her parents that their 'going for broke' would be paramount.

It took no more than a glance and a nod to let Gillian know that I would have to leave as soon as possible. Nicola was keen for me to try and forget about what had just happened and to stay on. I explained that things had been getting increasingly out of hand over the previous couple of days, and that I could not be sure what Sheila might have in store next.

"All it would take would be for her to cry rape at some auspicious moment, when I might have forgotten never to be alone with her in the villa. 'Auspicious' for *her*, that is: *not* so good for *me*. And if *that* were to happen, *then* where would I be?"

"Surely she wouldn't do *that*!" scoffed Nicola.

"Maybe not … if only as a result of limited imagination," I conceded, "but right now, I'd be a fool to put *anything* past her. And *besides*, causing a girl to cry, even Sheila, is not something that I'd want to get drawn into *ever again*. Deciding to come here *at all* was – as has now become apparent to me – hardly my *best* ever decision. In any case, you'll be *fine*," I asserted. "Gillian's cool anyway, and I think you'll find that Sheila will be at great pains to endear herself to you after I leave."

Chapter Thirty-Eight

The next morning, I paid the holiday courier £70 for a seat on the Friday flight back to Glasgow.

Aside from the Louden girl's sustained habit of door slamming, my last couple of days in Tenerife were largely tolerable.

I arrived back in Glasgow late in the afternoon of Friday, August 23rd, to find my mother mildly annoyed at having received a couple of 'silent' telephone calls earlier in the day.

"How many people of your acquaintance *alone* know this telephone number?" she asked me, shortly after I came through the door. In setting up a new BT connection just before leaving for Tenerife, I had secured an ex-directory number.

"Six."

"Anyone that you think might go in for this sort of thing?"

"No. Except, the Louden girl had a good look at my notebook one morning in Tenerife, and she wrote down a few things from it. She even wrote in the notebook itself."

"Why would she be so obvious?" my mother asked, looking perplexed.

"Overconfidence? Certainly not underestimation. I'm out of options. It'll have been the mother. I assume that the number was withheld in both instances?"

"Yes, I dialled 1471 both times."

"And …?"

"It was that electronic voice, saying, 'no number is stored'."

"Don't worry about it," I reassured her.

"What next?" she asked me.

"Now, *that* I'm not sure of. But worry never got anyone anything but high blood pressure and grey hair. Am I *right*?"

My mother made no reply. She just made her way back to the kitchen and to whatever she had been busy with in there.

The calls continued with an average frequency of four a day for a further nine days. The caller never spoke, or even breathed heavily. On a couple of occasions, when I answered, I heard a small dog bark in the background: but other than that, just silence for about ten to fifteen seconds before the receiver would be replaced.

Eventually, I got tired of the intrusion and in one instance, after a sufficient pause between lifting the receiver and affording any genuine caller time to speak, I said, "Hello, Mrs Louden."

Whoever was at the other end, immediately hung up. Thereafter, we received no further such calls.

The following week, while in Milngavie precinct, I bumped into a newly returned Gillian MacCallum.

"Listen, I just thought I should let you know that there are rumours flying all over the place. Do you know Rhona Ferguson?"

"No, but if it'll help limit any future imponderables, I would certainly like to hear what you might want to *tell* me about her."

"She was in the fifth year: red hair. She and Shiela are friends: as are their mums."

"I'm sorry, I didn't pay much heed to most people in the year: too busy watching my own step, I suppose. I can't picture her."

"Just another of the great unnoticed, huh? I sometimes wonder where you *live*, Brian."

"Just in *here*, a little way behind the bridge of my nose, I rather suppose," I said, indicating with my index finger. "Just like everyone else."

"*Whatever*! Between the four of them they've been setting about painting a fairly grim picture of you. And that's not *all*. Sheila's mum was round here last night. She was talking about having gone to the headmaster about you. *My* mum and dad wanted nothing to do with it, though. Look, Brian, I'm not sure ..." She either paused or simply ground to a halt.

"That's okay, I understand," I cut in quickly. " Gillian, I'm going to have to go. I don't want to leave my mother alone for too long."

That was the last that I ever saw of Gillian McCallum. She had been, I sensed, not a *bad* soul, but it was a great relief to have gotten clear of *all* of that.

Chapter Thirty-Nine

I am soft sift
In an hourglass – at the wall

From: *The Wreck of the Deutschland*, by Gerard
Manley Hopkins

It was not often that I received mail sent 'recorded delivery'.

It was from Norman MacLeod, the head teacher at
Bearsden Academy.

He wrote that he 'would be grateful if you [I] could call
at the school regarding a discrepancy in school records'.

He continued that it 'would be helpful if you could
clarify this matter as it may have an influence on your
progress in higher education'.

He ended by asking me to contact his secretary, so that
she could arrange a meeting at a time suitable to both of us.

I tried to make an appointment for later that day, but he
was not to be available until the following Monday.

It was the faint odour that alerted me first. Once I had sat
down, it took around half a minute of close range scrutiny of
the discernibly jaundiced skin, corneas and – most tellingly
– the patterns of tiny, black, ripped holes on the iris of each

336

(blue) eye, for me to know that in the absence of his having access to a Rife machine – a most *unlikely* circumstance, I thought – MacLeod was not long for this world: some manner of progressed malignancy; most likely a leukaemia.

Maybe it was the intensity of that scrutiny, or maybe my having declined to shake his hand, that led him, immediately upon sitting, to betray the manner of air of wary skittishness characteristic of a long-tailed cat trapped overnight in a rocking horse factory. As he shuffled a few of the papers on his desk, he made some attempt to control his nervousness by trying to convert it into a kind of animated bonhomie; but it was awkwardly stilted.

I realised then that he *knew* that he was dying.

Dr Watt, one of the assistant head teachers, was also in attendance. He sat a little off to the side of MacLeod's desk, and appeared more sombre and composed.

MacLeod did most of the talking and, as he began to speak, it quickly became apparent to me that he was interested in doing nothing more than going cursorily through the motions.

As I again held his gaze for a few seconds more before he spoke, *fear* came into his eyes.

There was no psychic link possible: not even distant kin of the Augmenter was *he*. *Had* there been such a link, I might have thought to ask him if it had all been *worth* it: for the constant trickle of orange juice and invariably *bad* coffee; the petrol; the tough bloodied steaks; the peculiarly anachronistic headmaster's 'Batman' cape that he liked to wear to swan about in the corridors; the series of disappointing little cars and the retirement flat; the inadequacies of his plans; his contingencies, every missed train, the failed picnics, every lie to a child … It had hardly been riches beyond the dreams of avarice, *had* it?

If he would serve any *at all*, a man can serve only *one* master. Had he even *known* whom he had served? Or, *fully* knowing, did he believe that the 'Light Bearer' would be willing and able to scrub clean for him his sorry shaded and burdened soul?

Maybe not quite as shaded and burdened as *some*, though. And it was not for *me* to dwell upon his being held to account: given the state he was in, there could be little doubt that he already *was*.

For the most part, I chose to sit and listen.

"I'll tell you what it's about, Brandon. I've been contacted by my employers. In recent years, they've started running compulsory checks on pupils of upper school age, who arrive from abroad and go on to study in areas such as teaching, medicine and related fields. You *know* the sort of thing."

"The thing *is*," he continued, "that they couldn't trace either a Professor William Lee or a Martha Hunt at these addresses you provided."

"I see," I said, just to fill in, and for the sake of (his) continuity.

"Now, as *I* see it, *all* of this could be cleared up quite easily if you could produce a *birth certificate*. *That* would do, wouldn't it, Dr Watt?" he asked of his, until then, silent colleague.

"Yes, that would do it," nodded Watt.

"That shouldn't be a problem," I affirmed, trundling out the words in an even and unconcerned tone. "It should be with my father's effects in London. However, I have a long-standing booking for a week's visit to Germany, from next Saturday, the 16th. After I return to Scotland, on the 23rd though, I could go down for it. Would you be able to give me until, say, the end of the month?"

"Yes, if you could bring it to us by then, that would be fine. Otherwise, you see, I'm obliged to write back to the people I work for and say, 'Well, this fellow has been unable to provide me with adequate evidence of his identity'."

I nodded.

"It would seem that for some time now, Brandon, there have been rumours about you circulating around the school. Now, *normally* I would pay no heed to gossip, but yesterday, my secretary put through a call from an anonymous caller ..."

"Mrs Louden," I shot back. I could not resist it.

He winced and tried to counter with something intended as a wry smile, but he did not quite get there. I flashed his self-same expression back at him. We both of us knew that his secretary would not have long entertained an anonymous caller.

"Mrs *Louden*." He ruminated upon the surname for a moment, as if it denoted something forgotten. "Why do you say *that*?" Then, not even waiting for my answer, he turned questioningly to Watt. "Mrs Louden teaches fencing at the school, once a week, doesn't she?"

Watt nodded his agreement for a second time.

MacLeod paused, and as he did so his face began to take on an expression of vacancy, as though a light had suddenly dimmed within him. Then – as such distinct manner of remarks are characterised in particular circles – he '*cracked out of turn*'.

"Anyway, all she said before hanging up was, 'Brandon Lee is Brian Lachlan MacKinnon, who attended Bearsden Academy in the late '70s'."

"She?"

"*She*?"

"Yes. Are you confirming that it *was* a *female* caller?"

MacLeod's demeanour seemed to darken for a moment, as he considered anew the soundness of my judgement, or possibly, his own.

"My dear fellow," I reflected mutely, "don't you know that it is judgement that *defeats* us? And how might it become each of us to be no judge at *all*?"

He had two items to show me, and he moved them both to a cleared area in front of him on the desk, where they then lay side by side. With the index finger of his right hand, he nudged the first of them towards me.

It was a piece of printed A4, oriented so that I could read it.

"There it *is*," he declared, "your personal report for university application. I don't suppose that I should even be *showing* it to you. I compiled it from the reports submitted by your various class teachers. I've never written a more glowing appraisal: *ten out of ten*, a *model* pupil. And I stick by what I've written there."

Next, he slid the second item across. It was a packed brown folder, with a photograph of me, aged thirteen, stuck to the outside.

"There *is* a resemblance, don't you think?" he asked, winding things down.

"There is, yes," I agreed impassively.

"And I'm willing to bet that my predecessor never wrote a more *commendatory* report for a student, than he did for Brian MacKinnon, at age sixteen," he added finally, as he first rotated, then opened the brown folder at the marked page, for me to inspect same.

"Until the end of the month, then" I said, looking up after my brief perusal of the written assessments.

Then, because I could not help but be annoyed by it all; and because the sun was shining; and because I was determined to keep my spirits up, I leapt up onto the tightrope that stretches between the junction of two named chasms: *high camp* and *theatrical indulgence*. And I set upon my face the most determined scowl that I could muster: without, of course, seeming to appear unduly impolite — a possibly *unique* hybrid study, couched somewhere between Lee Marvin and Derek Nimmo, yet embodying qualities of both.

"I just wondered if you'd be kind enough to let me see the letter from Strathclyde Regional Council."

"The letter?" replied MacLeod hesitantly.

"Yes."

He started back a little and paused to take stock for a moment before he spoke again, "I didn't mention a *letter*, Brandon. The contact that I referred to came in the form of a *telephone call*."

"Yes, of course," I agreed in as deadly and hushed a tone as I could summon. We regarded one another impassively for a few moments. Heaven alone knows what Watt must have been thinking. *I* certainly wasn't interested.

Then, suddenly feeling a little guilty at my inane provocation, it occurred to me that had he been provided with the appropriate knowledge, MacLeod could, even by *then*, have bought himself a few more years. *That* much was know-how that I *could* have furnished him with.

"Mr MacLeod, do you think that I might speak to you alone for a few moments?" I asked him.

Again, he seemed startled.

"I think that anything that you might have to say, Brandon, would best be heard by myself *and* Dr Watt."

"I see."

"Was there something important that you wanted to tell us Brandon?"

"No."

We were moving towards the door again. He was offering me his hand to shake and I was nodding towards Watt, when MacLeod spoke again.

"If my bosses were to send *letters* every time they wanted to communicate something to me ..."

"You'd be snowed under," I completed. Then, having once again declined to shake his hand, I said 'goodbye' to both men.

Later in the day, I thought that it might be the decent thing to do to write to MacLeod and outline how he could have deferred his own passing for at least those few more years.

I thought hard on it.

"If my sons did not want wars, there would be none."

— Gutle Schnaper Rothschild, wife of Mayer Amschel Rothschild

Then, I remembered my father: a man who, as an early teenager on a remote Scottish island during the second world war, had, in the absence of his *own* father – *himself* prematurely dead from cancer, which had originated at the site of a bayonet wound sustained in another useless stupid cull of humanity, instituted by hidden *hollow* men – had to feed his family *and* even worse off neighbours, by fishing, and shooting red deer, the carcasses of which he had had to carry – often for many miles – off the hill and back to the farm. And I thought of how, decades later, he had, with the heart of a Minotaur, rallied hard against the fate which one of MacLeod's cowardly club associates had had him brought

342

to: sucking in his last breath amidst a final outpouring of blood and bowel remnant.

Then I further remembered how I had had to remove myself from the girl I loved; and how that little abomination and author of my pain, MacSween – whose will MacLeod was now serving – had unjustly brought to bear this obscene, criminal, ongoing moratorium on my life.

Once again, I just could not seem to tap into that seventh consciousness centre.

Shame on me, maybe, but I was *all out* of mercy for any of those degenerates.

The journalist who telephoned me in August 1996, to say that MacLeod had died, and to ask if I had any comment, was not forthcoming on how he had obtained the ex-directory phone number; but he was just another of *many* involved in that particular criminal activity.

I declined to comment. However, someone later informed me that a comment – attributed to me – and along the lines of it having been 'a great loss' had nonetheless appeared on the following day, in his piece for whatever rag paid his wages of fetid sin.

I have a couple of acquaintances who live in and close to Würzburg in Bavaria, and they are involved in the running of a health clinic in that area. In the third week of September 1995, they were offering what had been advertised as a 'healthy vacation week', ostensibly for foreign (English-speaking) visitors. On a prior visit to the region, I had been given a tour of the facility, in response to my professed and genuine interest in the holistic approach adopted by medical practitioners there. There is indeed a long-standing and extant Central European tradition, which deems the treatment of the 'whole person' – rather than solely disease symptoms – as quite orthodox, and I was eager to observe at least certain elements of such philosophy in practice.

Before I flew out to Frankfurt on the 16th, I was moved to try to persuade my mother to accompany me to Germany for a second time. A feeling of apprehension in me prompted the effort. I had a vague sense of foreboding that something might happen while I was away.

"It'll be fine," I assured her. "The woodlands of the Spessart are reminiscent of parts of Scotland."

"But I don't like to be so far from the *sea*, Brian," she complained.

This was her given reason and I knew that she was immovable. My mother had lived through the horrors of World War II, and I realised that even if the sea could have been brought to Bavaria, the diplomatic skills of *Jimmy Carter* would still not have been enough to persuade her to *holiday* in Germany.

"I'd better *cancel*, then," I resolved aloud.

"You'll do nothing of the *sort*!" she insisted, continuing: "Don't start letting your life be ruled by the very self-degraded types who have already forced you into your current predicament!"

"Are you *sure* you have no German affiliations?" I enquired with a smirk; and then, with no immediate reply coming from her, I pressed a little further with "What about that *pal* of yours: *Ratzer*?"

With eyes narrowing, she betrayed only the faintest smile.

"Don't you worry about me, *or tomorrow*, son," she said after some further seconds had passed, "I'm sure that Dawn will check in on me at least a couple of times while you're away."

"I *guess* it'll be all right," I agreed, with an absence of any conviction. "But let's keep in regular touch throughout the week, *okay*? You've got the telephone number?"

"Yes. Rest assured," she smiled: broadly, that time.

"Look, I'm afraid that Dundee's a *bust*. But I think you realise that already, don't you?"

"I know that you had to try and get back what you are entitled to, and I'm proud of you for that."

"The iteration does become dispiriting though. *Here's* a thing: I've been reinvesting a good part of my cut from the profits on the trades since I started in June. There's enough now to get us away somewhere *warm* for the winter: somewhere *near* the sea, if you like. I was thinking *Portugal*, maybe? Best, though, if we go as soon as possible after I get back from Germany."

"Is that a long flight, son?"

"Four hours or so. With a good book, you'd hardly *notice* it. We could get some *heat* in our bones: and some of that good ocean *ozone* into our lungs. What do you *say*?"

"Alright, that's what we'll *do*," she replied, although she spoke the words in Gaelic. Her doing so exemplified an old private running joke, that by dint of being *way* overworn by repetition, could still sometimes raise a smile in each of us: something that she had decided that we both needed. Although I had always been – and remain – disinclined to speak that language, except to strangers, she had inferred, when I was around three or four years old, that I understood what was being said on those occasions when she and my father would switch to their mother tongue in order to hide information from me.

'… the bitch that bore him is in heat again'

— Bertolt Brecht

On the Monday night after my arrival in Germany, I took a call in my room. It was my mother, and as she began to speak at the sort of distressed pitch that I would otherwise never have associated with her, I realised that something awful had happened.

"I've just had the most terrible shock, Brian," she recounted, gasping. "That dreadful Alan Douglas ..."

"Who?"

"*Alan Douglas*, on BBC Scotland," she choked.

"Are you *all right*?" I demanded frantically, allowing personal concern to cloud my better judgement for a moment. Then I came back into focus. "It's okay, just relax. Take yourself a couple of big, slow breaths, and then tell me what it *is*."

"I can't," she insisted despondently. "I've got a tachycardia that isn't canny. I'm going to have to go out for some air. I'll try and make my way to the telephone kiosk at the Cross, and call you from *there*."

"Wait!" I commanded, but the line suddenly went dead.

Twenty unsettling minutes later, the phone in my room rang again.

My mother had made it down to the Cross.

"Listen," I cut in, before she could begin to speak. "Whatever's going on there, I'll get myself on the first available flight out of Frankfurt in the morning."

"No, *you* listen," she replied anxiously. "You must stay *put*, until I can assess this. Please, *do this* for me. Now, just give me a minute until I catch my breath."

After a few moments, she went on to relate Leslie Anderson's claims from the *Reporting Scotland* edition of that evening, which had been fronted by Alan Douglas.

"What shall we do?" she asked, sounding somewhat bewildered. She was still taking it all in.

"Go home. Try to get some rest, and otherwise just sit tight. And call me in the morning. Are you going to be all right?"

"Yes, I'm fine."

"Look, I really think that I should come back at once."

"*No*!" Then, after a pause: "Brian."

"What?"

"They had a video of you in a school *play* …"

Chapter Forty

Shortly after breakfast the next morning, I went straight to reception and settled my account, while explaining to the receptionist that there had arisen a problem at home, which necessitated my returning immediately. I had made an antejentacular call to 'Tom'. There was no impishness in the timing of it: just desperation on my part for information, wherever and *whenever* I could think to discover it. His ominous assessment of my situation, and his forewarnings, immediately set me on edge.

While I waited for the cab to Aschaffenburg Bahnhof, I went over to the seating area to the left of the reception desk, infused a peppermint tea and picked up one of the American newspapers. After a couple of minutes, a tall, athletic, dark-haired, Armani-clad woman, whom I estimated to be in her late twenties, walked up to the desk.

There were immediately apparent two qualities of aspect and mien, respectively, which did not square with the greater part of how she presented.

The shoes, or more specifically, the *soles* thereof, were just that bit *too* utilitarian for the boardroom. *Lactae hevea* — natural rubber outsoles; custom-made and treadless: just like *I* had on a pair of boots of my own. As to her *bearing*, there was something of the big, sleek, predatory cat about her gait: the narrow, yet still vaguely feminine, rolling haunches.

Being somehow *past* fear, I perversely indulged myself – if only throughout what amounted to a couple of nerve-racking seconds – in the onset of that secondary feeling experienced when watching footage of a polar bear or an orca taking a seal from an ice-floe: one may initially be repelled by the act, but in some sense, one nonetheless encounters in oneself at least a *scintilla* of admiration for the efficiency with which such top predators go about their ruthless business.

"So, maybe not a *breeder,*" I remember thinking. "But what interest should I have in this woman's *fertility* (or lack thereof), or for that matter *anything else* about her?" I puzzled. *That* was it: the much-dimmed ellipses radiating from her corona — so lustreless as to escape consideration. It was not that she was not a life *bringer*, but rather that she was a life*taker*.

In imperfect German that certainly was not her mother tongue, she asked straight out if there was a Brian MacKinnon staying at the clinic. In that moment when I heard her speak, there finally dawned upon me the chilling realisation that she was a *practised* killer.

Arising as insouciantly as I could, I walked past and behind her.
Green! Now it was *me* who was green-lit: but not in a *good* way.

"Herr *MacKinnon*?" puzzled the receptionist, as though trawling the depths of his memory for some vaguely familiar name.

As I passed behind the new visitor, I caught the receptionist's eye just long enough for my look of demurral – coupled with concomitant slight shake of the head – to register.

Just beyond where she stood, on the right and across from the automated sliding glass door entrance, there was an alcove, where I had stowed my suitcase for the interval before my planned departure. I slipped into that area.

I heard the receptionist reply, "Ja, aber er heute früh verlassen auf einem Ausflug."

It immediately became clear to me that any excursion (Ausflug) that I might *actually* have been about to embark upon was not going to be of a *leisurely* variety.

I did not hear the woman make any reply, but I heard her leave.

From my vantage point in the alcove, I was able to observe her turn left and down the hill outside. Re-emerging into the corridor, I saw her make her way towards a black VW van parked about fifty metres down the street, where she exchanged words with two other male 'suits', who were stood in front of the vehicle. Even greatly lacking in experience, as I was then, it was clear to me that none of them were journalists.

As I continued to watch, a cab arrived outside, immediately in front of the short walkway to the front door of the clinic.

I waited until the driver had opened the door and begun to get out; then, taking the chance that it was for me, I picked up my case and headed towards him.

I did not look down the hill to my left

"Mac … *Kinnon*, ja?"

The elderly German driver pronounced my name to me a little awkwardly, but nonetheless with a sense of recognition, as he moved – thankfully lightly on his feet, given his advanced age – to the rear of his cab, and took my suitcase.

We were less than a minute off the slip road and – with gratifying rapidity – onto the Autobahn, when I noticed the VW van again: tucked in three cars back.

At around that point, *Bernd* (as his name turned out to be) finally piped up with expression of some interest in why I had been looking over my shoulder quite so often since we had set off. So, with the omission of my certainty that our pursuers were other than *journalists*, I briefly explained my reason for that behaviour; and then I made him an offer of double his usual fare if he could take five minutes or so to try and lose them in the town, before circling back round to the train station.

He was *game* was old Bernd, and to save what might - as I then reasoned - have turned out to have been crucial seconds when it came time for me to alight, I passed him the cash immediately he gave me his estimate.

"Sie sind ein Amerikaner: ein berühmter Schauspieler, vielleicht, Ja?" he enquired eventually, regarding me with an eyes-narrowed, conspiratorial, sideways glance.

"*Schottish*," I replied, looking back again; then adding, "und weder berühmt noch ein Schauspieler."

My fitting into neither of the latter two categories seemed to disappoint him for a moment, but he appeared to revel in the 'serious' driving part once we reached Aschaffenburg.

For the Frankfurt trains at Aschaffenburg, you descend from the concourse (either by stairs or by lift) to an underground walkway; and then up again, via one of a series of side stairwells, to your platform. When I walked in through the main doors of the station, I had three minutes to get to my train. Once inside, I picked up my heavy case and I *ran*: eschewing the lift, which would only have slowed me down anyway. I got to the train with about thirty seconds to spare.

Moving towards the doors of a middle carriage, I suddenly became acutely aware that I was being *observed*. I did not pause, but as I reached the threshold, I looked back to the top of the platform stairs: nothing, *no one*. But *still* the nerves and muscles of my back were tingling and writhing; the fine hairs on the back of my neck *bristling*.

Discomposed – and further irked at having been rendered so – I kicked my case towards the closed doors on the opposite side of the passageway. Then, turning again, I eased my head gingerly… *haltingly* past the still-opened doors. Steeling myself, I surveyed first right, then left; but I could distinguish no likely candidates.

Moments later, as I settled into my seat, I sensed my heart briefly palpitating and my hands clammy.

"*Ten*: relaxing and going deeper; *nine*: becoming more content and peaceful; *eight*: going deeper with each count, *seven*: …" I began, silently to myself. Then, through the carriage widow, I glimpsed the face of the woman who had come to the reception at the HG Naturklinik, in Michelrieth, less than an hour before.

I had sight of her anguished features only briefly, as my train pulled out in the midst of what was an extraordinarly 'kinetic' skirmish at the top of the stairs leading onto the platform. There was one tall lithe figure at the centre of it, but he was moving *very* quickly between antagonists, and I did not see more than his left side and back throughout what could have been no more than two full seconds.

> Charm'd magic casements, opening on the foam
> Of perilous seas, in faery lands forlorn.

From: *Ode to a Nightingale*, by John Keats

Slumping back down, I looked over at the old German man in the aisle seat across from me and to my right. He smiled.

It must have been my instincts kicking in and taking over that made me forget to continue with my 'calm down countdown' routine, as I drifted into a daydream.

I fell to remembering an old lady: a near-neighbour of my maternal grandparents, when they resided at *Normann's Ruh*, in Torloisk on the isle of Mull's North West coast. She had visited one evening when I was little, and had spoken of *another* lady – a tourist from Iceland – who had claimed to have seen 'Huldufolk' at The Glebe: a nearby area of land to where I would at certain times run off to play.

As those memories brought some modicum of comfort, a sense of peace began to draw into me.

Although I refer to it here as 'Glebe', *that* untrammelled *wild* place of forces and rhythms that exceeded the human, and which extended in a wide swathe, with its interconnecting paths and bostelling hidden holloways – flexing, circumradiant and impelling beyond the realm of the big woods, the burn and the bonny bright sandy bay at Kilninian – could no more be defined by the coarse cant of men than it could be disjoined or devitalized by stigmatizing vicarage walls.

"a wild dedication of yourselves
To unpath'd waters, undream'd shores."

From: *The Winter's Tale*, by William Shakespeare

Within that bidding expanse, there stretched and surged time-wrung intervals wherein all that is human was *far* from me. Yet, never did I want for a puckish preceptor.

And in that realm, even this *coureur de bois* emergent – as opposed to 'not quite a *proper* boy' – learned instanter to sauter while still treading lightly: a subtly-limned silken blur, pulsing between waypoint boles; and with eyes bent afresh, en route to an unshackled ataraxic potential of bridging pathway to those enabling 'undream'd shores'.

Back on my seat on the train, I found myself recalling how – living in the city, as I more often than not *did*; and where people *locked* their doors – I had been fascinated by the custom of local visitors to the cottage, only *rarely* to knock on the MacLean's *never*-locked outside door. They would simply come in through the porch and tap gently on the living room door: announcing themselves as they stuck their head round, immediately in advance of entering.

'Gentler times', I mused to myself, and looked again towards the old German man diagonally across from me. But *he* was focussed on something – or some*one* – in the aisle behind me. He looked briefly troubled; then he stood up, grabbed his bag hurriedly from the overhead shelf, and promptly decamped: presumably, for another seat.

"And do you *still* believe that there are such creatures moving amongst humdrum humanity?"

As she sat down in front of me, I deduced that she must have been the source of the old man's sudden agitation and departure. I had never seen *quite* such a creature: willowy and fiercely-fronted. At first, I thought that it must have been *contact lenses* that lent such a predominant suffusion of lucent violet tint to the irises of her eyes, but it quickly became apparent to me that that was not the case. I suppose that she would have struck many as a great *beauty*, but it was not beauty that stirred anything in *me*.

"I don't know. Am I *looking* at one?" I ventured, seeking to provoke a reaction that I somehow *instinctively* knew would not be forthcoming.

Although I could not be sure whether it was just the unsettling sight of her, or some other cause that coincided with it, I began to feel slightly nauseated.

Continuing with her apparent mind read, she next conjured – from inside her coat – a circular silver hip flask.

"*This* will help," she instructed, first taking a short draught herself, then offering *me* the vessel.

I took one short swig. The concoction was *pube-straighteningly* sharp: like lime juice with ginger and something else that I could not identify, but which was decidedly not a *sweetener*. Neither was there in it any of that 'non-predictable hepatotoxin'.

She next produced a long, zippered, travel document wallet, placed it on the small table between us, and nudged it towards me.

"That is everything that you need for your revised travel schedule back to Glasgow. Do not deviate from the plan. Use the alarm on your watch to get as much rest as you can throughout the various stages of transit, brother."

"*Brother*? There's only *one* who regularly calls me that, and you are certainly not *he*: that much I *know*. And, although I'm tired, I also know that this is no *dream*. You don't seem so very far *removed* from him, though. Just *who* – or *what* – *are* you?"

"Auroi," came her gently spoken one-word reply.

The registering of that term came as a *very* odd experience indeed. On the one hand, I was *sure* that I had never heard it before, yet – and *bafflingly* – it did not strike me as anything but *familiar*.

I contented myself that it must just have been the tiredness.

"Well, *Auroi*, why bother trying to save *me*? My life's buggered nine ways from next Tuesday. Why don't you just make sure that my *mother* is okay: *there's* a good sort!" I enunciated, no doubt betraying my continuing unease.

"In undertaking to stop your pursuers at the top those platform steps, one of my colleagues just risked *exposure*. We would not *do* these things if we did not hold your life to be of value."

I sat back and regarded her for a little. This was *truly puzzling*. On the one hand, there was no doubt in *any* part of me that I ought to go with this schedule presented by this very *strange* stranger, yet I wanted nothing to do with *her*.

"Why '*exposure*': he was *one* against at least *three*? Aren't you more concerned for his *safety*?"

"No."

"Well, *I* hope that he was okay … *and* the individuals he appeared to be pulverizing.

"Who *were* they: the ones that were after me?"

"Contractors, UK-based."

It was 1995. I had never before heard the term 'contractors' used in a context like that, and my first thought was that it may have been a malapropism arising from English not being her first language: she had a curiously marked accent that I could not for the life of me *place*.

However, *she* was not one *given* to committing errors.

"Set to what *task,* exactly; and by *whom*?" I demanded. But there came no reply: just a steady penetrating stare.

"Look, I want to know just what they had in *mind* for me," I persisted.

"Just follow the revised travel schedule!"

If she wasn't going to volunteer anything further, then I wasn't for humiliating myself by asking her again.

"You know, I'm surprised that the likes of you doesn't *often* draw attention."

"'*All* that we see or seem …'" she enounced, softly as silk. Only the continued absence of any mirth in her expression kept me mindful that *her* reticulation was more akin to duralumin.

With that, we continued to regard one another in uneasy silence for what must have been at least another five minutes. At one point, an attendant with a trolley passed by our seats and asked us if we would like coffee, but, mutually engrossed, we both ignored him.

Finally, I found myself disposed to speak again.

"I'll give you your *due*: that opening line, *especially*, was impressive, but since then you've pretty much been all incomplete declarative statements and unhelpful silences, *haven't* you?"

At that, she began to stand up. Sensing peril, I did the same and skipped swiftly out into the aisle. I fully realised that this was a dangerous creature. If she *was* going to *do* for me, then although I was – again, *strangely* – without fear, my preference was that it should have been in more open space, where I might have had a chance to fight back. So I *kept* backing up: through the sliding door of the carriage and into the vestibule.

'*Preternatural*' strikes me as the appropriate term to describe how fast she was. She had me pinned against the wall next to the door of the aforementioned space almost before I could even react to her movements. Her right hand and fingers locked round the left side of my neck and head, as she pressed her left hand against my upper chest, over my heart.

It felt as though, like some evolved reptile, she was making close assessment of my nature. Yet, with *my* purportedly tripartite brain, I could not – even by *then* – gain any perspicuous reading of *her*: not by a *long chalk*, it still seemed.

I guessed that it was something about my *will* that stopped her in her tracks. The gravitational pull of the sun was maybe too much even for her; so *why*, she surely wondered, not for one such as me?

"Why did you go against *yourself* … *transmute* your evolutionary imperative thus, when otherwise you struggle so …?"

Of a sudden, she released her vice-like grip, with a fleeting look of amazement, which quickly flowed into one resembling amused excitement. As she moved in closer, I imagined that it was either to kill me or, as seemed a comfortingly levitious alternative in that deadly moment, for one of those continental 'kiss on both cheeks' farewells.

But instead – and to my further surprise – she moved straight to kiss my lips. I froze as hers met mine in the lightest brushing contact; and immediately thereupon – and with room to manoeuver my head restored – I recoiled from it, disgusted.

It was, if anything, in our *not* kissing that she was – if only in small measure – *revealed* to me: cold, unremitting, Delphic and damaged.

Seemingly indifferent to my aversion, she then moved her lips towards my right ear.

"What were *her* kisses like?"

In that split second of fresh comprehension, I wanted not to answer her. But maybe it was *pique* that got the better of me.

"Generous and passionate; glorious and *true*: so, not like yours *at all*. An *eternity* with her, and I would still be to the Wonder. *You*, I already want to be rid of."

"And now she is *quite lost* to you."

As the look in those eldritch eyes of hers became more intense and crazed, I could feel her mining, deeper – wantonly and uncaring – into the landscapes of my memories. Finding the seam that she had sought, she chose her words – words not her own – carefully … cruelly: "*Ah, diddums!*"

The speed of thought

With all of my God-given speed and *will*, I contained the entirety of the emotion of what would otherwise have given rise to an unavailingly abusive response. I doubt that sign of any of it even reached my *eyes*. I just smiled indifferently at her as I spoke.

"Do you know what a *deoch an doris* is?"

'AS I PASS through my incarnations in every age and race
I make my proper prostrations to the Gods of the Market Place …
… But we found them lacking in Uplift, Vision and Breadth of Mind,'

From: *The Gods of the Copybook Headings*, by Rudyard Kipling

She moved her head, with rapid jerky motions: down and to the side; then, more smoothly, she returned her gaze to mine before intoning, "It's Celtic for a final drink taken before parting."

"Do the Irish have it *too*? I may stand *enlightened*. I suppose they *would*: their Gaelic is practically the same. Or was it just a term invented for a *song*?" I found myself, unexpectedly and distractedly musing. "Anyway, that little nip we just … well, I won't say *enjoyed*. Let's make that *our* 'deoch an doris'! I'll follow your '*revised travel schedule*' only because my best instincts, which I seem – *foolishly*, I might add – to have been paying scant heed to this past while, tell me that it is *somehow* the *right* thing for me to do. But *you*, girl … or *whatever* you are. *You* can tell whoever sent you, that if they are planning further encroachments into my life, then they really should do me the courtesy of conducting themselves as would the *dead*. And that certainly wouldn't be difficult for *you*, *would* it? I mean, you have little trouble playing the *ghost*, *do* you?"

Carrying a serious back injury that was not diagnosed until three years later, I have scant idea of how I moved quickly enough to deflect – never mind *anticipated* – the blow, which next she aimed towards my vagus nerve; or of how I used her momentum to slide past her; or even of *why*, instead of making a run for it, I turned back towards her and decided to finish what I had to say, as her fist slammed into the wall.

"A few moments ago, you sensed something with just a little too much *heft*: a scale of *will* beyond your own. And you had to *back off*. You were befuddled at the *actuality* of it. It made *all* but no sense to you; and in *that*, I had the *measure* of you. You see, I didn't sign on for *any* of this; and if you can't just *stop* MacSween and whoever he acts for, then you are of no use to me whatsoever. And I'll be damned if I'm going to be made currency in *your* or *any other* party's shared interests."

It was my chance to close in on her, and maybe close her *out*.

"There can be no words for the enormity – the sheer *immensity* – of the dimensions of the rat's *fundament* that I could not give about *any* of you. One of your near-kind hanging around, invited or otherwise, is more than enough to cope with: so, you take a *hike*."

She looked taken aback. I used the pause to try and finally, literally, *turn* her.

"Go *on*, now!"

Reorienting myself through 180°, and facing away from her, I spoke once more:

"Hey!"

Before continuing, I waited for the merest sound to confirm that she was still there. I could not be sure, but I thought that I heard her halt.

"As one so gifted, oughtn't you to think about bucking up your ideas? The *Poe* quote quite *became* you. The role of rapist thug, though? *That* sits *not* so well."

A moment later, I *knew* that she was gone.

With her departure, I suddenly did not feel tired any more. Maybe it had been that peculiar drink: but I neither knew nor cared.

Having first taken a moment to compose myself fully, I returned to my seat, unzipped the wallet and began to examine its contents. Instead of a few hours flying time from Frankfurt to Glasgow, this alternative (and tortuous) schedule had me a further four *days* in transit.

As I arrived at Frankfurt Hauptbahnhof, I noticed that it was just eight minutes until my next connection. And it was a bus, to boot.

"Eight *bally* minutes:" I lamented, "one more '*fun run*' towards another regimenting tyranny; only, *this* time a tyranny of the internal combustion engine. *Ah* well, what if the *Tomorrow's World* of yesteryear *did* promise us all jetpacks? It still just doesn't *do* to grumble: well, not *too* much anyway!"

Aside from several payphone calls to my mother – which I would have made in *any* case – at the various stopover points, I stuck to their schedule. Doing so probably saved my life.

Chapter Forty-One

The night that I arrived by taxi at 11 Whitehurst, the scene was gruesome. It was dark and raining, but I could still see cars parked far back in three directions from the junction of Whitehurst and Stirling Drive. And all of a sudden, most of them were belching out their occupants. I understand that such a phenomenon is referred to as a 'media siege'.

Already beginning to buzz with characteristic self-righteousness, and possessed of temporary synthetic rage, the approaching swarm of journalists looked like what it *was*: a suddenly excited and untangling collective of chimeras — simultaneously a pack of snapping wolves aroused by the prospect of rounding on individual prey, and a flock of indoctrinated and conformist sheep: each primed to think and write equivalence of a pre-prepared, received 'wisdom'.

Seeing the commotion, my mother came out with an umbrella. That was an added worry, but I could at least by then *fully* comprehend why she would have been glad to see me (and, as I would learn later, grab her first breath of fresh air in several days).

One old reprobate with white hair and herring breath, stuck to me, limpet-like, all the way to the door. I tried not to listen as he identified himself and whatever screwed-up 'comic' he drew wages from. All that I clearly remember of his harangue is his not quite impassioned – yet repeatedly *bayed* – plea that '*the people have a right to know*'.

I imagined him repeating this line to himself, as an alternative soporific to counting sheep; and, all the while, believing nothing of the sort.

"Just a few more and I can doze off, sufficiently convinced that my life has some tangible worth: *the people have a right to know, the people have a right to know ...*"

"And I'm sure that you always tell them just what your bosses think 'the people' *ought* to know," I thought. But I refrained from wasting my breath on giving voice to what *he* already knew.

As my mother stepped ahead of me into the house, the canopy of her outsize golfing umbrella got caught in the doorway and, briefly, I was stranded on the step. That was just time enough for one of the quicker photographers to kneel by the side of the door and click away with his camera.

"I don't think that you're supposed to come into the garden, like this," I remarked, but he payed no heed.

Inside, I noticed that my mother did not look in very good condition. She had not been able to leave the house since her walk to Bearsden Cross, on the Monday, five nights before. Furthermore, on the night before my return, she had risen in order to check the lock on the door, after the latter had been hammered on for the umpteenth time; and she had tripped over the latest pile of letters on the floor. In falling, she had knocked her head and come to, cold and shaking, only after some two hours.

"It was funny," she said, "but when I got up and found the light switch, the first thing I did was to look at one of the letters at the top of the pile. It was from one of the tabloid newspapers, and it was offering £35,000 for your story. 'Too bad I don't have an old-fashioned fireplace here', I thought. 'I could get a rare old blaze going with this stack of wastepaper.'"

"I'm sorry mum. But I *told* you: 'Toxic by association'. You should have gotten *shot* of me, before."

"Don't you *ever* think that way: I'm *proud* of you!" she countered, with alacrity.

"Are you okay for food?" I asked.

"Yes, Louise brought me some."

"Nobody else?"

"No."

"It could be a few days until we get out of here. Can you *cope*?"

"Yes. How are you going to handle this?"

"I'll use *The Herald* newspaper."

"When?"

"I'll call them tomorrow," I said, looking round the corner of the curtain. As I did so, a barrage of flashbulbs lit up the garden. "There's a letter that I've been working on since the day before yesterday, and I'll have to finish that first."

As I sat down on one of the living room armchairs, a flashbulb camera appeared at the window: followed from below by the hand which supported it. The room filled with five or six consecutive bright flashes. The *Sunday Mail* of September 24th and the *Daily Record* of the following Tuesday and Wednesday featured a number of the resulting – and illegally snatched – photographs.

"I'm off to bed, son," intoned my mother wearily. "You'd better close those curtains."

"Yeah."

Chapter Forty-Two

'To understand the actual world as it is, not as we should wish it to be, is the beginning of wisdom.'

— Bertrand Russell

The medical school office at Dundee had had their letter prepared and waiting. It was dated 19th September 1995, the day after the *Reporting Scotland* item.

It had arrived with the early morning post of Wednesday 20th, and my mother had relayed its contents to me on the telephone.

Dr Almond, the faculty secretary, wrote of,

'... recent reports in the press and on television and radio, suggesting that you [I] supplied the university with false information when you applied for entry to the medical course in 1994.'

The inevitable moral absolutist in a sea of already-obfuscating relativism, he continued:

'... If this is, indeed, true, then the Dean would not be willing to re-admit you to the medical course, as falsification of documents is a serious matter in a prospective medical practitioner.'

He concluded:

'... If you consider this unfair, and wish to put an alternative point of view, you should get in touch with me as soon as possible. If I have not heard from you by 27 September (*sic*) I will assume that you do not intend to contact me.'

'If this is, indeed, true, then the Dean would not be willing to readmit you.' I turned the words over in my mind. "Well, that's *that* then," I concluded. A telephone call would simply have been a pointless exercise in self-humiliation. I would have to put my response down in writing and make sure that it was more widely read than by just another 'autonomous body entirely responsible for its own internal administration'.

That response, which I first forwarded to the Dean of Dundee University medical faculty, and then to Norman MacLeod at Bearsden Academy, was later printed – in a form considerably less than faithful to the original – in *The Herald*.

"As far as I am concerned that is an end of the matter."

Sir Norman Fry, MP (David Walliams), *Little Britain*

Any remaining faint glimmer of hope, though, was totally eclipsed by the remembrance of my having identified (in late 1992) Dennis McDevitt – *still* the Dean at Dundee in '94 – as one of MacSween's creatures. Other than making me more wary than ever, however, *that* had been – and continued to be – of little help to me. By the mid-nineties, the 'interconnectedness' and iron grip control of the elements of a Power Infrastructure that certainly served *anything but* the common good, were long-since (at least fifteen years prior to that time) well-established in Scotland.

McDevitt's reply was exactly as I had expected.

He began by acknowledging my letter of 25th September 1995, and continued by indicating that he was

'... sorry that we are having to conduct this correspondence, on a matter which I know is of the utmost importance to you, in the glare of publicity. In particular, I find it entirely inappropriate that you have chosen to communicate with the university through the intermediary of The Herald newspaper.'

I wondered how he imagined that I might otherwise have managed to get my letter to him: even in the absence of an ulterior motive on my part.

He went on, this amoral 'familiar' of MacSween, knowingly letting himself off the hook of his own making, and readily grasping the opportunity to enable himself to pose as a moral *paragon*:

'... I have carefully considered your letter and consulted informally with other colleagues. It is clear that your place in the medical school at Dundee was obtained, by your own admission, using false information. Even now (*sic*) your letter to the medical school and your account in The Herald omitted important facts which might have been thought to be to your disadvantage – to the extent that the University of Glasgow found it necessary to hold a press conference to correct the public record.'

I could not then – and I cannot *now* – discern any such 'important facts', which 'might have been thought to be to my disadvantage'. But if Professor McDevitt might, upon reading this, finally care to point out what these 'important facts' might be, I would be interested to learn what he claims that they are.

As for Glasgow University's having found it necessary to 'correct the public record', I would consider 'lie through their teeth, in order to cover their shame *and* the tracks of a little wretch in their midst' to be a more honest and accurate expression of their public pronouncements at that time.

Now firmly established atop what seemed to me to be a rather spurious moral pedestal, the Dundee Dean chose to remind me that '... The public expect the medical profession to demonstrate both knowledge and integrity and we are, therefore, obliged to take these standards into account when selecting candidates for training.'

Finally, there was his uninspired, dispiriting, but wholly expected decision:

'... Taking all these circumstances into account, I have to inform you that I am not willing to readmit you to the medical course in October 1995.'

Chapter Forty-Three

"Who's calling, please?"

Shortly after we admitted him to the flat, Ron Mackenna had taken over the task of answering the telephone. During those periods when he was interviewing me, he would disconnect it at the wall.

"It's the local police. They want to speak to you," he said, with his hand over the mouthpiece. "It's a back-covering exercise over the 'two passports' claim."

"But all the media outlets, save for BBC Scotland – the outfit that first broadcast all that vile rubbish – have indicated that those were bogus and unfounded claims. It should be MacSween and his associates – *and*, indeed, those Louden creatures – whom they ought to be pursuing *now*."

When a few seconds later, I spoke with the detective sergeant at the other end of the line, he was less forthcoming than Mackenna's assertion might have suggested. He and another detective wanted to interview me at Milngavie Police Station on the following day. He would not say why.

After a while, adjectives conveying feelings of outrage and disbelief tend to lose their power: just as the feelings *themselves* fade upon repeated provocation, like a muscle or nerve membrane which has entered its refractory period after an extended span of activity. What was happening, just *was*. That is perhaps the best perspective from which to view subjective reality in a society where common decency has been obliterated from public life.

Mackenna next suggested, with some force of conviction, that I take a solicitor to the interview with me. My mother was in the room with us at that point, and she spoke up immediately,

"Why would he need a solicitor? He's done nothing illegal."

Mackenna, however, was not willing to let the matter go.

"I have a lot of experience in these sort of things, *believe* me! I'm studying *law* at the moment *myself*. You'd really be better off in there with someone who knows the ropes, Brian. We could *provide* someone for you. I can get her on the phone right *now*."

"Oh, who might *she* be?" I enquired of him, while doggedly distancing myself from considerations of either tragedy or comedy.

"Gillian Wade. She's with Bannatyne, Kirkwood. We use them all the time. They're *very good*."

I had been sitting down, and in sensing that Mackenna was puffing himself up for more – and more forcefully delivered – harangue, I suddenly stood up and bluntly insisted that he and his entourage, which had grown by one person per day over the previous three days, step outside for fifteen minutes, as there was something that I wanted to discuss privately with my mother. She, in turn, had the presence of mind to recognise *that* as a propitious moment to demand that, as per our original agreement, there could be no more than two of them in the small flat at any given time.

Pre-Babbage: The Antikythera Mechanism

In 1901, a Greek sponge diver working off the isle of Antikythera, found the remains of a 2,000-year-old clockwork mechanism. Over a century later, detailed X-rays of the mechanism (generated via a technique called linear tomography) led to the suggestion that the device was an astronomical computer capable of predicting the positions of the sun and moon 'in the *zodiac* on any given date'. Later analysis, though, suggested that the device was more sophisticated (in terms of its function) than the original investigator (the late Derek Price, a science historian at Hale University) had thought. Rather than contradicting Price, however, this later analysis reinforced the evidence for his theory of an ancient Greek tradition of complex mechanical technology. After the knowledge of this technology was 'lost' at some point in Antiquity, technological artefacts approaching its complexity and workmanship did not appear again in Europe until the development of mechanical astronomical clocks in the fourteenth century.

The Antikythera Mechanism, as it is now known, was originally encased in a wooden housing about the size of a shoebox, with dials on the outside and a complex assembly of gears within. Around 30 separate gears have been distinguished.

To comprehensively convey, in detail, the correlations involved in the interpretation of the cosmos by the ancient Greeks; the early Egyptians before them; the considerably-evolved and technologically advanced race of *humans* that existed some ten millennia before *them*; and the Gnostic Christians who emerged after all three of those races, would require an entire text, which I have no interest in compiling. For the purpose of all that I am minded to convey *here*, however, I provide what Americans might call the 'short version'.

From time to time, while in the proximity of people looking into the clear firmament of the late evening or night, one might hear an enraptured effusion along the lines of, "Oh, the moon and the stars – how unbelievably many stars and countless Milky Ways!"

The 'interpretation' referred to, two paragraphs back goes as follows:

The material macrocosm provides the 'memory bank' for every person, because his/her small world is stored there as a 'likeness'? The material macrocosm and, beyond *that*, the *finer*-material spheres – also called cosmoses – store all the important contents of our five integrants: feeling, sensing, thinking, speaking and acting. According to the movements and connections of certain planetary constellations, these send to the person only what he/she (the *micro*cosm) entered into the macrocosm.

From a scientific point of view, energy can be converted into one form or another, but it is never 'lost' (destroyed). Extending that axiom usefully into considerations of spirituality, one might think of 'energy' not merely in the rigidly categorical terms of the physics lab (Potential, Kinetic, and their various forms), but in terms of the 'vibrational frequency' of subtler forms of energy, which we perceive ('feel', 'sense', 'think') and exude or emanate through our words and actions. For example, the 'high' energy that you might feel after just having done – in quiet and dignified fashion – a good deed for a stranger, with neither hope nor expectation of reward, versus the 'low energy' that you might feel were you to see someone ahead of you on a quiet street drop a twenty pound note, and then pocket it for yourself rather than run after them and return it.

What each person sends out – positive or negative – comes back to him/her. Consequently, the 'echo' in the person, i.e. that which befalls him/her, is the 'word' of the stars, which, as already stated, store the inputs of each person and, according to the planetary or star constellation, sends these back in segments to the person. Furthermore, every energized (energy-bearing) consciousness aspect communicates with the same and similar aspects: because *like* always attracts *like*.

Even though a person might from time to time hear or read that each of us is the 'microcosm in the macrocosm', and a part of the material cosmos, he/she may brush this aside, thinking, "Well, so *what*?"

Authoritative groups, such as NASA and the ESA, the creators of Star Trek, and authors of much other science fiction – plus the 'scientific' community as a whole – promulgate and countenance *no alternative* to the outlook that the stars and planets are just *there*: another 'new frontier' to be explored by us, *ever* further, as our technological advancements permit.

Nonetheless, the aforementioned civilizations interpreted the 'signs' of the stars as signs of the *zodiac*.

To any interested Active Dreamer, there becomes available related detail which lends itself to 'interpretations' *beyond* the dreams of the many. Sadly, this availability has never gone unnoticed by a select few of those individuals who bind themselves to the worst forms of wickedness.

"I'm an astronomer, not an astrologer"

— Stephen Hawking to *The Theory of Everything*'s
Eddie Redmayne

At this time of writing (August 2015), how could one give credence to the notion that the 'word' of the stars is reflected in each person, i.e. that it radiates back and becomes apparent in the person, according to the planetary constellation in which some of our 'inputs' are stored?

Steps to the future via the past

My own current position in life is that of one who, having once sublimated his own biological imperative, became – and remains – a (largely) disinterested and apolitical observer. I do, however, note here – and with both sadness and some amusement – the ubiquitous (and spurious) polemic raised repeatedly by Masonic hedge fund-acquired (and managed) politicians and commentators courted by the modern media, that calls for any directional changes that do not concur with 'received wisdom' are unreasonable demands for a return to the 'bad old days' of the *past*.

And as we all must *surely* know, the bright and brave present in which we now live is – and *always will be* – so much better *in every respect* than the past.

Ought one to be *entirely* dismissive of *everything* that is *past*? And, if *not*, then how might one see clearly that which is relevant *for the present* … and that which is *not*? I am inclined (*just*) to put forward here the notion that – given what already is, for almost *all* people, the *overwhelming* sophistication of established Power Infrastructure propaganda – the jettisoning of base *human* thinking may be the only answer. As to what one might replace that with: that is something which exists *beyond* one's human self, but which can be sought by first going *within* that 'self'.

That much stated, this late-coming Original Christian is disposed further to add – for any and all *inclined* to such an undertaking – only that one ought to select one's path with the *utmost* care: for one's *own* sake.

Once we were sure that we were alone – and with my bedroom door closed over – my mother was quick to speak first.

"You oughtn't to have anything to *do* with their solicitors."

"Let's come *back* to that!" I urged. Just now, it seems almost trivial alongside something that has begun to trouble me profoundly. That photograph of me as a newborn ... the one that appeared in the papers over the last couple of days ... where you have your nurse's uniform on and are holding me in your arms. Can you remember how *that* came about?"

"The professor at the Unit ..."

"Forgive me, but where were you in your career path in the summer of '63: Queen's District, Maternity, Surgical or Dermatology Sister?"

"I was a Sister in Surgical at The Western. A call came down from the professor that the *Daily Record* and *The Herald* newspapers wanted to do a short piece, with photographs, of me with my new baby. I recall that he said that it would highlight ... something about the good work that we did, and the human beings behind the uniforms."

As she paused, an expression of dolour came upon her.

"Those were *different times* back then, or at least they *seemed* to be. I didn't ..."

"I know," I interrupted. "*Calm* yourself: you did *nothing* wrong. I am keen to know, though, if there was anything ... *anything at all* that seemed *untoward* about that day. Will you tell me as much as you can remember?"

She proceeded to cogitate for a few moments.

"I remember the *reporter* most prominently: a tall, arrogant, terse man with sandy-blond hair. He was particularly brusque with the photographer: repeatedly ordering him to take all manner of close-up shots of your head. When I suggested to him that a simply framed photograph of me holding you was surely as much as they would need, he just ignored me."

"Anything *else*?" I urged, almost reluctantly, as I felt an uncomfortable chill pass through me.

"Well, the professor had requested that I bring along your birth certificate. That did seem a little *odd*, but I brought it anyway. He [the reporter] was *very* interested in *that*: particularly the precise time of your birth and what my mother's maiden name was. When he pressed to go over those details with me for the *third* time, I became *so* annoyed with him that I asked him if he was *deaf*. That didn't please him *at all*. To avoid things becoming any more acrimonious, I swiftly brought the encounter to an end. I mentioned it to the professor the next time that I saw him, but he seemed indifferent."

It was then, just as she stopped talking, that my mother must have noticed that I had sunk down despondently into a chair. It suddenly felt as though the creature on the Aschaffenburg-to-Frankfurt train had successfully delivered a whole *array* of blows to my liver. It was hardly the case that I had not long-*suspected* it on some level. There had been plenty of hints and indications here and there, but there had not until *then* been anything in the way of what I might have considered as appreciable, linking and corroborating *evidence*: permitting me to conflate what had oftentimes appeared as not a *great* deal more than accretive auguries.

"What's wrong? Are you all right?"

"Mum, *I* didn't come with *instructions*, did I?"

"No," she replied, with a note of regret in her voice, "babies never *do.*" Then, with a short perplexed laugh, she quizzed, "Why on *earth* would you ask me *that*?"

"I'm so *sorry!*" I offered back immediately and with a deep sense of regret for having absent-mindedly voiced such a stupid question. "It was just something that an unpleasant fellow once said to me to try and wind me up. Please forgive me!"

I let my head sink into my opened hands. I did not want her to see my face. She may have known a little less than *I* did, but I was sure that she had the gist of it too. She had *never* been a creature to be underestimated.

I found myself doubting that if Barrie had written a third work featuring his mischievous, anageric, flying character, then anything quite like *this* could conceivably have been the manner of the boy's eventual induction into adulthood: neither married to darling Wendy (Darling) and sharing with her the triple realisation of the joys, disruptions and restrictions that the arrival of their first born would bring; nor daunted into intense introspection by the dawning prospect of a further quarter century of mortgage repayments; nor even jolted *out* of that state of being by first experience of some other, commonplace, domestic Sturm und Drang … but *boxed in*, immobilized and sodomised in the pitch dark by a discounted and unseen Hook, just as the steadfastly abiding youth had, at the seeming last-ditch, sought frantically for any prospect of serving up Mr Smee and his proliferating motley crew the justice that they richly deserved.

"*Where*," I wondered, mixing literary sources, "is one of those Brobdingnagian crocodiles when you need it?"

I hoped – as I have always hoped – that nothing save the fleeting memories of any that I loved would mark my eventual passing from the world, but there next came to me – with accompanying *sickening* dismay – the image of a headstone with my name and the subscript acronym 'FAB' marked upon it: with the 'A' and 'B' representing 'At' and 'Birth', respectively.

"Sit there! I'm going to *get* you something." declared my mother; and with that, she headed off, first towards her room; and a little after that – as I could discern – she went into the kitchen.

After a few seconds of being alone, my eyes were drawn to a barely perceptible space between two books on the second from top shelf of my bookcase. The two tomes were both Folio Society editions: *Journal Of The Western Isles* by Johnson and Boswell, and *Russian Short Stories*. It had not been laziness that had sustained my disavowal of alphabetisation, but merely my liking for exercises in visuospatial recall.

Between the two dust covers was wedged an envelope, which bore my name (*handwritten*), plus the address of my parents' old flat at Jedworth Court. It had arrived there with the mail, one morning towards the end of 1990, and three days after an assault and robbery on my mother, by two men who had alighted from a car, as she was walking near Bearsden Cross. She, I and my father had later that night returned from the Accident and Emergency Department of The Western Infirmary, only to discover that in our absence the flat had been broken into: although there had been no visible signs of a *forced* entry, other than a trio of spent matches on the hall carpet, just beyond the inside doormat; plus two cupboard doors that had been left open. A far more horrifying vagary, which I had happened upon just before the police had arrived (for the second time that day), was that the image of my mother's head had been 'cut out' from a family photograph that had rested on a shelf in the living room.

My father had sat my mother down on a chair in the kitchen, and I had heard her command: "*Leave me!*" She did not care for being fussed over when unwell, or otherwise out of sorts.

It had therefore been just as I was peering at the disfigured reframed photograph that my father had entered the living room and had had his first sight of the peculiarity that had caught my attention.

There had been no mistaking the seriousness of his intent as he had looked at me implacably and shook his head. I had understood that it was not a development that my mother was to be made aware of. He had nonetheless informed the *police* of it: an unfortunate move, which inevitably had led to my mother being apprised of the discovery. I had been surprised at how well she had handled it, but I had thereafter discerned that she had been very badly shaken as a result of all that she had gone through that evening.

The A5-sized envelope that had arrived three days later contained a sheet of card, which was just a little smaller than its paper casing. On one side, there was – firmly glued – the image of my mother's head from the photograph; and on the other side there was a very neatly inked symbol, which I can here describe only as a *sigil*: because that is what it *was*. Moreover, it was a sigil that I had seen before: although not in the 'waking world'. The message had been clear enough to me, and I had likewise known that it would have been unfathomable to any but a few individuals who might have been empowered to provide help in the matter. Moreover, I had reasoned that there would have been precious little chance of anything but *trouble* from members of *either* group. I had therefore kept the matter to myself.

After an investigation that I carried out in late 1992, I had kept – folded inside the same envelope, and against the side of the card with the marked sigil – the contents of an envelope that I had taken from MacSween. Retrieving and unfolding it, I once again turned my attention to the wording, while my mother was out of the room, that day in September of 1995.

The typed communication, dated for 6th September 1980, headed: 're: Brian Lachlan MacKinnon', and addressed to MacSween, was unusual in four respects.

Firstly, the language employed was concise and authoritative. This was unusual because, from what I had surveyed (which was a substantial amount), many of MacSween's *received* communiqués were the (subtextually) haughty-yet-biddable sesquipedalian delineations of middle- and upper-middle class men, who, although adequately educated, had been weak and stupid enough to fall into his resistless grasp. *This* letter, however, was from someone higher up the food chain. Indeed, the *sign off* – which was its second notable peculiarity – spoke as *much* to that as did its prose style.

Following upon its final (third) short paragraph, there was no typed 'Yours sincerely,' or printing of the sender's name; but just a clear signature: 'Master M'.

When I had first discovered the letter, one day in late '92, appended to a copy of my birth certificate, it had been the 'Master' part that had quickly caught my eye and – with memory of the television show, *Doctor Who* – it had brought a rueful smile to my face.

However, the letter's third 'unusual' aspect quickly wiped that smile away.

It was an instruction to 'eliminate' me.

It would seem to be a characteristic of the great majority of killers – and *would-be* killers – that they *will not* countenance the use of the K-word, lest it make too clear the awful nature of the thing itself. I understand that in certain

381

recently 'revised' versions of their Bible, they have changed even the sixth commandment to 'Thou shall not *murder*': something to mull over when the next carefully choreographed atrocity-cum-Illuminati photo opportunity hits a city just that bit nearer to yours than did the last one. In *these* times though, 'mulling over' is most likely as much as you will ever be able to do with regards to *that*.

As to the fourth unusual aspect? Well, that was *everything else*, i.e. the letter's remaining content.

Beyond the listing of the scores (158 at age nine and 162, aged ten) that I had achieved in the Intelligence Quotient tests I had taken at primary school, it was the abbreviated, jargonized and red ink-underlined and encircled content that was of *particular* interest to me: 'RhD –ve … poss early (or next gen) trans to Chr 46+2 Chrst consc.'

I had just wanted one more look at it: before refolding it, slotting the card *inside* the two folded sheets, and sliding the old envelope's newly configured contents into a fresh envelope, on which I wrote 'Professor Roddy MacSween'.

Every room is a cell
Every birth certificate
A passport to hell

— The last three lines of a poem in a student magazine, found on a chair that I occupied throughout a lecture in The Boyd Orr building, one morning in October 1980.

The nonesuch had shielded me, and also, in some degree – as I sensed to be the case – my *parents*, from all but the initial jolts of MacSween's vile hostilities and persecutions. However, since my unfortunate decision to 'defend' myself quite as *offensively* as I had done one night, over two years previously, my sometimes visitor's *apparent* involvement in my life had become more *specific*. And although I knew that I would receive no aid from him in relation to my adopting such reactive conduct, my remaining pride urged me to do *something* to demonstrate my unwillingness forever to 'turn the other cheek'.

Hemmed in and cornered as I then was, I had no qualms about trying anything that I could think of that might turn MacSween's vile occultist hoodoo back on him; and maybe even enlighten a couple of his nosy lackeys, in the process of the return to him of his stolen 'trophy'. But while I was to all intents and purposes *alone* in this, he and *his* were legion. I therefore did not put much stock in the success of this belated 'vulpine' plan to unnerve him.

Shortly after I had completed writing the name, my mother came back through with a glass of a homemade fruit wine from a bottle that I had bought her – by way of a *joke* – at a country fair we had gone to the year before: my mother was teetotal. As I rarely imbibe – and on such occasions, only *very little* – and because she was very disapproving of the practice, she had never before served me up *any* sort of alcoholic drink.

I therefore became conscious of myself smiling, only seeming moments after I had been sure that I would never smile again. In lifting the glass from the low table, I spoke unguardedly to her.

"You know, I once told someone else I truly loved, that I loved them; and then I made rather a *hash* of things. That's why … What I mean is, I *am* grateful that …"

"I know."

"Look, mum, I know that it's a damned *cheek*, but do you think that you could do a couple of other things for me?"

"What do you need?"

I looked at her in silence for a few seconds, and then, smiling again, I said "*Okay*. Well, first up, would you mind ignoring an envelope with *MacSween's* name on it, which I'm going to leave on one of the living room side tables. Mackenna – or whoever he brings back with him – will *take* it at some point?"

"Alright."

"I doubt that it'll remain there long, so ignoring it oughtn't to turn out to be a *sustained* effort. Could you also try and buy me, say, an *hour* tonight? Tell them that I desperately need sleep, and not to disturb me. What I *in fact* need to do is to slip the cordon for a little while. I'll use the bedroom window: *both* ways. I have to check the car at the front, and then I need to get down to the payphone at the cross: to call Jerry."

"What about your *back*? I know you're still having trouble with it."

"*You* saw the headlines: '*Peter Pan*', wasn't it? Don't worry: there's still some of the rubber and magic of youth left in my muscle and bone! And *should* it desert me … well, maybe I can try to channel *Walter Mitty* and *imagine* the damned tasks to completion!"

She studied me for a moment.

"And I'm not *sure* about Jerry: he drinks *so* much. Can you *trust* him?"

384

"He has troubles of his *own*. And *besides*, I'll just be looking to pick his solicitor's brains. He's *not* so bad, that funny American."

"*Brian*, I'm not going to ask you *how* you're going to be able to check the car: given that it is parked behind the hedge at the front, and surrounded by well over a hundred people. But *why* do you need to check it?"

"I'll make you two predictions. *One*: tomorrow morning, perhaps in the course of the hour or two before we are taken from here to Milngavie Police Station by Mackenna and his buddies, the numbers out there will substantially diminish. There will remain, at most, a small compact group of photographers: either at the corner of the hedge, or further out, in the middle of the grass at the centre of the square. They will be set up nicely for a photo opportunity as we make our way out to the transport. You'll probably also be able to pick out a few individuals – *muscle*: security types – out at the road entrances and exits: to keep anyone else away; and *two*: we won't be able to get to the police station under our own steam, anyway: because they will have already done something to the car. If I'm right – and I'm increasingly certain that I *am* – a *lot* more resource has been directed to this than might generally be thought. But what does '*generally*' matter? It's only what *we* know *specifically* that might help *us*. *Right*?"

A fleeting expression of perplexed distraction, followed immediately by one of alarm, appeared upon my mother's face.

"Should we even be *discussing* these things, here? I mean, what if they've '*bugged*' the place."

"Do you mean the one they put at the foot of my bedframe or the one behind the bookcase?" I asked, leaning down to slide out, from under the coffee table, an old shoe box containing the recently smashed remains of two, antenna-topped, electronic transmitters, each about the size of a *Milky Way* chocolate bar. "I haven't found any others anywhere else in the flat, but the door to this room is closed, so we should be okay."

She gave out a short sigh of relief

"You should have said something at the beginning. You're *terrible*!"

"*Sorry*, I didn't foresee you're thinking of that. Nor did I want to *worry* you with it. 'Terrible', 'incorrigible': what does it matter, when you're just trying to keep your head above water? *Anyway*, better ask our charming visitors back in now. I'll post the remains of their hardware back to their editor, next week."

"Sorry son, I didn't mean it *harshly*."

"I *know*," I assured her. "Just as I know *she* never did either. I apologise: I guess I *am* a little tired."

"That's hardly a *wonder*! Couldn't we just ask them to *leave*? And shouldn't you give those things to the *police*?"

"Getting rid of them now would only extend our incarceration time here. As it stands, I reckon on a few more days at the most. By then, they'll have squeezed about as much as they *can* out of it. As to the *police*? It's a moot distinction. In matters like this, they are *unfailingly* revealed as merely a blunt instrument of those types that are behind my predicament: a predicament that I'm so *very sorry* that you now find yourself embroiled in. The police would only seek to use the discovery *against* me."

"You're my *son*," averred my mother distraitly. "I couldn't be anything else *but 'embroiled'*."

Chapter Forty-Four

"Who, sir? Me, sir? No, sir?"

Sir Percy Blakeney (Leslie Howard)
The Scarlet Pimpernel

I had a pair of black leather, French-made, short boots, with tread-free natural rubber soles that had already done service for far more taxing tasks. With *those*, an old pair of trousers, a black military style peaked cap and a hooded top that I had once bought in a charity shop, I was set.

It was an overcast night and a constant light drizzle was coming down, when, as an *eel*, I slid out the back window. Then, ascending the phylogenetic scale, I made like an urban fox through three back- and two front gardens, before finally emerging as an upper primate onto Iain Drive, near its entrance into Whitehurst.

I merged with the crowds out on the *left* side, in terms of the perspective afforded by the view from the living room window of my mother's flat. Gradually, I eased my way towards the car. I was quickly able to discern that at *least* the front offside and rear nearside tyres had been deflated or, possibly, *punctured*. That was *that* then!

"Do you *know* him?"

It was a young male reporter. Although I did not look *all* the way up at him from the flimsy sanctuary afforded by my attire, I nonetheless found myself sizing him up as a possible threat. However, my initial concern quickly diminished. He was a small and feeble chap, and there was something seriously wrong with his movements: a problem with his pelvis. Congenital? The result of an injury? I couldn't afford the further interest.

"Naw, mate. He wis a couple 'a years ahead 'a me."

At this, he began to engage himself in an effort to dislodge a voice recorder, which was wedged tightly into one of the pockets of his photographer's waistcoat. As he did so, I faded right and back and into the unrelenting, thronging, night-time crowd; then, inexorably, *left* again, before egressing the area the same way that I had entered. Back on Iain Drive, I started to jog the half mile or so down towards the payphone at Bearsden Cross.

It was after nine, and there was always the concern that Jerry may have drifted off into a drunken stupor. He answered at the fifth ring.

"Hey, it's me!"

"I *figured* I'd hear from you sooner or later; but if you're calling from *your* place, it could well be …"

"I'm in a payphone at Bearsden Cross," I interrupted.

"How did you manage *that?* You're supposed to be *under siege*! It's been live on TV for over a week, for *Christ's* sake!" Then: "*Nah*, on second thoughts, *don't* tell me. How's your mum holding up?"

389

"Okay … I *hope*. She's covering for me just now. It's a bit presumptuous, I know: but maybe presumption is only ever an attempt at forward planning. Anyway, I've not got much time, and I need to pick your brains: so, hear me out right quick, *will* you?"

> 'He who would do good to another must do it in Minute Particulars: General Good is the plea of the scoundrel, hypocrite and flatterer …'
>
> — William Blake

"Pas de *problème*, amigo! What do you need to know?"

"This increasingly seems incredibly well-organised, right down to points of detail: like a veneer of the *shambolic*. There's been an interview set up at Milngavie Police Station, tomorrow, regarding a 'claim' about my possessing two passports."

"But the TV news said that none of that was *true*," he came back at me, adding: "although there was no further word on any follow-up investigation to reveal who was responsible for it being misreported."

"*Still* think I'm a conspiracy theorist? They're keen to set me up with a solicitor from a firm called 'Bannatyne, Kirkwood' … name of *Gillian Wade*. Know anything?"

"*Bannatyne, Kirkwood, France and Company,*" he mused. "Now that *is* interesting! However, there's some other commentariat bullshit you might be interested in hearing first."

"Okay, let me have it!"

"I mean, there *is* quite a *bit*, and I *will* mail it all to you: but *two* things in particular … *Anyway*, first up is a guy called Geoffrey Scobie. I'll read it out. Okay. On the 20th, the day before the two passports/barroom brawling stuff was revealed to be bullshit, the *Daily Fail* [*Mail*] ran a short article. You ready?"

"Yeah … I actually remember Scobie rather *well*: small, rotund, and a puffy pockmarked face. He was a lecturer on the second year Higher Ordinary Psychology module that I undertook as part of that science course that I embarked on at Glasgow: to try to get back into Medicine. I remember one occasion when he turned up for his lecture with a clerical 'dog collar' and black gown on. The subject of the lecture was *stereotyping*; and he announced, *pompously*, that psychology was not the only subject in which he held a doctorate. Another time – one afternoon, just as the lecture was about to start, and the last-minute stragglers were heading for their seats – he suddenly turned on this *girl*, who was descending the central stairway and heading for a vacant seat at the end of a row further down. He hit her with this explosively splenetic and offensive outburst about the presumption of people like her, who felt that they could wander in at past the designated time for the commencement of his lecture. He ranted on at her for close to two minutes. The poor girl went white as a sheet, and soon crumpled into a seated position on the stairs. When he had finished, he coolly changed his tone of voice to announce, 'That was an example of *aggression*!' 'Aggression' was the subject of that day's lecture. Nobody laughed, and I observed the girl approach him at the end of the lecture and inform him that she was going to make an official complaint. My third, fourth and fifth mental images of him, however, are ones that I dearly wish that I could delete from my memory. It was when I was 'dug in' for longer than I had planned to be, while investigating MacSween in late '92. There were three … *compromising* doesn't quite cover it … *damning* photographs of him: one of them annotated. MacSween *does* like to photograph his patrons."

"I take it those were not of the 'posed' variety."

"No, they were almost certainly stills from a video recording: with the video concealed somewhere in the room. If only one could *unsee* such images …"

"You gave it all in to the *police*?"

"Yeah, beginning of '93."

"Where'd *that* get you?"

"Threatened with arrest at first; then the *high-hat*; then … *nowhere*."

Amidst the other odious nonsense of the *Daily Mail* article, Scobie was quoted as follows:

'For me, the key – the significant clue – to this whole sorry tale is the fact that McKinnon travelled on his holiday to Tenerife with two passports.'

Then, at the close of the piece:

'Both he and his mother could do with some sympathetic psychological counselling to work out their lives and their relationship.'

'Counselling': a byword for the nineties. It ranked alongside 'care in the community' and 'client' (historically, '*patient*') as a monument to a still ongoing era, wherein not only the misconceived, misnamed and long-term (and *knowingly*) mismanaged National '*Health*' Service itself, but also – and consequently – public confidence in health care generally, are being relentlessly strangled on the altars of greed and stupidity.

"It is *troubling* that someone like that can get column space, but he *is* just a *psychologist*," I concluded aloud at the end of Jerry's brief reading. "I mean, I'd have been no *less* troubled if they'd hired Paul Daniels for their required punditry. It amounts to nothing more than trifling doggerel, and there will no doubt already be printed much other fatuous tripe just like it. But *maybe*," I pondered "… maybe things are so much worse than one might *imagine,* that such contributions are as much as they *need* now. Is that *it?*"

"Nope! There's another one, and *it* could maybe be a little *scarier* for you: and certainly *very* scary in terms of the guy in question bringing the medical profession into disrepute."

"I rather think that the medical profession in Scotland has little *repute* left to '*dis*', don't *you*? But, pray *continue!*"

"Better *brace* yourself," he forewarned, "this one's *majorly* fucked up!"

"*Okay*," I replied resignedly, "go ahead!"

The quote was from *The Herald* of that day, September 27th, 1995, and it followed directly on from the supportive remarks (in advance of Dundee University's response to my letter of explanation) of Dr Brian Potter, the (then) Scottish Secretary of the British Medical Association.

The Herald had ended its little 'exclusive' thus:

'However, a contemporary of Mr MacKinnon's at Glasgow University said last night that the dons there may have done him a favour by excluding him from the course. Glasgow GP Dr John McKinnon revealed that one, possibly two, students from that year had committed suicide after being exposed to the sink-or-swim rigours of a hospital residence post.' (*sic*)

"That *is* interesting," I ventured.

"Prelates and preachers, amigo! It would seem that someone high up *does* have it in for you. You *know* this *McKinnon* guy?"

"No. I've encountered a few ill-intentioned '*Johns*' *hitherto*, but I've never heard of *him* before. Neither do I recall any '*McKinnon*' in my year at Glasgow. And while my heart goes out to *any* poor soul crushed by their circumstances, I'm glad I'm blessed with physical and psychological fortitude, the limits of which I know I'd not encounter amidst the demands of a hospital residence post."

Apollo in silly sad senescence

'I digress!' was more or less the *catch phrase* of one impressively inveterate and defiantly unrepentant old poseur, and roué – and Brian Sewell look- and sound-alike – whose lectures I rather enjoyed throughout part of 1987. He was reputed to be a 'world authority on cell adhesion'. When I heard the circulating story of his having been banned from the on-campus natatorium, for spending inordinately long periods 'posing in a pair of budgie smugglers' at the edge of the pool – in determined preference to actually getting into the *water* – his overall disposition suddenly made better sense to me: or at least it made me consider what could be, for some, the blurred distinction between *bon-* and *mal vivant*.

Tenaciously avoiding any 'sticky' puns, it now becomes *my* turn for a brief digression: simply to reaffirm here, at this time of writing, fifteen years into a new century, my continuing disaffection with self-slaughter: no matter *how* grim life might seem.

"Well, I figure he must have been well *paid* for it," inferred my friend down the phone line.

"... or maybe it was just an order from his Lodge Master," I offered in turn.

"Either way, I'd be surprised if *his* mortgage repayments won't be a thing of the past come next month."

"In any case, it isn't the first time I've been called a suicidal motherfucker, *is it* ... Jerry?"

He went quiet for a moment, before speaking again.

"Yeah, well we don't all have the Spiderman gene. That rock face was at least a 5.9. That's what ropes are *for*. Besides, that *free soloing* shit is for lizards and insects; and when *I* climb, I like to sweat through exertion, *not* because I'm worrying about the prospect of having to watch whoever I'm with fall to their *death*. You don't ..."

"*Okay*, I'm *sorry!*" I cut in, suddenly ashamed, *and* apprehensive that he might hang up on me. "*Harsh banter* — I guess it's just what guys *do*, isn't it?" I added, in supplication. "Maybe it has some *evolutionary* function: keeps the HGH gates open in the pituitary – just as would a well-formulated secretagogue – trickling down to the topping up of already high levels of testosterone: maintaining *matey manly* men in the *full bloom* of their manliness."

"I'm not sure what that *means* exactly," he replied, still sounding peeved, "but I gotta tell you: it *does* sound slightly *gay*."

That made me smile in the midst of all the havoc, and I realised that he was back with me.

"What about this matter of 'Bannatyne, Kirkwood, France'?"

"There was a guy I knew in my year, who did his traineeship with them. He's now an in-house lawyer for the brainwashing corporation [BBC]. There's a rumour that they administer a slush fund for *Glasgow University*, *The Herald* – *both* of which they have acted for – and *God knows* who else. *Listen*: from a professional viewpoint, I'm on a steep learning curve here too! But here's my best guess for what you can expect. As to *why* exactly, though, I haven't a *clue*: unless you have somehow fallen into the plot of a *Dennis Wheatley* novel. *Look*, if I'm right and they *are* planning to 'shield the ball' – for *whatever* reason – it's an absolute fucking *scandal*!"

"*Jerry*! *Tangents*: circling back *round* for now?"

"Oh yeah. *Sorry*! Short version. In *theory* at least, one way out of this for you is through litigation. It is incumbent upon any party that has defamed you to prove the veracity of their claims. Best as I can tell, several parties have already done *plenty* of that. However, although you *officially* have *three years*, the essence of any action that you might pursue successfully is *speed* … *plus*: the high level of public awareness helps. But that's as good as it *gets*. Whereas slapping quick warrants on one or two media sleazeballs is one thing, Scottish Civil Law, in common with that of many other countries, is *really* accessible only to the *rich*. To pursue even a *single* case of defamation to *any* sort of satisfactory conclusion will require a lot of money."

"How much do you mean by 'a *lot*'?"

"Amounts in excess of a hundred thousand."

"Not currently an option for me, I'm afraid."

"And before you ask, I know of no one in Scotland who undertakes that sort of work speculatively."

"No *pro bono publico*, huh? No provision for justice for all, *after* all, eh?"

"Damn *right*, amigo! Unless your Sean Connery or Lord Moneybags of *Inverasshole*, it's got nothing to *do* with justice. What it *has* got to do with is *scary monsters*: scary monsters fighting over the pieces of what they're programmed to perceive to be a fast-disappearing cake! As to the *one* they send in your direction, tomorrow? If I'm right, she'll have been instructed to do everything she can to slow you down."

"What if I were to demand another solicitor?"

"*Same* disappointing outcome. *Here's* some free legal advice: *fuck* the law! Hang around and suck it all in as you take the stoning, if you like: maybe the act of observing the infliction of your own pain will put a little more iron in your soul. But *fuck the law*!"

"I need *more* iron in my soul like I need more mercury in my fillings. And I hope that's not legal advice that you've started doling out *willy-nilly* these days," I chuckled half-heartedly. "Surely *you*, of *all* people, haven't gone all *anti-capitalist*, have you?"

"Very funny. Excuse me while I laugh up a *lung*! What's left of this country is fucked into a cocked hat. I've actually been giving some thought to going back to the States. *Look*, why don't you just *do over* what you've just *done*: get it *right* this time, then come clean once you've got the degree?"

And miles to go before I sleep

From: *Stopping by Woods on a Snowy Evening*, by
Robert Frost

"No, but the idea of writing a personal account has been suggested to me. It's not something that I in any way relish the prospect of having to produce, but I suppose it *might* be worth doing as a possible means of gaining a medical school place in one or other English or German-speaking part of the world, where decency and good sense still hold *some* sway."

"What's it like down there in the abyss?"

His question surprised me somewhat, as his questions occasionally did. I thought for some seconds before answering.

"I'm not *recognising* an abyss, but maybe those who get a glimpse of heaven in *this* life, *have* to see the other end of the scale at some point. And as to that '*heaven*'? It registered a little bit like those tumbling notes in the Adagio assai from Ravel's Piano Concerto in G major. You *know*: fecund and timely; and strangely … unexpectedly … full of the *world*."

"I don't know what you *mean* by that, but I'd be *shittin'* myself. You know, I have observed that when they at first encounter little or no restriction, those who have a *taste* for power will do ever-more-terrible things to hold onto – and, where they can, *increase* – what power they have. And *most* human beings are *far* from averse to holding power over others."

"I found that out too: *early on* in life. And it has been a lesson much reinforced ever since. 'Keep calm at all times!': that was something that my mother impressed upon me, even *earlier* on in life. It has always proven to be good advice. I do my utmost to keep to it."

"Do you even still *want* to live in the world?"

"*Damn right* I do!"

"*Why*? Just for the sheer *hell* of it?"

"No. Things will come good again. In that much I retain complete faith. And meantime, my one ongoing determination is not to *despair*."

"Well, it must have dawned on you that, for the time *being* at least, they've got you *fucked sideways*."

"All signs point *to* it," I sighed.

"Well, I gotta go. Those vodka martinis neither make nor drink *themselves*, you know?"

"Well, *there's* a gene that I may *lack*!"

"What's *that*?"

"For double expression of alcohol dehydrogenase: I *may* – much as I am *loathe* to admit it – metabolise alcohol only half as efficiently as *you* do."

It was a big fat whopper. Rasputin himself may have considered possession of my liver as an upgrade: that claimed status being attested to by *at least* five occasions (those when I have been *acutely* aware that I have been in serious trouble) of attempts having been made on my life – throughout the years since then – when *poisoning* has been the method employed. *True*, there are three compounds in particular, to which early on I saw the wisdom of rendering

399

myself mithridatic. *Mainly*, though, survival of those events has largely been down to hepatic efficiency.

Of Jerry, however, I had been moved to think, "Bless his good heart: I have to offer him *something* here!"; and knowing him as I did, such a comment concerning *booze* was the best that I could come up with in the moment.

"*Christ*, that must be fuckin' *awful* for you!" he piped up, sounding reinvigorated; then proceeded to enquire, "So, *why* does that thought make me feel so much *better* all of a sudden?"

"You're a sick puppy, Jerry," I chided, signing off with, "And I'm going to leave you now, to let you enjoy your next beverage. *See* ya!"

"Wouldn't wanna *be* ya!" I heard him whoop, just as I was replacing the receiver.

For the most part, I try to be impersonal. But 'Jerry' was someone that I could not help but be fond of. I had a coffee with him in February of this year (2015). A few weeks ago, I heard that he passed away suddenly in the early summer.

Ignoring the pain in my back, and the surge of guilt over having spent a deal longer than I intended with the phone call, I settled into a smooth slow run back towards the end of Iain Drive. Only the mysterious balm of glorious *night* could come anywhere close to the efficacy of *her* delicate powerful fingers, as, once, they eased the impossible tensions in my neck and upper back. *Night*, with all her magic. *Ave domina noctis*!

About a quarter of the way back, the sky opened up with a downpour of hard driving rain. I stepped up the pace and powered my way through it, back towards base.

With phylogenies renegotiated – and having returned to my bedroom – I stripped off, stowed my wet clothes and boots at the bottom of the wardrobe, and slid under the duvet.

Ten minutes later, the loyal, forthright, pragmatic telepath who had raised me, looked round the bedroom door and smiled. I opened my eyes wide and gave her a conspiratorial wink. Less than a minute after that Mackenna also took it upon himself to look in on me. Olfaction was all that was required for certainty as to *his* presence.

Chapter Forty-Five

'I am *in* the world, but not *of* the world
I do not work of myself, but it works through me'

From an Original Christian prayer

The following morning, with the 'left lying' envelope conspicuously absent from the top of the coffee table, my mother, Mackenna and I stepped out into a purposely – and temporarily – cleared road, and towards a parked Toyota Previa 'people carrier', provided to drive us to Milngavie Police Station.

My concern at that time was entirely for my mother, as, for my own part, I felt *atypically* '*removed*' from much of what was going on around us. Indeed, with the realisation – renewed as it was at the beginning of each new day – that both the Augmenter and any near-time prospect of finally getting back on my chosen, earned and never tenably-forfeited educational path, were *lost* to me, a walk out to a dawn *firing squad* would have come only as a blessed, merciful relief, in comparison to that bleak empty prospect of the shattering traipse from bed to bathroom. *Occasionally*, though, I would still take a *little* comfort in the thought that, given that it had been by God's good grace that she – and for that matter, my mother too – had come to *be*, then giving up

402

what yet existed of my base human qualities to my maker (as best as I could thereby *cognize* God), might be the *one* path that might lead to something worthwhile in the long run. I nonetheless sensed, though, that it might be a tough process. How far-fallen I had become, I could not tell. Who among us *can*?

As we pulled up into the car park at the rear of the police station, I decided that Mackenna was looking just too smug to tolerate any longer.

"I'm not sure that I need a lawyer in there with me *after all*, Ron," I complained. "Besides, there's the *cost* to consider."

"This is a *Herald* matter, Brian. *We'll* take care of any costs," he insisted. "Don't you worry about *that*: it'll be *fine*! Gillian and her firm do a lot of work for us. She knows her *stuff*."

"Yes, but what about the question of *conflict of interest*, Ron? It might at least be best if I asked for a *duty* solicitor."

He seemed quite nonplussed by those remarks, and struggled for a few entertaining moments for any form of reply, until finally: "Look, just *hold on*, Brian … *Ah, here* she is *now*!"

"Does my bum look big in this?"

—Arabella Weir

The 'Gillian' to whom Mackenna had referred was Mrs Gillian Wade, of the Glasgow-based firm, *Bannatyne, Kirkwood, France & Co.*; and she had just teetered – on vulgar brown spike stilettoes – from a taxi across the car park. Whatever the 'stuff' that she knew *was*, it did not encompass elegance or poise.

She wore 'matching' brown mini-skirt, brown jacket and brown bowler hat. I first tried to console myself with the thought that she may just have arrived from a meeting of the *Avengers* Appreciation Society. Then, I recalled the old adages about there being 'no accounting for taste,' and 'not judging by appearances'. Judgement, however, was *one* thing: *gut feeling* was another.

As soon as we were introduced, she wanted first to speak with Mackenna in private. To this end, they moved off together, a little way from the van.

"This immediately seems more than a little *irregular*," I thought.

The two policemen wanted to speak with me in connection with a 'false passport' case that they were investigating in Liverpool. I very quickly made it clear that I knew nothing about *that* or any other case of criminal fraud. I also stressed that I had never possessed – or had made application for – more than one passport in any name other than my own, in either the UK or any other country; and that the false and malicious claims suggesting otherwise – as first broadcast by BBC Scotland, over a week previously – had quickly been refuted by both BBC Scotland and all the other media outlets that had repeated them. I noted further, for the record (both theirs and mine) that: (i) whereas I was aware that several other media outlets had apologised publicly for rebroadcasting the aforementioned false claims, BBC Scotland had not; and (ii) prompt investigation and prosecution of the Louden family, who had first promulgated these spurious and fraudulent claims – plus ensuing investigation of those who had suggested and facilitated their course of action – would prove to be sagacious means of bringing to a just end this ongoing profligate waste of public money. Lastly, I made explicit reference to the dossier that I had handed in at the same police station, in early 1993.

They paid no heed whatsoever, and took my passport anyway. They held onto it for over a month.

Throughout my time living in Glasgow, I have often heard reference made to the police – even by members of the *professional* classes – as 'The Filth'. While I cannot condone such references or the attitude from which they arise, I can in *some* sense understand why both betide.

I retain (at a location that I will not disclose here) audio recordings (on 'microcassette', for the historians amongst you) of the entire interview, and of my earlier interviews with Mackenna.

On that afternoon, my outrage muscles were no longer refractory. There was no question that these policemen were a disgrace to their profession: and even the fact that they were also rather *dim* could hardly have been advanced as a tenable excuse their deplorable behaviour.

Throughout the taped interview, Mrs Wade said nothing. Back in the van, she produced her own mini tape recorder and proceeded to switch it to 'record'. I had kept mine hidden in my pocket throughout much of the afternoon.

"What are you doing?" enquired my mother, in a defensive attitude. "Why are you ...?"

"Oh, that's just for *us*," interjected Mackenna, stuffing his face with chips. "For '*The Herald*', May."

The driver had already scrunched up the wrapping of *his* half-eaten fish supper, and was starting up the engine. My mother had treated both of them to lunch while the interview had proceeded inside the station. I contented myself with the assertion that she would have had *some* worthwhile cause for contributing to their ongoing Roman holiday. I tried to catch Wade's expression, but she would turn no further in my direction than to the extent that she was able to glance surreptitiously and obliquely towards the half of the vehicle where I sat. Mackenna had the grim, grey look of a bomb disposal man working pessimistically against a countdown.

The Previa pulled away and I made one last attempt to observe Wade's demeanour. She looked round boldly. *That* was enough.

"Oh *no*," I thought, "you're a *very* bad pony. I would *never* bet on *you*!"

As we left the police station, I let it be known to Mrs Wade that I wanted to make an official complaint about my having been questioned *at all*. Unsurprisingly, she was vigorously opposed to that idea. I did not suppose that it would have proven to have been a worthwhile pursuit anyway.

At the first of our subsequent meetings, Mrs Wade was all enthusiasm and assurances.

"I'm obliged to inform you, though, that I act for *The Herald* – as I believe you already know – and the *Daily Mail*," she said. "You don't intend any actions against either of *them*, do you?"

"I certainly do intend to challenge the *Daily Mail* on a number of issues, Mrs Wade," I replied.

"The thing is, you see," she went on, "that they apparently have a tape from Mr Roy, the landlord at Tayport."

"Neither I nor my mother have anything to fear from Mr Roy," I affirmed. "We acted scrupulously. Mr Roy, on the other hand, misrepresented in his capacity as landlord."

"Yes, well, maybe we'll leave that one until 'the second round', so to speak," she added, reddening noticeably. "And before I forget, Ron has instructed me to draw up a contract between you and him in relation to the book of your story."

"I'm afraid you are again misled, Mrs Wade," I replied, a little irritated by her ridiculousness. "I have no interest – nor have I ever *entertained* or *expressed* any interest – in having Ron Mackenna ghost write *anything* for me. I am perfectly capable of doing that myself, should I decide to do so. And *besides*, the man can barely produce intelligible copy for the parochial inane rag that employs him."

By November 14th, Wade's 'enthusiasm' had gradually diminished to the following order:

She began her letter by referring to 'your [my] letter of 7th November'. She had been '... unable to reply to your [my] telephone calls as I have been absent from the office due to ill health.'

She was '... still quite prepared to proceed with the defamation actions which you are suggesting and consider there to be substantial merit in much of your claims but there would be a considerable advantage in waiting for the media attention to die down further before issuing writs.' (*sic*)

She continued that, '... It can never be in your benefit to conduct litigation in the glare of publicity and as there is still considerable interest in the actions proposed by your mother, I do not wish to give the impression that you are attempting to seek further attention. I think that no matter how difficult it might be, we should concentrate our efforts on keeping the media interest as low key as possible. I have been contacted by a number of newspapers over the last few days looking for a story in respect of your mother's action and I have advised them that I am not in a position to comment as I owe duty of confidentiality to her and that I am not prepared to co-operate. I would suggest that you refer all calls which you may receive from the press to me and I will give them the same answer. Given the fact that you are defending your reputation which you say has been ruined by the press coverage, you must give the media as little chance for speculation as possible at this stage.' (*sic*)

Layperson I may be, but surely the issuing of writs at or before that time, would have been the measure necessary to silence the media, while legal proceedings went ahead.

Mrs Wade saved her most extraordinary advice for the latter part of her letter. She wrote: '... Having considered the matter fully, I am also very seriously disinclined to mention the issue of the passport. I am not quite sure if you have fully appreciated that the police, in handing you back your passport, have not given up their right to proceed against you, as the Fiscal cannot possibly have made up his mind in the time given. I would therefore hate to pre-empt any further action by suing, in the meantime.'

A month thereafter, a bill for £473.11 was rendered by *Bannatyne Kirkwood*, to me (plus another to my mother). I paid both immediately. *The Herald* had, of course, *not* 'take[n] care of any costs: this, in spite of Mckenna's earlier assurance to the contrary.

Chapter Forty-Six

One day in the early spring of 1999, my mother and I packed our remaining (essential) belongings into the car, and we 'hit the road', leaving 11 Whitehurst behind for good. MacSween had intensified his delegated reign of terror to such an extent that being divested of most of our individual assets had seemed – to *both* of us – a matter of little consequence, in light of the miracle of our both having remained alive up until that point.

In 1996, I had bought two diamonds with the profits from my trading; and it had been the subsequent auctioning of those, plus a percentage of the money from the sale of the flat – that *small* percentage which had not just 'disappeared' from my mother's bank account, one day a couple of months prior to our departure – that had provided us with the means to decamp.

We had agreed to head south for England. There did not seem to be any particular reason as to why it should be *England*. Petrifying – as great swathes of it rapidly were – under layers of either quick-setting, Blairite, mineral concrete or industrial agriculture, there was little in its *modernity* at least that held anything much in the way of attraction for either of us as a place to bide for long. But there just did not appear to be anywhere *else* anymore; and it offered escape from the *parochial*: a necessarily larger crowd in which to hide. Aside from a six month rental – which, as it would turn out, we would use only as an occasional overnight base – in a little Scottish backwater called Helensburgh; plus a few requisite (for the purposes of escape and evasion) 'jaunts' around Ireland and the near continent, England would turn out to be where we would spend much of the following few years: never in any *one* place for more than a few *days*, though; at least not after two early – and unsavoury – experiences of our having been caught up to by MacSween's murderous hireling myrmidons.

Leaning across to take something out of the glove compartment, just after I had pulled over (a little short of the junction of Whitehurst and Drymen Road), I noticed the right side of my face in the rear-view mirror. A mere two months before, it had been beaten to not far short of a *pulp*: with extensive damage to the orbit and mandible. Now, only the jawline showed even the slightest sign of being not fully restored to normal. Even *I* could not tell that my nose had been broken. I wondered briefly at this newly bestowed capacity for regeneration.

Then, in the next split second, I was moved to concern at the sight of the much more *slowly* healing scars, just in from the hairline – and extending to the right temple – of my mother's forehead; and on the bridge of her nose.

Perhaps it was because I was unappreciative – or because I did not care even for *indispensable* 'gifts', when they came without discernible exposition – that there reacted a part of me as might have some ancient smilodon: aggrieved at having been pulled under the tar, and finding himself with some *kick* left in him. That near-forgotten, interminably benumbed part of me that countenanced emotion, reawakened and battled hard for the surface.

410

Remembering was *easy*. What I sought was the accompanying *feeling*, as I recalled how the Augmenter would sometimes press *her* nose to one side: squidging it over, as though she wished it just that bit more perfect. I had told her once that she had no *need* to do such a thing, and that she – *and* her nose – looked lovely … '*just right*'. But not wanting ever to be responsible for pushing her towards the wrong side of laudable self-possession, I had repeated neither the reproach nor the compliment.

As I sat, with the car engine at idle, some unconscious and calming impulse inclined me to scry through and beyond the reflective surface of the rear-view mirror, and thence towards repeated experience of an event past. By *whatever* hidden process, my doing so finally (if still only *temporarily*) brought the longed-for freedom from that long-induced *numbness*.

"*Psst!*" she would sometimes call in my direction, when she sought my attention surreptitiously, or when that attention had (rarely) wandered in a crowd of others. I 'heard' that call again as, one day in the summer of 1993, I flew up the stairs to the flat where an audience with her had been arranged.

I had, throughout parts of the previous two years, desperately and imprudently tolerated the attentions of one of her friends, in the increasingly forlorn hope that a meeting like this might eventually be engineered. '*Brother*' — that is how the nonesuch would address me. If that is what I *truly* was, then I had hardly proven worthy of the familial title. My latter-day conduct in relation to the girl I loved – and, indeed, towards her friend – had been anything but *exemplary*.

Although my eleventh hour had seemed to me to have come and gone around a year before – marked as it had been by a meeting with the (Scottish) Adviser of Studies at The University of Edmonton – *hope* does have that habit of

411

springing eternally in the human breast: and I am no less than human.

The ubiquitous interloping 'friend', at last perplexed and resigned, may well have finally delivered as go-between, but if *this – unexpectedly* as it had come – *was* to be hope beyond hope, it had come a year too *early* for me. The Augmenter had recently graduated, but neither of us was yet free of Glasgow; and I had by then embarked upon that course of particularly risky action, which as far as *I* was concerned, meant that there could not be *any* perception, in the mind of *any* potential gossip, of a renewed association between us for at least a year further. Maybe Sartre was onto something with his assertion that 'Hell is other people ...': and not *just* 'at breakfast'!

Two nights previously, I had had a hard lesson on the value of living in the present.
I had gone out for a late-night walk from the flat at 11 Whitehurst, where, since my father's death towards the end of April of 1993, I had stayed with my mother.
As I had turned off Drymen Road and onto the top right side of the narrow first part of Ralston Road, a large dark Ford saloon had screeched round the corner behind me. Lost in contemplation of prospective challenges throughout the coming days, weeks and months of my return to Bearsden Academy, I had – in that indulgence – fallen from the percipience that fear can exist only when you contemplate the future; and that violence is *always* fear-driven.

Neither had I noticed any car following me.

As soon as their vehicle had mounted the pavement just ahead of my position, and three of its four occupants had piled out, moving in coordinated manner revealing of intent to crowd me and – as I had quickly foreseen – drag me *inside*, it was '*fangs out*'.

Microcosm and macrocosm

At this time of writing, deluded, weak, Luciferian men of the same ilk – still expressly, cohesively and (in the lower orders) *semi*-cohesively grouped; and pre-armed with remarkably sophisticated protocols for brute force mass-corralling and culling – exploit fear on a *grand* scale, by engineering confrontation between (and within) two broad cultures: each 'armed' with its own adulterated 'good' book, a part of which egregiously abrogates its essential message for *each individual* to live a peaceful productive life in the spirit of *goodwill* towards all those around them.

In view, however, of the relentlessly attritive sequence of unjustified humiliations that I had had to endure over the course of more than a decade, my impression had become that, *forced* to this distasteful necessity of advancement by deception, I had been let down by my Guardian; and, indeed, just let down *generally*. Now, I had this one last possibility, which I had had to recreate for myself: *all* by myself. And I was not about to let that odious wretch's goons beat intelligence of it out of me. It was not that I had nothing to lose, but rather that I had a very specific *something* left to hang onto; and suddenly *fearful*, I had not been for relinquishing it without a fight.

With my decision having been made, I had known that there would come no assistance from any quarter: no more slowing down of the world for my convenience; just my own mortal will, prowess and speed.

Two of them had come towards me, while the third had circled round behind. I had charged towards the two in front: a move which had provoked an instant look of surprise in the one closest to me. As he had begun to raise his right hand, I

413

had hit him in the throat with the pointed knuckles of the half-clenched fist of my own right hand. Then, having shifted my weight to my left, I had followed through, via my centre of gravity, to the open palm of my left hand, which I had slammed into the left side of his shaven head: smashing *it* into the head of his companion, who had been positioned in that instant, a little behind him and to his left. Continuing to use the first man's body as a weapon, I had then grabbed the fabric at the top of his jacket and had made use of it to pull myself forward while simultaneously launching him into the man who had gotten behind me.

Having passed my first attacker, I had hit his reeling companion squarely on the point of his chin with the heel of the palm of my opened right hand: projecting the blow at a steep upwards angle. He had fallen immediately.

Then, with just enough space to perform a tight circling motion of my own, I had used my momentum to step-rebound off the side of their car, thus projecting myself a few feet higher into the air, for a swing kick aimed at my third would-be assailant's head, before he had fully recovered from his impact with the confederate I had launched towards him. I had known immediately – simply by the 'feel' of the strike – that he would be of no more threat to me.

In common with war, small scale violence can also go wrong for *anyone* involved, *anytime*.

With the proviso that everything that I had just done was contrary to a basic tenet of my creed, I had thereupon made my one *tactical* slip-up of the encounter: I had neglected to look down early enough as had I descended. This error had arisen from my sudden preoccupation with the driver of the car making to get out of the vehicle.

As a result, I had at the last moment been unable to avoid landing on the forearm of the first-struck of the three assailants. His arm had come to lie at an angle between the road and the kerb, and I had felt it snap under my left foot as

414

I had landed. The fallen man had given out a moan. I had doubted that he was fully conscious. There had been no doubt as to *my* state of consciousness, though, as an agonizing jolt of pain had gone through the right side of my back at the completion of my landing.

My next sight of the tall overweight driver, as he had alighted from their vehicle, had been of the back of his head and of his right hand holding what appeared to be an old-fashioned, hardwood, policeman's truncheon: vertically upright and pressed against the frame of the side window.

The mere *sight* of such a weapon had been enough to adrenalize me anew, and I had, in a final headlong bound, traversed the roof of their car, and kicked him frantically and repeatedly to the ground before he had even gotten fully upright from his seated driver's position.

The bludgeon, at around eleven or twelve inches long (including the grip), had bounced a little along the tarmac: clunking resoundingly in the process of settling. I had immediately picked it up and walked around behind the driver, as, still conscious, he had begun to try and right himself up onto one knee.

I had felt relieved that I had dealt so swiftly and thoroughly with him: for although he had seemed unfit, I had seen immediately that he was a hugely powerful brute of a fellow, who – had he had managed to overpower me – could easily have killed me.

I had stood behind him: watching silently as the searing pain had returned to the right side of my back; and he, having come to a kneeling position, had proceeded to spit blood and saliva onto the road.

Incongruously, I had remembered something that had momentarily been baffling in its advent: image of the outrageous, pouting Frank N. Furter, as played by Tim Curry in that film of which the Augmenter was a fan.

415

Maybe it had simply been that I had not even wanted to give the driver the benefit of hearing my undisguised voice; but more likely it had had more to do with my having noticed his right hand moving out of sight and towards the left side of his chest, that had led to my having declared, in as confidently camp a tone as I could muster, "*Ooow*, that's a *big* one! You weren't going to *hurt* me with that, *were* you?"

He had stumbled forward a little again and the right hand had shot back down once more, to provide the still-required steadying support.

He had spoken with what I perceived to be an east London accent.

"You know," he had said, coughing "I read somewhere that humour is really just a form of perversion." Then, after more spluttering – which had worried me greatly, because I had sensed strongly that it was being, if not entirely *feigned*, then at least *exaggerated* – he had laughed: "Perhaps we are all just *perverts* now!"

Noticing the right hand once again seeking out its left-side destination, I had grasped that the laugh too had been insincere.

Deferring my eventual reply, I had moved in rapidly and silently, and swung his own cudgel heavily across the back of his skull: just north of the inion. Delivery of that final blow had left him crumpled: prone.

Pithy though my delayed rejoinder of "*I* might be!" may have *been*, I doubt that anyone but *I* heard it.

I recall having stared at the stick for a further few seconds, and wondering how – were I to have had the hardihood to 'fittingly' insert the hardwood – MacSween might have reacted to the spectacle of having *that* lever 'at his disposal'.

Having then gone down on one knee *myself*, to recover fully my *own* composure, I had surveyed the edges of the

416

mayhem that I had wrought: limp limbs; the top of a head, visible at the front edge of the obscuring vehicle; blood. There had been no desire for a detailed look: just a growing sense that there would be no '*early trans*', or even further, near-term, prodigious aid for me. *Every* life matters. And no matter *what* they may have had in mind to inflict upon me, I had had no moral right to have let myself been drawn into acts of violence.

Eventually heedful of the possibility of another car appearing from either direction – and at *any* moment – I had picked up the period baton, departed the scene, and disposed of the weapon over a wall at the bottom of a nearby garden.

I had not bothered to check what it was that he had been going for on his left side. It had been of no further interest to me.

Nor had I even bothered to *run* back towards the flat. Under normal circumstances, I would – almost inevitably – have been in what a Canadian acquaintance would have designated a '*shit ton*' of trouble; and, certainly, I would have had *welcomed* arrest: just for the chance to have brought all that I had endured (up until that point) to public attention. But I had by then realised that that was *one* thing – after my remarkable experience at Milngavie Police station in January of that year – that, *extraordinarily*, I had become unsusceptible to.

On my return to the flat some fifteen minutes later (although it had felt *so* much longer), I had experienced a strong sensation of being 'overheated', to the unsettling extent that I had thrown off my clothing and settled into a curled-up position on top of my bed: *refolding* my inner self in the darkness of the moonless night. Indeed, *such* was my disquiet, that it had felt almost as though I was inhabiting not my *customary* room, but one more closely resembling a bedchamber in one of those uncanny depictions by Gottfried Schalken.

I had just stared at my forearm for a while: *unthinking* in any sense but that of ouroboric self-reflexivity — not so very unlike the man chasing his own hat in *Miller's Crossing*.

"You get what get!" had been the invading human thought that had eventually come to command my attention: stealthily in the silence.

"*No!*" I had remonstrated, unaccepting and with greater, oppugnant, quelling hush. Then, with eyes still opened, I had wept profusely until dreamless sleep had eventually taken me.

Hightailing it up those stairs two nights later, though, all such considerations – plus any attention to excruciating back pain – were swept from my mind by sheer *elation* at the prospect of seeing her again. Ascending, *soaring* – equally in spirit – I found myself thinking of Sam Shepard in that (fast and) loose depiction of the career of the test pilot Chuck Yeager. I had not much enjoyed *The Right Stuff* throughout any but a few of its final minutes: when he purloined the rocket-like Lockheed NF-104A jet and seemed to head straight up for the sun — "*'Stretch it! Stretch it! Come on! Come on now, you can do it!'*"

In remembering, I shared in that sense of one freed at last to hie up again from a desolate stifling terrain, towards the near-but-far, brightening, quickening star; and at last – and for *good* – to *hold* … embrace. That is how, *unfailingly*, she would inspire me: gravity-cheating, death-defying; heart-lightened and vision-refocused in every glimpse of an abiding sunrise. All the other faces – every other little twinkling star – would inchmeal *fade* to background glitter: framing her august pre-eminence. And in certain *timeless* moments, the rest of the world would simply disappear.

At the door to the flat, I spoke quietly to myself her given names. As ever it has, the saying of them brought that joyous sense of lingering ease that I would experience when we were together. *More* than that, it was the unique and *absolute* certainty of coming *home*: which was wherever *she* was. And I felt, with *such* a sense of urgency, that I just *had* to find a way back for us. And even if I could not quite put it all together on the spot, then – given how she had surprised and delighted me so often in the past, with her wisdom and insight – *surely* she would reveal hitherto withheld comprehension of the extent of my predicament, and come up with something: *anything* that would give rise to a workable solution for us.

We were quickly left alone together in the room where I found her again, sitting on the sofa, smiling benignly, her legs tucked up beneath her: that super-smart, witty, and breathtakingly, heartstoppingly (and heart*resettingly*) beautiful Leo, who had so *impossibly* – yet seemingly effortlessly – delivered me from my deep-den, seven-year reticence, back up towards the sunlight: *her* sunlight.

"*I adore you*!'": it was something that we had declared to one another on a couple of occasions over those ten months or so of '88/'89. *Then*, taking brief pause to consider the fluidity of the sentiment that could ensue, when even a *hint* of the grandiose was attached to repetition of the expression – toppling everything into absurd mawkishness – we would both burst out laughing. I *did* adore her, though: in the very *best* sense. And that meant that, at this imposed culmination, only guileless candour would be bearable.

Attempting to abandon my silly pride as best I could, I began by mentioning my father's passing a few months before.

Suddenly, there were tears in my eyes. Not because of grief at the event that I was describing: I was *glad* that his pain was over, and I have never been inclined to 'hang onto' the dead, for fear that such clinging thoughts might contribute to restraining them on their onward transformative journeys. My tears were tears of sadness that, in view of all the extant and mounting danger that I was in the midst of, I could even be *contemplating* forestalling or imperilling her further, on account of nothing more than my own selfish desire. And besides, in view of my end-of-night '*niagaraishness*', immediately following my barely curbed actions less than two days previously, another bout of unchecked weeping – and the bellyaching that inevitably would have accompanied it – just would not *do*.

It was my last chance, then.

Could I have but *heaved* my heart into my mouth once more, and told her how I missed her, and how I had come to love her above *all* else: above breath, above *life*, and with every fibre of my being; and how I detested the destructive impediments to what I desiderated most: our being together again, and for good …

… But to love is not to burden, forestall *or* imperil.

There have been times when I have found myself resolving that there is no such thing as bravery: just *pride*. But I hope that it was the *best* of me – *something* truly courageous in me – which, in that clear-headed moment, swayed me to appreciate that I could not … *must* not declare my true feelings. Had my feelings for her been of a *lesser* order, then I might have found myself able to let slip and say more. Instead, I stated bluntly that I wanted her to have a good life … a *great* life, but that it could not be with me. In that moment – although I knew that I would continue to be lost without her – I meant what I said with all my heart.

420

Even with the full force of my human ego promptly rushing and pressing back against the fleeting divinity that is most commonly still referred to as superego, *unerschütterlich* had held true as a character trait. It would be a useful attribute in my chosen profession, were that pathway not still withheld from me; and all in all, I hold still that it served the greater good that day too.

Like the lone, ejected, earthward-hurtling test pilot – a latter-day Icarus who had encountered calamity over 104,000 feet up in the stratosphere, just as he had gained *his* unclouding view of the empyrean – *my* head *too* began to feel as though it was on fire. But my *heart* – the heart that somehow she had imbued with new vigour – kept true and steady, and I held fast to grimly realised purpose, as, for a second time, I bore that which seemed to be unbearable.

As we had sat together on the upper deck of a Glasgow bus, one day in the early part of 1989, she had intimated how as a result of the umbilical cord having wrapped itself around her neck in the womb, she had sometimes experienced dreams of being choked. Aghast at my having hurt and confused her again on that last day some four years later, I too – although nightmarishly *awake* – began to suffer in a fashion perhaps not so dissimilar.

There suddenly came over me awful sensations of shame and suffocation: with the latter feeling intensifying rapidly, as remembrance of the daily-renewed heartbreak of the previous four years engendered dawning realisation of the harrowing prospect of interminable estrangement.

Her view – expressed only minutes after my once having told her that I loved her – that it didn't really matter who you ended up with ('Just someone to cuddle in bed with, at night.') was *one* 'confirmation bias' – one developing *notion*

– that I truly *had* intended to disabuse her of: not by *argument*, but by the actualisation of a lifelong devotion.

Here was *epic* failure!

A broadside composed of nothing but 'Egads!' would have struck me as mild rebuke in comparison to her flashed look of severe disapproval, had I not already been in the throes of falling into a state of despondency. Then, she struck out at me with an aggrieved anguished '"Tut!"', followed by quick trenchant account of a PhD student, who had been chatting to her at the bus stop she used; and of how he had been asking to go out with her.

In her own way, she too had proven *unerschütterlich*. Only at the last had there come this sign of reproach, in response to the irresistible, petrifying veil, which I was permitting to descend between us; and which could only set us upon divergent paths.

Life has its eras, and the best one by far that I had ever known was now, finally, petering out before my eyes. With her goodwill withdrawing and disappearing from view; the remaining shimmering red bonds between us rending and the portals closing, words were suddenly revealed as having become naught but unintended weapons, and I realised that although propriety required me to say *something* else, the *least* would be the better.

Shocked, etiolated, *blank*, I asserted aloud that there would be *lots* of men seeking her attention, even as consecutive pulses of unworthy sexual jealousy and further shame scorched me more. Then, fighting hard to hold onto my composure as I made a beeline for the door, I abashed myself anew by blurting out that hideous old chestnut about hoping that we would always be friends. I knew, though, that in view of all that was hovering over me, and all that might very well descend – as, indeed, it later *did* – she *had* to be clear of me. And, of course, by no *rational* system of assessment could one *iota* of blame have been attributed to *her* for being quite at the end of her tether with me.

But *still*, it felt *fundamentally* wrong: as though I had gone against *all nature* — just as it had felt when I had distanced myself from her four summers before. And in that moment of fading and disintegration, the overwhelming presentiment was such that I surely did not care to *exist* anymore.

Guilt and despair make for an egregious and noxious little combo that I would not wish upon *anyone*: not MacSween, nor even his infernal master. The Augmenter had been *all too briefly* the best friend and inimitable companion I had ever had. I am, however, without complaint about that brevity. Whenever the sadness of regret comes upon me, I do my best to counter it with *gratitude*: gratitude that ever she came to me. And with that appreciation, I offer up whatever I can give of my remaining base humanness.

A *perfervid* depiction? Maybe.

Prototypical? I don't know: I haven't read many memoirs.

Hagiographic? Not unduly so.

And certainly not *fawning* — *that* quality was *never* in me. *Had* it been, then who *knows*: it might have been linked to further weakness that would have had me buckling, and seeking to indulge myself in a little more precious time with her: time and events that would certainly have compromised her *further*. It was just that before I met her, I had never dreamt that another person – another *soul* – could have come to mean so much to me; and for one thus smitten, this is simply as *true* an account as I can give.

I am of late and in this incarnation fifty-two years in the world; and I shall fight no more. If my penance is not yet done, then it will yet have to *do*. And when I am inclined to wonder what greater good has come of my being dropped in this cold, damp little country on the northwest shoulder of Europe, I remember the times I had with her.

Startlingly, the recusant, rocketeering, movie airman, possessed as he was of the titular 'right stuff', had walked away from *his* catastrophic event. Strong and (sometimes) resourceful as I can be, I *know* that my physical survival from that day to this has not been by my own might alone.

Finding myself abruptly reprojected to my seated driving position again, at the roadside in 1999, I promptly experienced an image of her flashing that momentarily fixed, censuring, simian grin that she had shot my way a couple of times when I had overstepped the mark with boisterous teasing. It was one of only a couple of behaviours that would remind me that she *was* only human.

It dawned on me immediately that I had been *shown* this: it was not what I sought to recall. It had been *he*, my once-invited 'guardian', who had intervened.

Then, he let me 'see' a little more than I had bargained for.

"Mawage."

— The Impressive Clergyman (Peter Cook), *The Princess Bride*

I had long known *really*, but for the sake of my sanity, it had been that one thing I would sometimes flinch from, when, a few times each day, I would encounter it head on: that inflooding mix of raw heartache and dejection at the loss of her affection, and the apparently unalterable prospect of life without her — something not so very far removed from the lot of each tenth, decimated legionnaire: some deep and, arguably, self-inflicted and deserved wound that may never be mended.

Such is life, though: hazard-fraught and occasionally lacerating.

I thought, with briefly mounting rage, of those who had gotten between us. And then, all of that just *faded away*. They were not feelings borne of love. And I *did* love her: the augmenter of my own heart. I *knew*, for all the good it would do, that I would *always* love her: the human being and the spirit being, out there in the 'big wide world', living life as best as she could: as she *ought* to be living it.

But it was by then *way* past 'check-out time', and in the *moment* – wherein one *always* ends up finding oneself – I just had to let it be: let thoughts of her go.

'*Soul*, awaken in the consciousness of Christ!'

From an Original Christian meditation

Picturing a white energetic flame between my shoulder blades, in my fourth consciousness centre, which is the Centre of Justice or Earnestness – also known as The Redeemer Centre – I thought about giving myself up to it, but I found that I was still not ready to go there; and, no doubt aware of that remaining disinclination, my visitor adjusted me back to how I had been those few years past.

"Are you alright?" my mother asked me. "You look a little pale."

"Yeah, my directional sense just got a little bit messed up for a moment, there," I answered, "but it's alright now."

At the junction with the main road, I indicated right for the city, and the South.

"Did you notice the grey Mercedes?" I asked her. "It was parked about a hundred metres back from the flat again this morning."

"No, I *didn't*."

"Well, it pulled out right after *we* did, and it's just pulled *in* again: a little forward of where our car was parked. I'm guessing even *those* lowlifes are already aware that we know what they're up to."

"Oh."

"I may to have to take a few detours and drive a little *erratically* here and there for a little while before we hit the motorway. Can you *cope*?"

"I have every confidence in you."

"Well, that makes *one* of us at least."

I pulled out onto Whitehurst again, and forgetting about *tempus* – *or* how *fugit* it can be – I turned right (and south) at the junction with the main road. Had I been afforded any inkling of the agonies that would be visited upon us in the years that were to follow, I'm not sure *what* I might have done.

I infer that it was in foreseeing those ordeals, and/or in consideration of much of what had happened up until then, that my spectral guardian had upped – and would continue to become more proactive in – his involvement in the matter of our survival. That encompassed the furnishing of the means for some considerable improvement in (amongst other things) my *driving* skills.

To *light* and guard, to rule and *guide*

Inside my Active Dream, I close my eyes and I say:

"When I open my eyes, I shall have moved from this place into a location where the flow of time has changed. At this island in the river of time, one night of terrestrial sleep shall last …" and I say how long I want to stay. Then, I continue, "At this place, which I will find pleasant, relaxing and comforting, there will be a Guru with the wisdom of Solomon, the patience of Jesus, and the gift to show mankind the light and make it understood. This Guru will hold all the knowledge of the Akashic Records on the subject of …" and here, I state as precisely as possible what it is that I want to learn.

After reciting this, I open my eyes, and I find myself in a lovely location, with a person who can and will teach me what it is that I want to know.

If at any point I want to leave, all I have to do is cover my eyes with my hands, think of where I want to be, and say, "And so to leave this Guru and this time stream, returning to my normal space/time with the speed of Hermes." Then I open my eyes, and I am back in normal Active Dream space.

Epilogue

Into my heart an air that kills

From: 'Blue Remembered Hills', by A. E. Housman

It took no more than ten minutes to lose the Mercedes, along the side streets of Bearsden.

I pulled over into a quiet spot close to where nearby Kessington met the 'green belt', and quickly checked the car for any attached tracers. There was just one, which had been fixed up under the nearside back wheel arch. As I briefly regarded the tricksy little device in the palm of my hand, I reflected on how neatly – and seemingly *irrevocably* – the society in which I had grown up had come to be set on slow autodestruct. Then, picking up a large stone, I smashed the damned thing and threw what was left of it into the low scrub in front of the trees.

Wasting no further time, I swiftly got back into the car and drove us both, via the back road, towards nearby Milngavie.

We ended up in the tiny car park beside the *Classic India* restaurant, at the beginning of the Ellangowan Road, below the level of the precinct. Once parked in the invisible-from-the-road corner space, I asked my mother to hang tight while I ran up to the sandwich shop. I had reasoned that it might have been judicious not only to get something to keep us going throughout the long drive down the M74, but also to give our erstwhile pursuers a head start towards *nothing* along that same motorway.

Just across from the sandwich shop in the precinct, there stood – and yet stands – a Masonic Lodge. Perhaps five or six thousand people pass it every day. I doubt that more than a *couple* of those passers-by even notice what it *is*. En route back to the car, I paused and scrutinized its front doorway.

I knew that I could not risk leaving my mother alone for long, but I was temporarily rooted to the spot. Long-separated from most of what mattered to me, I felt vaguely light-headed, alone, wounded: almost as if I might, on an instant, simply 'pop' out of existence.

As the smilodon gave his last futile kick and disappeared entirely under the tar again, I considered how, a little while before, I had not been prepared to align my consciousness with the intuited white flame deep in my chest; but now, perfused with a rapidly heightening fear, which seemed to reach my core, I nonetheless found myself praying: "Inner Christ of God, Christ-God Spirit: grant me renewed strength and the wherewithal to prevail!"

As I began to settle, I looked again at the lettering above the main entrance. It read: 'MILNGAVIE: "LODGE ELLANGOWAN" No. 716', and was flanked on either side by small inconspicuous 'square and compasses' symbols.

There had come to my mind a simple four-word Latin expression that would have sat appositely atop the identifier.

sic transit gloria mundi

'sic transit gloria mundi' means 'thus passes the glory of the world'.